Contemporary Sociology
an international journal of reviews

_____ 600 _____ **words**

due by _____ 1-16-87 _____

D1163368

CAMBRIDGE STUDIES IN LINGUISTICS
SUPPLEMENTARY VOLUME

General Editors: B.COMRIE, C.J.FILLMORE, R.LASS, R.B.LE PAGE,
J.LYONS, P.H.MATTHEWS, F.R.PALMER, R.POSNER, S.ROMAINE,
N.V.SMITH, J.L.M.TRIM, A.ZWICKY

The urbanization of rural dialect speakers
A sociolinguistic study in Brazil

In this series

Supplementary Volumes

* Issued in hard covers and as a paperback

THE URBANIZATION OF RURAL DIALECT SPEAKERS

A sociolinguistic study in Brazil

STELLA MARIS BORTONI-RICARDO

Department of Letters and Linguistics, University of Brasilia

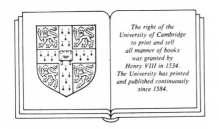

The right of the
University of Cambridge
to print and sell
all manner of books
was granted by
Henry VIII in 1534.
The University has printed
and published continuously
since 1584.

CAMBRIDGE UNIVERSITY PRESS

CAMBRIDGE

LONDON   NEW YORK   NEW ROCHELLE

MELBOURNE   SYDNEY

Published by the Press Syndicate of the University of Cambridge
The Pitt Building, Trumpington Street, Cambridge CB2 1RP
32 East 57th Street, New York, NY 10022, USA
10 Stamford Road, Oakleigh, Melbourne 3166, Australia

First published 1985

Printed in Great Britain at the University Press, Cambridge

British Library cataloguing in publication data
Bortoni-Ricardo, Stella Maris
The urbanization of rural dialect speakers : a
sociolinguistic study in Brazil. – (Cambridge
studies in linguistics : supplementary volumes,
ISBSN 0068-676x)
1. Portuguese language – Dialects – Brazil
2. Urbanization – Brazil
I. Title
469.7'98 PC5443

Library of Congress cataloguing in publication data
Bortoni-Ricardo, Stella Maris, 1945–
The urbanization of rural dialect speakers.
Cambridge studies in linguistics supplementary volume.
Bibliography: p.
Includes index.
1. Urban dialects – Brazil. 2. Portuguese
language – Brazil – Dialects. 3. Sociolinguistics – Network
analysis. 4. Rural-urban migration – Brazil.
I. Title. II. Cambridge studies in linguistics.
Supplementary volume.
P40.5.U732B63 1985 469'.01'9 85-18983

ISBN 0 521 30404 0

To the memory of
Maria Aparecida Bortoni

CONTENTS

ACKNOWLEDGMENTS

This present book is a revised version of my 1983 doctoral thesis
presented to the University of Lancaster. I am deeply indebted
to people in Lancaster and in Brasília who have contributed to
it, in particular to my supervisors, Roger T. Bell and
Christopher N. Candlin. I have also received valuable critiques
and comments from Lesley Milroy, Marilyn Martin-Jones, Roberto
Cardoso de Oliveira, Lytton Leite Guimarães, Anthony Naro,
Antonio Salles, Augustinus Staub, Ulf Baranow and Hildo Couto;
and the warm support of Maurício F. Ricardo, Marilda Cavalcanti,
Luzia and Luís de Castro and Maria Helena Kubrusly.

Throughout the development of the work, I had the efficient
collaboration of the following research assistants, students of
the University of Brasília. For the fieldwork: Ricardo Lobato,
Roberto Patrocínio, Márcia Damaso, Bráulio Porto, Aliris dos
Santos, Tulia Vogensen and Neuza Carvalho. For the transcription
and coding: Niviene Maciel, Ilza de Borja and Ruth Alves. For
the computer processing: Luiz Soares e Maria Inez Walter.
Terezinha Bublitz has worked as an efficient secretary during
all these stages and also patiently typed this final version.

Thanks are especially due to the following bodies:
The Ford Foundation for awarding me the research grant 739.0817.
55/62;
The Conselho Nacional de Desenvolvimento Científico e Tecnológi-
co - CNPq - for awarding the research grant 40.0778/81 and
financing the last year of my graduate studies;
The University of Brasília for institutional material support.

My warmest thanks go to my **parents, Geraldo and Maria**
Aparecida and my sister Márcia and to my children Larissa,
Clecio José and Ana Karina for their actual help, confidence

and understanding.

Finally, I am very grateful to my informants of Brazlândia who so generously shared with me their thoughts, their food and shelter with my regret that I can help them so little.

When we approach the study of modern national languages from a
sociolinguistic perspective a major trend that must be acknowl-
edged is the transformation of geographically based rural dialects into urban social class based dialects. Labov (1972a:300)
has observed that the growth of vertical stratification in languages is related to the decline of local dialects. Such linguistic phenomena are the consequence of a mass exodus from the
rural hinterland to the urban areas. In Europe the process had
begun during the late Middle Ages, was well underway in the
seventeenth century and was definitely established in the
nineteenth as a result of the Industrial Revolution. In developing countries like Brazil the phenomenon is more recent and,
in contrast to what happened in Europe, urbanization was not
necessarily preceded by industrialization.

To understand how urbanization takes place, and, more specifically, how countrymen and peasants are transformed into city
dwellers and industrial workers, has been a major concern of the
social sciences in this century, but surprisingly, the study of
the concomitant linguistic changes does not seem as yet to have
secured to the same extent the attention of the linguists. The
traditional dialectologists were aware of the relation of urban
to rural, though they tended to comment with regret on the
'destruction' of the rural dialects by the town; but most modern
linguistic consequences of urbanization pertain to the broad
area of language maintenance and shift in bilingual or multilingual societies and are built on the foundations laid mainly
by Weinreich (1953) and Haugen (1956).

The transformation of rural dialects into nonstandard urban
varieties - which we shall be referring to as 'urbanization of

rural dialects' - is at the very heart of the processes of language change and language standardization in Brazil. The migration of rural masses into the cities, the introduction into the
countryside of an urban way of life together with technology[1]
and a high level of interregional population movement are nowadays main characteristics of Brazilian society, and must be
understood in the context of a developing country which has
only recently emerged from a predominantly agrarian economy and
is beset by serious regional imbalance and by a perverse and
accelerating concentration of income.

   The rural migrants who are establishing themselves in the
cities are illiterate or semi-literate and speak regional rural
dialects of Portuguese which show a surprisingly high level of
uniformity - if one considers the huge size of the country - and
which tend to merge with nonstandard urban varieties. Any assessment of nonstandard Brazilian Portuguese should therefore take
such a merger into consideration. Approaching this complex
sociolinguistic situation is not an easy task however. Most of
the available sociolinguistic methods that deal with language
variation and change have been developed to suit the characteristics of (1) multilingual or multidialectal societies, (2) creole or post-creole communities and (3) nonstandard dialects in
developed countries where literacy is close to universal. None
of these is entirely adequate in the Brazilian situation. Brazil
is a monolingual nation and non-Portuguese speakers are quanti-
tatively irrelevant. Dialect differences, even though they imply
actual situations of cross-cultural communication, do not
preclude intelligibility. To treat the Brazilian Portuguese
variation as a post-creole continuum is not appropriate either.
The large gap between the standard language and the rural
varieties can possibly be accounted for by the influence of a
pidginized language on the latter during the first centuries of
colonization. If this hypothesis is correct, however, we have to
concede that this early pidgin has undergone a relatively rapid
decreolization process, since there are no Portuguese based
pidgins or creoles in Brazil such as exist in other former
Portuguese colonies.[2]

   As regards the sociolinguistic tradition of studying non-

standard dialects in industrial nations, some revision is also
required if it is to apply to the Brazilian situation. Firstly,
as Gumperz (1980:137) points out, the method of correlating
linguistic variables with social groups begins with the assumption that social groups are identifiable and known. In the case
of the modern capitalist nations this is an issue much in dis-
pute in the social sciences. In the case of a developing country
which was overwhelmingly agrarian until World War II, an effective identification of social classes in the society as a whole
appears an almost impossible task. Secondly, the maintenance of
nonstandard varieties in advanced industrial societies is directly related to the raising of minority group consciousness
(Ryan, 1979), a phenomenon that does not seem to have achieved
any prominence in Brazilian society as yet.

   We decided four years ago to examine the effects of the
rural-to-urban transition in the speech of a group of rural migrants. In view of the actual complex dialect contact situation
resulting from population mobility, as well as problems of
theoretical and methodological adequacy, we were faced with the
following questions. Which are the main factors at work in the
maintenance of rural and/or nonstandard varieties in Brazil?
Could their preservation be viewed simply as a result of illiteracy and spatial or social marginalization? As the population
gradually gains access to formal education will the dialects
recede? To what extent is there an ideology of prestige operating among the so-called marginal population?[3] Would this
population be **eager** for assimilation? To what extent is the
homogenization trend in the urban society subject to opposite
forces, on the one hand standardization pressures and, on the
other, the maintenance of nonstandard forms as signs of group
identity? Could the changes that take place in the repertoires
of the rural migrants be described in terms of sociodemographic
indicators such as duration of residence in the urban environment? Coming down to specific linguistic variables, is there a
trend towards elimination of verbal inflections or are the
speakers rather adding the verbal endings as they come under the
influence of formal education?

   The present book is aimed at answering these and other

related questions. In the case of a few of them, we come close
to satisfactory answers, but concerning many others, all we can
do is shed some light on their intricacy.

When we started the research we intended to carry out a
typical correlation study in which the frequency of a few selected nonstandard linguistic variables in the speech of a group
of rural migrants would be examined in the light of (1) duration
of residence in the city, (2) years of schooling, (3) stability
of employment, in addition to the commonly used parameters of
sex and age. But as we became more acquainted with a migrant
community we began to realize the weakness of some of these
parameters as predictors of dialect change. The large range of
variation in the repertoire of the adult migrants, which is
typical of fluid systems undergoing rapid change, did not appear
to be consistently conditioned by any of these sociodemographic
factors. At that stage we were already convinced that we needed
a methodological procedure capable of dealing with individual
differences and of capturing the subtle systematic patterns of
variation. In sum, it was a situation that in the old days would
be recognized as the most unpredictable dialect mixture; but, of
course, we knew that the migrants' linguistic behaviour was
amenable to some degree of prediction. We only needed the adequate analytic tool. This adequate tool was in fact the analysis
of the migrants' social networks.

A social network is simply the set of links of all kinds
among a set of individuals.[4] The interest of network analysis in
social science lies not in the attributes of the people in the
network *per se*, but rather in the characteristics of the linkages in their relationships with one another. Such characteristics are viewed as means of predicting and explaining the
behaviour of the people involved in them (Mitchell, 1969, 1973).

By the mid 1970s, Gumperz had already stated that network
position 'is a function of actual communicative experience and
also varies with education, occupation, generation cohort, political values and individual aspiration for mobility. Accordingly members of the same family and neighbourhood background
group may show different language usage practices' (Gumperz,
1976a:13-14).An analysis of the migrants' personal networks was

therefore employed as a means of assessing variability in individual linguistic behaviour in the community. It provided the criteria for establishing a basic distinction between insulated and integrated networks. The former represents an early stage in the rural-to-urban transition, and tends to be restricted to the migrant's extended family, pre-migration acquaintances and neighbours. The latter, in contrast, is more heterogeneous as far as the link recruitment framework is concerned. In an integrated network the links are activated in a larger range of social contexts. The working hypothesis related to these concepts is that the more advanced the migrant is in the process of transition from an integrated network, the more exposed s/he is to the mainstream urban culture and language and the more s/he will be committed to an effort towards assimilation of prestigious ways of speaking, which represents a movement away from the original rural dialect. Two network indices, the network integration index and the network urbanization index, were used as the yard-sticks that provided the quantitative assessment of the process.

Field research was conducted in Brazlândia, a satellite town located 43 kilometres from Brasília. Four linguistic variables were selected as indicators of the evolutionary trend of the migrants' dialect: the vocalization of the alveopalatal lateral phoneme $|\lambda|$ in intervocalic position, the reduction of final rising diphthongs and the subject-verb agreement rule with first and third person plural.

It should be noted, however, that our main concern was not with investigation of these variables *per se*, but rather with their capacity as sensitive indices of the whole process of adaptation of the rural population in the urban milieu. We felt with Gumperz (1972) that 'speech community studies are essential for the study of ongoing processes of linguistic change, for the development of linguistic indices to the study of social phenomena and for most areas of applied linguistics' (Gumperz, 1972:13).

Labov (1972a), accordingly, emphasizes the utility of sociolinguistic studies in the assessment of social changes. He says: 'variation in linguistic behavior does not in itself exert a powerful influence on social development, nor does it affect

drastically the life changes of the individual; on the contrary,
the shape of linguistic behavior changes rapidly as the
speaker's social position changes. This malleability of language
underlies its great utility as an indicator of social changes'
(Labov, 1972a:111).

This book represents a synthesis of quantitative sociolinguistic methods (the analysis based on the network paradigm is
supplemented by more traditional analysis of aggregated scores)
with an ethnographic study carried out during long-term participant observation in the community. Both the urban dialectology
and the linguistic anthropological methodologies aimed at providing an effective account of the language-network relationship, and, ultimately, of the peasant-urbanite transition phenomenon.

I give here a brief statement of the content of each chapter.
Chapter 2 is a description of the sociolinguistic situation in
Brazil. Chapter 3 is concerned with the description of the
phonological characteristics of the migrants' rural dialect, the
Caipira dialect. Chapter 4 provides a review of different traditions in the application of network analysis, with emphasis on
sociolinguistic studies. In chapter 5 the process of rural-to-
urban migration and its linguistic consequences are looked at
more closely. Chapter 6 focuses on fieldwork strategies and
includes ethnographic and sociodemographic information on the
migrants' community. In chapter 7, the different quantitative
methods used in the analysis are discussed in detail. Chapter 8
consists of the quantitative analysis of the four linguistic
variables. Chapter 9 is concerned with reporting and discussing
the problems of miscommunication between the informants and the
fieldworkers. And, finally, chapter 10 presents conclusions and
suggestions for further studies.

Notes

1 These phenomena are commonly referred to as 'peasantization
   of cities' and 'urbanization of villages' (Halpern, 1967).
2 For a full discussion of this hypothesis, see Guy (1981).
3 The peasantry and the rural migrants, which are the fastest
   growing segment of population in Latin America, are regarded
   by some social **scientists** as a marginal population, on the
   grounds that they lack formal articulation or insertion in

the urban industrial process of production. For different
views on the issue, see Lomnitz (1977), Berlinck (1977),
Schüly (1981), Oliven (1982).

4 The concepts that are being defined rather roughly in this
chapter will be more carefully dealt with in the next
chapters.

2.0 *Introduction*

This chapter, which is divided into three sections, contains a
description of the current sociolinguistic situation in Brazil.
In the first part the characteristics of the national speech
community are discussed and the large range of variation of
Brazilian Portuguese is approached from the perspective of a
dialect continuum that ranges from the stigmatized rural varieties to the formal urban standard.

In order to shed light on these sociolinguistic phenomena, a
review of the relevant historical and sociological facts is
provided in section 2 which, together with section 3 (which
deals with the Caipira culture), has the additional purpose of
establishing grounds for a closer understanding of the rural-
urban migration process and its linguistic consequences, our
main object of investigation.

2.1 *The Brazilian speech community*

Brazil has a population of one hundred and twenty million people, unevenly scattered throughout its large territory (the
demographic density is 14 inhabitants per square kilometre) and
it is by and large a monolingual Portuguese-speaking country. Phenomena of bilingualism are restricted not only to the remnants
of the aboriginal Indian tribes that have survived the gradual
ethnocide which took place during the historical process of land
occupation, but also to groups of European and Asian immigrants.
The immigrants settled in Brazil in large numbers: the European
group from the first half of the nineteenth century until World
War II, and the Asian from the last quarter of the nineteenth
century until a few decades ago.

It is difficult to assess accurately the size of the indigenous population in Brazil, but it corresponds to no more than
0.2 per cent of the total population. Among the existing 211
different Indian groups, 46 (21.8 per cent) can be considered to
be isolated, i.e., without systematic contact with the mainstream society (Cardoso de Oliveira, 1981). Of those that live
in contact with the mainstream society, approximately 120,000
have undergone different degrees of acculturation and their
linguistic repertoires range from monolingualism to an unstable
bilingualism that tends to favour Portuguese at the expense of
their mother tongue.[1]

As for the immigrants, the contingents that established themselves in metropolitan areas, mainly in the eastern and southern
regions of Brazil, tended towards assimilation to the dominant
language within a lag period of one or two generations; whereas
those who remained isolated in typical closed network systems
were more conservative and slow in the acquisition of Portuguese, which for some of these groups is still a second language
learned in school.

The characterization of the national population according to
the broad, large-scale category of speech community poses some
extra problems besides those inherent in the concept itself, for
the Brazilian speech community presents features of traditional,
stratified societies as well as of those which are modern,
personal-achievement-oriented. (For a discussion of such a typology based on criteria of repertoire range, access and fluidity, see Fishman, 1972.)

As usually appears to happen in traditional societies with
broad diversified repertoires, the varieties of Brazilian Portuguese could, for analytical purposes, be displayed along a dialect continuum ranging from isolated rural vernaculars at one
extreme to the urban standard of the upper classes at the other.
On such a continuum, adjacent to the highly stigmatized vernaculars, there are nonstandard varieties that might be labelled
'rurban'. These varieties are spoken by lower-class illiterate
or semi-literate people who live in the cities, but who, in
most cases, have rural backgrounds, or by the population living
in modernized rural areas. The criterion of social stratifica-

tion, therefore, partially overlaps with urban or rural background in explaining linguistic variation, since the larger part
of the lowest social stratum is made up of the peasantry and the
rural migrants. In other words, the distribution of several linguistic variables differs both on the basis of social class and
on the basis of rural/urban origin. Using the term proposed by
Wolfram and Fasold (1974:79), one would say that stigmatized
variants of these variables are 'socially diagnostic items' with
a general significance related both to lower-class and to rural
origin.

Interestingly enough there seems to be no variation in Brazilian Portuguese associated with ethnic background. In Brazil
the social process of integration, which embodies the linguistic
process of acquisition of the standard code, is basically related to social mobility and not directly to ethnic differentiation. It should be noticed, however, that most of the Negro and
mestizo population belongs to the lower-class and generally has
less opportunity for social mobility than the white population.

As compared to the standard extreme of the continuum, the
rural and urban varieties are marked by a large number of rules
that cut across phonology, morphology, syntax and semantics.
This broad range of variation does not preclude intelligibility,
but it does imply communication problems among different segments of the society, even though it has been national policy to
emphasize the homogeneity of Brazilian Portuguese and overlook
the disadvantages of the nonstandard speakers. Evidence of miscommunication due to dialect differences will be discussed in
chapter 9.

Most of the nonstandard features of the language are characteristic of a gradient rather than a sharp stratification, to
use again the terms employed by Wolfram and Fasold (1974).[2]
According to these authors:

> All socially diagnostic variables for a given population
> do not correlate with social status in the same way.
> Differences in the discreteness of the correlation have
> led us to distinguish between what we have labelled
> 'sharp' and 'gradient' stratification. Gradient strati-
> fication refers to a progressive increase in the fre-
> quency of occurrence of a variant when compared for
> various social groups... [when] none of the groups shows

a significantly greater frequency discrepancy than the
other... But there are other variables which indicate a
sharp demarcation between contiguous social classes...
In the case of sharp stratification, we find clear-cut
patterns of correlation in terms of major social classes;
whereas gradient stratification does not show the same
discrete distribution. (Wolfram and Fasold, 1974:79-81)

The gradient nonstandard features of Brazilian Portuguese
occur in the speech of every social group, in varying degrees,
irrespective of urban or rural background. Considering the
social dialects displayed along the continuum that ranges from
the extremely isolated Caipira varieties (placed at the left-
hand end) to the urban standard (placed at the right-hand end)
one will observe that the gradient variables show a progressive
decrease in frequency from left to right. In the vernacular of
the illiterate and isolated rural population some of these
features are almost categorical, whereas in the urban standard
they are stylistic markers that are likely to occur in colloquial registers only.

The sharp nonstandard features, on the other hand, are subject to much stigmatization, according to the publicly accepted
norms, and characterize the Caipira varieties *vis à vis* the
urban standard. They define, therefore, a sharp distinction between rural and urban speech.

The classification of the variable rules as sharp and gradient is not an easy task, however, considering the existence of
what we have labelled rurban varieties, that is, the language
spoken in metropolitan areas by lower-class illiterate speakers
with rural background, or in rural areas open to modernizing
influences.

An accurate classification would require extensive linguistic
surveys of the correlational type, i.e., in which the frequency
in the occurrence of the variables is correlated with sociodemographic indices (including social class), as well as information
on the degree of stigmatization associated with each variable.
Such studies are rarely available. Nevertheless an attempt is
made in chapter 3 to distinguish between sharp and gradient
phonological nonstandard features of the language. The classification is tentative and is based on qualitative and quantitative

analysis of the dataset of the present research as well as on information gathered from referred sources, two of which are briefly reported in the following paragraphs.

An investigation carried out among lower-class adult speakers in São Paulo (Head, 1981) revealed an interesting four-level pattern of social marking in their evaluation of several phonological variables. The highest degree of stigmatization was ascribed to three variables: the vocalization of $|\lambda|$ (see 3.2.3), the occurrence of $|r|$ instead of $|l|$ as a second member of a consonant cluster (see 3.2.3) and of retroflex $|\dot{r}|$ instead of the lateral $|l|$ or the back semivowel $|w|$ in syllable or word-final position (see 3.2).

The degree of stigmatization associated with loss of final $|s|$ (see 3.2.1.3) and realization of syllable-final or word-final $|r|$ as a retroflex was revealed to be 'medium to high'. A 'medium' stigmatization was associated with the reduction of the nasal diphthongs ($|\tilde{a}\tilde{w}| > |u|$ and $|\tilde{e}\tilde{j}| > |i|$) in verbal forms (see 3.2.1.2) and the assimilation of the $|d|$ in the sequence $|nd| > |nn| > |n|$ (see 3.2.5). Finally, the loss of morphemic -r in infinitive verbal forms was evaluated with a 'weak' stigmatization (see 3.2.1.3).

The second investigation was carried out at the University of Brasília (Bortoni-Ricardo, 1981) and was designed to examine the perceptual correlates of the internal constraints in the subject-verb agreement variable rule in Portuguese as postulated by Naro and Lemle (1976). In the formal standard language, subject-verb agreement is a categorical rule, but in nonstandard varieties the singular and the plural forms of the third person have merged at the expense of the latter (see 8.3). The experiment demonstrated that university students consistently perceive the lack of the third person plural inflection, but sixth-grade adult night school students do not. Moreover it was shown that the nonstandard variant of the agreement rule acquires different degrees of social import in different syntactic and morphological environments. The perception of the feature varies according to the frequency of the rule. As a conclusion it can be stated that the lack of subject-verb agreement is in some cases a gradient feature, but in those environments in which it is more perceptible - and less frequent - it is clearly a sharp feature.

The diversified repertoire range of Brazilian Portuguese is maintained as a consequence of the social cleavages which restrict the access of a considerable part of the population to the oral and written standard. The speakers of low prestige varieties, most of them illiterate, have limited access both to the actual standard and to the referentially acquired norms of prestige usage.

In a social setting where literacy is universal, the idealized standard, used as a frame of reference, may reach a high degree of uniformity in contrast to variation in actual spoken performance. The isomorphism of referential and social evaluation, which has been found in New York for instance (Labov, 1972a), seems to be implemented by the action of corrective agencies such as the schools and the media. In the case of an illiterate population, the function of the standard as a frame of reference is likely to be less systematic, since the speakers' access to the evaluative norms will vary according to their relationship network, degree of exposure to the mainstream culture, to the media etc. (Bortoni-Ricardo, 1981).

On the issue of a diversified repertoire range, it is instructive to note Fishman's observation:

> The result of such frequent and easy role shifts [in modern democratic speech communities] is often that the roles themselves become more similar and less distinctive or clear-cut. The same occurs in the verbal repertoire as speakers change from one variety (or language) to another with greater frequency and fluidity. The varieties too tend to become more similar as the roles in which they are appropriate become more or less alike. (Fishman, 1972:34)

In contrast to what takes place in more industrialized and more egalitarian societies, limited access to the standard code, due to illiteracy and social or geographic isolation in Brazil, tends towards the preservation of deep dialect differences if one compares the extremes of the continuum.

Thus far we have seen that the Brazilian speech community presents at least two traits of traditional societies, namely, a large repertoire range and limited access to the standard. But, unlike those societies with a marked verbal compartmentalization, in which status is based to a greater or less extent on ascription, it exhibits a relatively high degree of dialect permeability and fluidity among those individuals who are integrated in the mainstream culture.[3] The capacity of nonstandard speakers to move along the continuum is frequently parallel to their opportunities for social mobility.

The standard language in Brazil is clearly a class-related phenomenon, in the sense used by Giles and Powesland (1975) when they distinguished this category from the context-related standard. Whereas the latter is not necessarily associated with a societal segment and is appropriately selected in situations marked by formality, the former, defined as the variety which is used by the most prestigious social classes, is considered correct and appropriate irrespective of the context. In Brazilian Portuguese any morpho-syntactic feature that does not fall within the scope of the actually used standard is simply viewed as 'bad Portuguese'[4]. However, the degree of stigma associated with nonstandard features varies greatly even within the same grammatical rule, as was seen above in the case of subject-verb agreement.

Apart from typical rural or regional features which are highly stigmatized, such as the retroflex syllable-final or word-final $|\mathfrak{r}|$, a generally accepted standard pronunciation does not seem to exist, at least for phonological rules that do not intersect with the grammar. Although the Rio de Janeiro accent is rather prestigious in a large area of the country, there are, in addition, many regional standard pronunciations (Rodrigues, 1967) and, furthermore, European Portuguese accents lack prestige in Brazil.

Given the complexity of the situation, we shall use the term 'accents' in the present work to refer to the different regional pronunciations and the terms 'dialect' and 'variety' to indicate language variation that embodies morpho-syntactic and morphophonemic rules, as in the case of the Caipira dialect *vis à vis* the standard language.

2.2 *Historical background*

A brief historical survey of the colonization and urbanization processes in Brazil should provide a better understanding of the current sociolinguistic situation as well as help to explain the character of the standard variety as a class-related phenomenon.

Brazil was discovered by a Portuguese fleet in 1500 and colonization started soon afterwards with the establishment of a few villages on the coast. The language that prevailed in the colony until about the end of the seventeenth century was the so-called *língua geral* - a lingua franca developed among the Tupi Indian nations along the Atlantic shore and adopted by the colonizers, especially by the Jesuits engaged in christianizing the natives.

The main characteristic of this early period was the existenceof an unstable bilingualism, the prevailing *língua geral* co-existing with, on the one hand, the Portuguese of the administrative elite and the clergy and, on the other, the pidginized varieties of Portuguese spoken by the bilingual aborigines and the colonizers' descendants. A good written record of this pidginized Portuguese, collected in 1620, is provided by Silva Neto (1950/1977:34-5).

The pidginization process was accelerated by the arrival of slaves brought in from Africa with whom the Portuguese and their descendants and the christianized Indians lived in close contact in the villages and in rural areas. The slaves were classified according to whether they did or did not speak one of the Portuguese-based African pidgins and they did not constitute a linguistically homogeneous group. Moreover, as the slave trafic lasted for about three centuries, there was permanent interaction between first, second, third and other generations of slaves born in Brazil and those that had recently arrived from Africa. They formed a fast-growing segment of the population: in the sixteenth century there were about 100,000 Negro slaves in the colony; two centuries later their number had increased to 1,300,000 (Silva Neto, 1950/1977). Goulart (1975:272) points out that from the beginning of the colonization until 1851, when trafficking in slaves was definitely prohibited, the impressive number of 3,500,000 to 3,600,000 slaves were brought into Brazil.

As the number of speakers of pidginized Portuguese increased, the *língua geral* gradually receded and was finally displaced by the end of the third century of colonization. In some localities, however, especially in the Amazon Basin, it gave way to Portuguese only in the late nineteenth century (Wagley, 1971: 14). It is interesting to observe that the Tupi-based *língua geral* in Brazil has disappeared; whereas in Paraguay, Bolivia and Peru, Guarani, Quechua and Aymara have, respectively, been maintained in the repertoire of those communities in a situation close to that of a stable diglossic bilingualism. In fact, the *língua geral* could hardly be considered a symbol of ethnic cohesion for it was not the language of any specific group but rather a supra-ethnic code, not paralleled by any homogeneous culture. The very term 'Indian' was a supra-ethnic category imposed by the colonizer, and there was no one 'Indian' culture to act as a defence against the displacement of the many different aboriginal cultures. Contrary to what has happened in other Latin American countries where the indigenous population is large and belongs to recognized homogeneous ethnic groups, the Indians in Brazil were split into a number of culturally, linguistically and racially heterogeneous groups, which were either exterminated or pushed westwards. Those that remained merged with the non-Indian population, losing their identity. Freire (1936/ 1968:356-7) observes that among the *caboclos* (Indian descendants) at the beginning of the nineteenth century the main concern was to look 'white'. They had rejected the cultural traits of their elders and adopted the Portuguese language, religion and way of life. Vestiges of the *língua geral* are nowadays found in toponymics, anthroponymics and in a small number of lexical items borrowed by Brazilian Portuguese.

Throughout the eighteenth century, the so-called 'gold cycle' (the exploration of alluvial gold in the hinterland) and the 'cattle cycle' determined the gradual occupation of the interior of the country and brought about a considerable increase in Portuguese immigration. According to Elia (1975:303), the country's population in 1690 totalled no more than 300,000 people, but only one hundred years later, after the gold rush, it had reached three million and the Portuguese court was worried about the possible transference of a large proportion of the population of the country to the colony.

This increasing number of Portuguese speakers in Brazil increased the availability of the superstrate language among the pidginized Portuguese-speaking communities. This fact, together with the prestige of the elite's speech, seems to have contributed to halting the evolution of the pidginization process. Bickerton (1977:55) observes that in situations of contact that give rise to a pidgin, the difference between arriving at a pidgin and arriving at a standard language lies in the availability of target models and interaction with speakers of that target language. Ferguson and De Bose (1977), pointing to some preconditions for pidginization, accordingly claim that it is not likely to occur when there is a high ratio of target language speakers to non-native target language speakers.

This is probably what happened in Brazil. As the number of European Portuguese speakers increased and the settlers penetrated into the hinterland, forming what Silva Neto (1950/1977: 76) has called a 'mobile linguistic frontier', the pidginization process was inhibited. Even so, the descendants of these pidginized language speakers developed nonstandard varieties of Portuguese such as the Caipira dialect. Such dialects were preserved with much vitality in the hinterland areas beyond the reach of the standardizing influence of the few littoral cities which began to have an effect at the beginning of the last century. Dialects like that of Caipira retain the marks of the rephonologizing process of the earlier stages and have preserved archaic traits of Portuguese. Their inflectional systems have undergone much reduction, especially in the case of redundant patterns of opposition such as that of subject-verb concord and concord within the noun phrase.

The phenomenon of language standardization in Brazil is partially explained by the demographic factor mentioned above, i.e. the increase in Portuguese immigration, but it is also related to (1) Portugal's permanent policy of language institutionalization, (2) the social stratification of the colonial society and the consequent prestige of the elite, and (3) the trend towards urbanization.

In the first period of colonization, Portugal's acceptance of

the use of the *língua geral* was probably motivated by pragmatic
considerations, as the number of Portuguese citizens in Brazil
was very limited. But this policy did not last long and was
definitely abandoned in 1757 with the expulsion of the Jesuits
from Portugal and the colonial territory; after this date a
number of decrees and laws were published with the purpose of
institutionalizing the Portuguese language in the colony. To
take just one example, on 30 September 1770, the Prime Minister
Marquis de Pombal signed a charter that imposed a unique official normative grammar on both the kingdom and overseas schools
(Dourado, 1981). This was a reaction against the growing influence of the many grammatical simplifications and changes that
had taken place in the overseas dialects.

The concern with strict rules of grammar has indeed been a
characteristic of the small literate urban elite. The command of
the morpho-syntax of Metropolitan Portuguese has always conferred status among those groups eager to embrace European cultural
patterns and the European way of life. As Cunha (1977:13) points
out, such a feeling among the Brazilian elite was summarized in
the famous utterance: 'We do not go to Europe, we go back to
Europe.' Especially for the **mestizos**, **knowledge of the standard**
seemed to be a passport for social mobility.

The national literature reflects this cultural dependence. It
was not until a century after independence that Brazilian writ-
ers started to adopt syntactic variants that are typical of
Standard Brazilian Portuguese but which deviate from the rules
of European Portuguese (Lessa, 1966/1976).

Language standardization in Brazil is closely related to the
relatively recent trend towards urbanization. In 1808, harassed
by Napoleon Bonaparte's army, the Portuguese court fled to
Brazil, and Rio de Janeiro, an insalubrious town of 50,000 inhabitants, was made the capital of the kingdom. This fact represents a landmark in the country's urbanization history. In a few
years the city experienced a rapid development and **became a**
centre of diffusion for the standard language and for a cosmopolitan culture.

During the process of urbanization in Brazil - and the co-
occurring language standardization process - two periods must

be distinguished. The first period was not accompanied by any
industrialization and started with the social and political
changes that took place in Rio de Janeiro at the beginning of
the nineteenth century.[5] By 1822, when the country became independent from Portugal, the city of Rio de Janeiro already demonstrated the type of social stratification typical of urbanized
communities and its population had adopted the habits and customs of bourgeois societies. The trend did not reach São Paulo
until approximately thirty years later (Pereira de Queiroz,
1978). But it should be noted that in the case of both cities
the adoption of an urban mode of life, which produced in Brazil
a deep cleavage between the hinterland folk culture and the
emerging cosmopolitan littoral cities, antedated by several decades the development of industrialization in the country. The
industrialization process only began in the late 1940s and this
date is generally considered to mark the beginning of the second
period of urbanization.[6] In view of the above, Pereira de Queiroz (1978:57-61) explains that the lack of an industrial base
meant that during the nineteenth century and the beginning of
the twentieth century only a few cities developed a stratified
social system. In the smaller cities, especially in the poorer
regions, the uniformity and homogeneity of the urban and rural
modes of life were maintained. This sociologist observes, however, that the diffusion of the European bourgeois mode of life
in these wealthier capitals determined a transformation in city-
country relations. A gap emerged between the urban civilization,
directly influenced by European customs, and the traditional
rustic civilization. The cities took on a position of clear
superiority *vis à vis* the smaller cities, towns and countryside;
and their inhabitants, irrespective of social status, considered
themselves superior to the country strata. The city's sense of
superiority led to a growing rupture with the country, and this
was to be further increased with the development of industrialization, which caused a very fast population growth in some
cities.

Some hinterland areas were affected by modernization, but
many others could not follow the trend and have preserved their
traditional way of life. Hence, Pereira de Queiroz (1978:61)

concludes, 'the existence of two parallel societies in Brazil, co-occurring almost independently of each other. In each Brazilian region, these processes occur at different moments, in different places.'

Profound regional differences are indeed an important characteristic of present-day Brazil, but, despite that, industrialization has led to a major trend towards urbanization throughout the country in the last few decades. Such a trend can be defined as a complex of changes encompassing the entry of technology into the countryside, the mass exodus from rural areas, diffusion of the mass media, improvement of the means of transportation and the relative integration of village communities in national society.

Table 2.1 gives a clear picture of the urbanization trend in the country.

Table 2.1. *Growth of the total population and urban population in Brazil*

Year	Total population	Urban population	% of urban population
1872	9,930,478	582,749	5.9
1890	14,333,915	976,038	6.8
1900	17,438,434	1,644,149	9.4
1920	30,635,605	3,287,448	10.7
1940	41,236,315	12,880,182	31.24
1950	51,944,397	18,782,891	36.16
1960	70,967,185	31,990,938	45.08
1970	93,204,379	50,600,000	56.00
1980	119,098,992	80,478,602	67.60

Source: IBGE: Instituto Brasileiro de Estatística

According to the 1970 census, one third of the country's population was not living in its birthplace (Oliven, 1982); and it has been estimated that the percentage of population growth in urban areas due to rural migration in the period 1960-70 was about 42 per cent (Costa, 1975).

In analysing the urbanization trend it is also instructive to examine statistics of the evolution of literacy in Brazil. Access to literacy is, of course, an important factor both in the process of social mobility and in acquisition of the standard language variety. Table 2.2 shows the evolution of literacy in Brazil from 1940 to 1980.

According to these statistics, approximately one in four Brazilians between the ages of 15 and 70 years is illiterate. Yet it should be noted that these statistics do not include the population below 15 years, a considerable proportion of whom either did not go to school or left before learning to read and write. Moreover, the data do not include those people who, though they were actually registered in school and claimed to be literate, never reached a level of functional literacy. For these reasons it is very likely that the number of functional illiterates is much higher than the official figures show.

Table 2.2. *Evolution of literacy in Brazil*

Year	Population over 15 years of age	Illiterates over 15 years of age	%
1940	23,639,769	13,279,899	56
1950	30,249,423	15,272,432	50
1960	40,187,590	15,815,903	39
1970	54,336,606	17,936,887	33
1980	74,495,000	19,352,000	26

Source: IBGE

2.3 The Caipira culture

In a narrow sense Caipira denotes the rural population of the hinterland of São Paulo. According to Cândido (1964:8), Caipira refers to the 'universe of the rustic culture of São Paulo' and identifies a way of life, never a racial type. At present the term, which has a Tupi etymology: *curupira*, is not restricted to the area of *Paulista* historical influence[7], but refers to the rural and traditional population of Brazil in general. As an adjective, the word is used to describe the isolated and backward way of life of the rural dwellers as opposed to the urban way of life.

During the sixteenth, seventeenth and eighteenth centuries the inhabitants of the coastal settlements of São Paulo were engaged in a movement of land exploration westwards, in the enslavement of Indians or in the search for gold. The main result of this movement was a considerable expansion of the

colony's territory as well as the development of certain types
of culture and social life, the Caipira culture, in great part
as the result of the mobility of those colonizers. Cândido
(1964) explains: 'the social life of the Caipiras assimilated and
preserved the elements conditioned by their nomadic origins. The
combination of the indigenous and Portuguese cultural traits
followed the wandering rhythm of the settlers, and preserved the
characteristics of an essentially hunter-gatherer economy, the
unstable structure of which depended on the mobility of the
individuals and the groups' (Cândido, 1964:20; translated from
Portuguese).

Their economy was based on subsistence agriculture and, as
there was no well-established system of land ownership in most
areas, the Caipiras maintained the habit of geographic mobility
as they searched for fertile unexploited soil. This permanent
demographic movement spread the Caipira culture with local var-
iations to the states of Minas Gerais - especially to the southern and western areas - and of Goiás and Mato Grosso.

The main feature of this culture was its segregation from
urban influence, a cultural isolation which established and
maintained social forms based on the closed subsistence economy
and on practices of mutual solidarity. The Caipira population
was scattered over a large territory either living in huts,
located far away from each other, or in small settlements.[8]
Whether they lived close together or far apart, however, the
families of a community were linked by the feeling of common
territoriality, by the ethics of solidarity, mainly manifested
in the neighbours' participation in agricultural tasks, and by
traditional religious and leisure activities. All this represented the fundamental structure of Caipira sociability (Cândido, 1964, especially chapter 4).

The trends towards urbanization and industrialization, discussed in the previous section, have deeply affected the cultural isolation of the Caipiras. Firstly, the introduction of
manufactured goods into the countryside has changed the pattern
of the population's minimal consumption needs and its closed
economy has had to be gradually integrated into the regional or
general economy through increasing trade relations.

Secondly, socio-ecological factors have had an influence. The growth of the population and the institutionalization of the land ownership system has led to a more sedentary life (since there are now no more easily available fertile lands), to the development of an agriculture to cater to the city dwellers and, consequently, to a stronger dependence on the urban hegemony. In view of this new state of affairs the rural population has been forced into some sort of adjustment or has had to opt for migration to one of the urban centres.

Oliven (1982:67-9) indicates four main processes that have fostered the rural-urban migration. The first is the penetration of capitalism into the rural economy, the result of which was the proletarianization of the poorer workers who were driven to the cities. The second is the introduction of sanitary improvements, resulting in a decrease in mortality rates and a consequent increase in population which is not absorbed in its place of origin. The third is the expansion of agricultural frontiers with the colonization of western areas formerly inhabited only by the Indians. And finally there is the attraction that the urban way of life has for the rural population, with the expectation of better life conditions: a phenomenon brought about by the spread of the mass media to the rural areas.

The linguistic consequences of the changes in urban-rural relations will be dealt with in chapter 5 with emphasis upon the process of migration and the consequent urbanization of the migrants' Caipira dialect. For the moment it should be recognized that the Caipira dialect is gradually merging with non-standard urban varieties, in a process embedded in a larger matrix of social changes, at the expense of the loss of many typical features. Amaral (1920/1976), the first dialectologist to describe the Caipira dialect, provides a definitive assessment of the phenomenon:

> At the time when there were no great differences between the Caipira and other varieties, *caipirismo* existed not only in the language, but in all manifestations of our provincial life. A few decades later everything began to change. The replacement of the slave arm by paid manpower removed a great part of the black population from daily contact with the whites, modifying thereby one of the factors of our dialectal differentiation. The genuine Caipiras, the

ignorant and backward countrymen, began to be pushed aside, to be thrown to the margins of collective life, to have an increasingly smaller influence on the customs and on the organization of the new order of things. The population grew and mingled with new elements. Means of communication were developed everywhere, trade increased, the small communities that had lived in isolation started to develop different types of relationships among themselves and the province came into permanent contact with external civilization. Education, which had been very limited, was enormously expanded. It was impossible for the Caipira dialect not to suffer from so profound a change in the social milieu. (Amaral, 1920/1976:41-2; translated from Portuguese)

Notes

1 Their situation of bilingualism is unstable because in the process of acculturation the Indians are likely to lose their mother tongue and adopt Portuguese. Fishman (1972:102) observes that in the circumstances of an unstable maintenance of bilingualism, one variety will displace the other over a period of time. The mainstream language will ultimately replace the language of home and neighbourhood.
2 Wolfram and Fasold (1974) used the terms 'sharp' and 'gradient' stratification in a way similar to the terms 'sharp' and 'fine' stratification coined by Labov (1966) in his The Social Stratification of English in New York City.
3 The issue of integration in the mainstream is a rather complex topic which will be tackled in chapter 5.
4 It is not easy to define what 'the actually used standard Portuguese' is. There is indeed a wide gap between the language taught in school and described in the normative grammars and the language spoken by the educated groups. Since 1969 an extensive survey has been carried out in several major cities with the purpose of recording and analysing the oral language of adults with college education (Cunha, 1985). So far only partial results are available.
   Despite the lack of systematic empirical evidence, the language, without any doubt, performs its function of 'frame of reference' (Garvin, 1959), that is, educated speakers have criteria to evaluate the 'correctness' of the language. Access to this ideal standard, which functions as a frame of reference, varies considerably, as was explained above, according to social and educational parameters.
5 Pereira de Queiroz (1978:60) has convincingly argued that this phenomenon should not be considered a real urbanization - which is intimately related to industrialization - but rather as the cultural diffusion of a western bourgeois mode of life that is eminently urban. The adoption of such external models, however, is conditioned by the availability of economic resources. In Brazil these resources came mostly from the development of agriculture and only those regions economically privileged, e.g. São Paulo, could afford it.
6 Southall's (1973:89) distinction between economic and social

industrialization is very useful for a closer understanding of the phenomenon:

> It is necessary to distinguish economic industrialization from social industrialization, and, of course, varying degrees of either. A city which is economically industrialized is one whose prime function is industrial. A city which is socially industrialized is one whose prime function is not industrial, but whose whole fabric and population presupposes and depends upon the technology and products of industrialization brought to it from elsewhere. While in the West industrialization was first economic and later social, in the rest of the world it was usually the other way round. (Southall, 1973:89)

7 *Paulista* is the toponymic of the State of São Paulo.
8 The Caipira culture is being discussed from a historical perspective. Yet it should be borne in mind that, although in many regions of the country there have been profound changes in these conditions, the description still holds for other regions.

3.0 *Introduction*

The purpose of this chapter is to discuss phonological aspects
of the Caipira dialect. A brief description of the Standard Brazilian Portuguese segmental phonology, and a few remarks about
the phonology of European Portuguese concerning some aspects
that differ from the pronunciation in Brazil are provided in the
first section as a frame of reference for the description of the
Caipira dialect in the second section.

Most of the studies that deal with the subject are based upon
the language as it is spoken in Rio de Janeiro. The present description is based upon the dataset collected in Brazlândia. In
the case of the many phonological and morphophonemic variable
rules which occur in the data, only the standard variant of each
variable was considered for the purpose of this description. The
nonstandard variants - some of which are specific features of
the Caipira dialect - will be discussed in section 3.2.

It is worthwhile noticing that in the case of Portuguese, in
contrast with most other European languages, 'there is no generally accepted phonetic standard to which one might refer' (Almeida, 1976:349). This assertion holds not only when one compares the standard variety of Metropolitan Portuguese with overseas standard varieties, but also when one compares different
accents within the scope of the Brazilian territory. The Rio de
Janeiro accent is rather prestigious in a large area of the
country and has been recommended as the preferred pronunciation
for the lyrical chant and the theatre. This recommendation is
not necessarily followed and indeed there are many regional
standard pronunciations in the several regional zones of influence throughout the country (Rodrigues, 1967).

The first description of Brazilian Portuguese phonology
according to the principles of modern linguistics was provided
by Mattoso Câmara in 1953. His work, with minor changes in sub-
sequent works (1970, 1975), has been seminal to all phonological
descriptions put forward since then. The description of the segmental phonology of Standard Brazilian Portuguese, included in
this chapter to be used as a frame of reference for the description of the Caipira dialect, is mainly based on Mattoso Câmara
and therefore follows an essentially structuralist model. It
should be noted also that all Portuguese examples are given in
broad phonetic transcription and, unless otherwise indicated,
different members of one phoneme are represented by the same
letter.[1]

3.1 *The phonology of Standard Brazilian Portuguese*
In contrast to European Portuguese, Brazilian varieties are
spoken with a relatively slower rhythm which has been analysed
as the preservation of an archaic feature of the language in
Portugal (Melo, 1971). An early grammarian of the sixteenth
century, Fernão de Oliveira, describing the pronunciation of the
language spoken at the Portuguese court stated: 'Mas nós falamos
com grande repouso como homens assentados' |'But we speak with
great repose as tranquil men'| (Fernão de Oliveira, 1536/1975:
39). It was probably in the seventeenth and eighteenth centuries
that the language in Portugal started to acquire a rhythm in
allegro with relevance to the stressed syllables (Silva Neto,
1950/1977:148; Mattoso Câmara, 1975:32). Naro (1971) points out
that the Portuguese language had probably undergone a series of
profound sound changes between the last quarter of the seventeenth century and the first quarter of the eighteenth century.
His conclusion is in accord with Franco de Sá's (1915) claim
that several phonetic changes, including deletion of pretonic
|e|, took place in European Portuguese in the first quarter of
the eighteenth century.[2]

   In terms of the taxonomy put forward by Pike (1945), European
Portuguese seems to be evolving from a syllable-timed rhythm
towards a stress-timed rhythm, with prominence of consonants at
the expense of the quality of unstressed vowels.[3] According to

Pike (1945:34), in stress-timed languages the sentences are
naturally divided into rhythm units beginning with a stressed
syllable and including any number of unstressed syllables. These
units recur at regular bursts of speed, irrespective of the number of syllables they embody. Consequently the syllables of
longer units are crushed together.

Brazilian Portuguese, on the other hand, when compared to the
European varieties, seems to be farther from the stress-timed
type, and consequently closer to the syllable-timed type.[4] In
the latter case, Pike explains, the syllables are pronounced at
more-or-less evenly recurring intervals and, as a result,
phrases with extra syllables take proportionately more time, and
syllables or vowels are less likely to be shortened and modi-
fied (1945:34).

Vowel modification and reduction which are consequences of
the syllable crushing tendency in stress-timed languages are
productive phonological processes in European Portuguese. An
extremely accurate phonetic description of such a variety was
provided by Viana (1883/1973). Even though no phonological
criteria were used, the author distinguished between 'full
vowels' ('voyelles pleines') and 'reduced vowels' ('voyelles
réduites'), which are indeed positionally conditioned variants
of the former, in unstressed syllables. The vowel system was
thus described by Viana (1883/1973:108):

'Voyelles pleines'	a		e	e		i		o	o	u
'Voyelles réduites'	a̤			e̤(i)		i̤(e)				u̦

a̤ was described as similar to the initial sound of the English
word <u>about</u>. It occurs in pretonic and in final unstressed syllables.[5] e̤ occurs in pretonic and in final unstressed syllables.
In the former position it neutralizes with i̤ in certain environments, but very often is simply deleted.[6] u̦ occurs in unstressed syllables.

Vocalic reduction and neutralization of this sort are not as
productive in the language in Brazil as in European Portuguese.
Vowel reduction does occur, however, affecting the four-level
opposition of vowel height. The reduction $|e| > |ə| > |\phi|$ does
not obtain. In other words, the reduction processes in Portugal

consist of narrowing and centralizing rules, whereas in Brazil
the narrowing rules are more productive.

3.1.1 *The vowels*
There are seven oral syllabic vowels in stressed position (figure 3.1), characterized by two oppositions: (1) front and back
articulation, and (2) low, medium grade 1, medium grade 2 and
high elevation of the tongue.

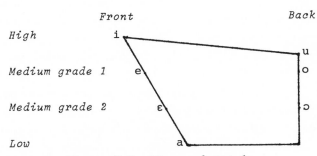

Figure 3.1 *Stressed vowels*

This system undergoes a process of neutralization in unstressed syllables. The opposition between medium grade 1 and 2
disappears in pretonic and in non-final unstressed syllables
(figure 3.2). In final unstressed syllables the system is reduced to three phonemes with the neutralization of the front
vowels, pronounced |i|, and of the back vowels, pronounced |u|,
and the central vowel pronounced |ɐ| (figure 3.3).

Except for |ɛ| and |ɔ| all the stressed vowels have nasalized
allophones whenever they are followed by a nasal consonant in a
contiguous syllable.

The high vowels |i| and |u| have non-syllabic allophones that
will be represented by |j| and |w|, respectively.

The final unstressed vowels are sometimes devoiced when they
follow a voiceless consonant.

There are five nasal vowels in the language which, with the
exception of |e|, which does not occur in final unstressed syl-
lables, all occur in stressed and unstressed position (figure
3.4).

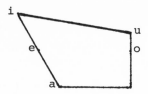

Figure 3.2   *Vowels in pretonic syllables*

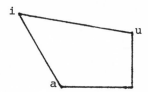

Figure 3.3   *Vowels in final unstressed syllables*

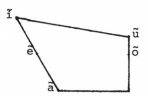

Figure 3.4   *Nasal vowels*

These nasal vowels have phonemic status and must be kept distinct from the nasalized allophones of the oral vowels. In the
latter the degree of nasalization varies and it is conditioned
by a nasal consonant in the following syllable (Mattoso Câmara,
1953/1977:70).

The process of vowel neutralization in unstressed syllables
is indeed more complex than Mattoso Câmara's analysis seems to
suggest. Unstressed vowels, in pretonic position especially,
seem to be undergoing a process of change, probably related to
earlier stages of the language.

The evolutionary course of final unstressed vowels in Brazilian Portuguese is probably further advanced than that of the
pretonic vowels. In modern European Portuguese the vocalic sys-
tem is reduced to |ə|, |α| and |u| in final unstressed sylla-
bles. In Brazil, as was described above, it is reduced to |i|,
|ɐ| and |u| in most varieties. Some regional varieties still

keep final |e| and |o|. By the time Amaral (1920/1976) described
the Caipira dialect in São Paulo, the occurrence of these vowels
was registered. A more recent survey of the same dialect (A.N.
Rodrigues, 1974) has shown that the phenomenon persists, but not
categorically.

The tendency of modern Brazilian Portuguese to raise final
vowels has been interpreted as the preservation of a sixteenth
century feature of European Portuguese (Carvalho, 1969; Melo,
1971) but the issue is not generally agreed upon.[7]

Several linguists have investigated the vocalism of old and
modern Portuguese but the subject is controversial, mainly because their interpretation is based upon scarce evidence from
orthographic transcriptions and comparison with contemporary
similar phenomena.

Herculano de Carvalho (1969), in accord with Hart (1955),
states that the realization of final unstressed |e| and |o| was
|i| and |u|, respectively, in sixteenth century Portuguese. Naro
(1971) challenges this interpretation and argues on the basis of
a voluminous set of orthographic and comparative data that six-
teenth-century Portuguese had raised variants of |e| and |o| in
final position, which, however, were not realized as high as
present-day Portuguese |i| and |u|. According to his analysis,
by the middle of the eighteenth century the raised variants |ę|
and |ǫ| had already evolved to |i| and |u| in the common lan-
guage. By the end of that century these pronunciations were
common in received speech. At the beginning of the nineteenth
century the present **pronunciations** |ə| and |u| were consolidated.
According to Révah (1958), final |e| was realized as |e| until
the end of the eighteenth century, when the present pronuncia-
tion |ə| developed, but this author admits that the change |o| >
|u| is an earlier phenomenon which started in the fifteenth
century.

In summary, the present realization of final unstressed
vowels in Brazil is viewed by some researchers as the conserva-
tion of an archaic feature of European Portuguese, and by others
as an independently developed phenomenon. Among the latter
group, Naro (1971:637) claims that the process has an acoustic-
articulatory teleology and must have occurred independently in

Brazil, Portugal and other lusophone regions. According to
Naro, the origin of vowel raising in word-end position is to be
found in 'phenomena characteristic of pre-pause position - namely, the typical decrease in the average energy content of the
acoustic waves which constitute the stream of speech after the
final stressed syllable of a normal declarative utterance. Since
narrower vowels are in general less intense than wider vowels,
raising is a natural consequence of decrease in energy.'

The analysis of pretonic vowels is even more controversial.
As was mentioned earlier, in modern European Portuguese the back
vowels are consistently pronounced |u|, whereas the front vowels
merge in an |ə| which fluctuates with |i| in some environments
and in others is simply deleted. The weakening rule affecting
the front vowels (e > ə > φ) has never reached the language in
Brazil, but the raising rule does not apply categorically, and
in fact, pretonic vowels are the *locus* of much variation. Pre-
tonic |e| and |o| in most varieties vary with |i| and |u|, re-
spectively. In some varieties the vowels |ɛ| and |ɔ| also occur
in this position.

When the language started to be exported to Brazil, in the
mid-sixteenth century, the raising of final unstressed vowels was
further developed than that of the pretonic vowels. In the former
case, raising seems to be a phenomenon of pre-pause position and
has nowadays probably completed its evolutionary course both in
Portugal and in Brazil, with slightly different end-products. As
for the pretonic vowels, the process seems to have been slowed
down in Brazil, whereas in Portugal it was probably fostered by
the tendency towards a stress-timed rhythm.

Several factors may have contributed to slow down the process
of pretonic vowel raising in Brazil. Firstly, it is a well-known
linguistic fact that the transference of a language from one
place to another slows the drift down. Transplanted languages
are then likely to be conservative. In this specific case, the
phenomenon can be easily understood. The Portuguese came from all
regions of the country, including the islands. It should be noticed also that colonization took place during a period of three
centuries. Considering that the pretonic vowel raising rule must
have started at a certain time, at a certain place, in the midst of

certain social groups, it follows that the rule was at different
stages of evolution in the repertoire of the successive groups
of settlers who came to the colony. Once in Brazil, these Portuguese with varied dialectal backgrounds lived in contact with
Portuguese based pidgin speakers and the aborigines. Such a
situation favoured the merger of Metropolitan dialect features
at the expense of many innovations.

Secondly, an opposite trend of pretonic vowel lowering has
started in the northeastern region of the country (Silva Neto,
1950/1977; Melo, 1971). The area where this rule is productive
has not yet been well delimited, but it includes all the northeastern states and the north of Minas Gerais (Houaiss, 1958),
with some local differences.[8] The rule of vowel lowering and
lengthening ($|e| > |\varepsilon|$, $|o| > |\mathfrak{o}|$, $|a| > |a{:}|$) has not been
fully studied, but it seems to be constrained by a complex set
of phonetic conditioning factors, since the rule has not simply
replaced the raising rule but, instead, co-occurs with it. It is
indeed an important isogloss that separates the northeastern
accents from the more prestigious central and southern accents.

For Herculano de Carvalho (1969:96-7) the preservation of mid
vowels in pretonic position in Brazilian and creole varieties
ought to be considered as the most faithful reflex of the older
Portuguese pronunciation. According to him, the raising rule
which took place in the sixteenth century in Portugal is comparable to the current process affecting pretonic vowels in the
present-day Brazilian situation.

Révah (1958) considers the pretonic vowels as the point of
essential differentiation between the Portuguese and the Bra-
zilian pronunciations. As regards the pretonic $|e|$ in the lat-
ter, the author admits that it corresponds to the sixteenth-
century pronunciation in Portugal, but he interprets the occurrence of both mid vowels in the Brazilian pronunciation as the
result of a learned restoration due to orthographic influence.

Naro (1971) explains the raising of pretonic vowels in Portugal as a consequence of two processes, namely, generalization
to mirror-image form of the raised final vowels, beginning in
the mid-eighteenth century, and the confusion of several layers
of prefixes. The mirror-image convention (Naro, 1971:638) ac-

counts for the raising of mid vowels, formerly restricted to final position only as a result of decrease of energy, on both
sides of the stress within the word. This rule was fostered by
the confusion or contamination of the normal development in- >
en- with the erudite in-, and of eis- or es- derived from ex-
with ens- derived from ins-. The result was the alternation of
en- ∿ in- and of es- ∿ ens- ∿ ins- ∿ is- in initial position.

Another source of alternation, according to Naro, was the
prosthetic vowels |e| ∿ |i| added to the initial cluster of |s|
plus consonant.

The traditional philological literature in Brazil has regarded the raising of pretonic vowels as a consequence of a rule
of vowel harmony, i.e. the pretonic vowel is assimilated to the
following high stressed vowel (Sousa da Silveira, 1923/1964:281;
Silva Neto, 1950/1977:53-4).[9] The examples adduced in the literature are of the following types:[10]

(i) |e| - |i| : |i| - |i|
       |fe'lis| : |fi'lis| feliz   (happy)
       |pe'rigu| : |pi'rigu| perigo   (danger)

(ii) |e| - |u| : |i| - |u|
       |se'guru| : |si'guru| seguro   (safe)
       |ve'ludu| : |vi'ludu| veludo   (velvet)

(iii) |o| - |i| : |u| - |i|
       |kor'tśina| : |kur'tśina| cortina   (curtain)
       |mo'rĭga| : |mu'rĭga| moringa   (water-pot)

(iv) |o| - |u| : |u| - |u|
       |for'tuna| : |fur'tuna| fortuna   (fortune)
       |gor'dura| : |gur'dura| gordura   (fat)

The hypothesis of vowel harmony does not account, however,
for the frequent cases in which the raised pretonic vowel turns
out to be more distinct phonetically from the stressed vowel.
Examples of these are:

(v) |so'fa| : |su'fa| sofá   (sofa)
       |bo'neka| : |bu'neka| boneca (doll)
       |me'λɔr| : |mi'λɔr| melhor (better)

In view of such cases, Abaurre-Gnerre (1981:37) suggests that the phenomenon of vowel raising ought to be interpreted as a process of articulatory teleology that makes the segments more similar to each other, by decreasing the articulatory difference between the vowels and the adjacent consonants.

For Houaiss (1958) the variation of pretonic vowels is conditioned by three factors: vowel harmony, morphological regularization and a conscious restoration due to the influence of orthography. He observes that pretonic vowels are likely to be raised in words in popular use and to remain unchanged in uncommon words. Moreover, speakers tend to use the raised variants in informal styles and to 'correct' the pronunciation in formal styles. The mid vowels |e| and |o| are regarded as more acceptable and correct than |i| and |u|, respectively, in pretonic position.

Houaiss also emphasizes the role of morphological influence in the rule. As had already been pointed out by earlier philologists (Sousa da Silveira, 1923/1964; Silva Neto, 1950/1977), the pretonic vowels in derived words tend to remain phonetically close to the stressed vowel of the base with which they are paradigmatically associated, and are, therefore, less liable to be raised as indicated in (vi). Carvalho (1969:96) refers to the phenomenon as 'an etymological consciousness of the derivation'.

(vi)	Base		Derived words		
|'sɔrtʂi|	sorte	(luck)	|sor'tudu|	and not	|sur'tudu|
			sortudo	(lucky)	
|'korpu|	corpo	(body)	|kor'piñu|	and not	|kur'piñu|
			corpinho	(small body)	
|'foλa|	folha	(leaf)	|fo'λiña|	and not	|fu'λiña|
			folhinha	(small leaf)	

In verbal forms, however, the influence of paradigmatically related forms does not seem to be as relevant, as is shown in (vii):

(vii)	|xese'ber|	receber (to receive)	|xisi'bia|	recebia (received)
	|po'der|	poder (can)	|pu'dʑia|	podia (could)
	|vẽ'ser|	vencer (to win)	|vĩ'sia|	vencia (won)

The aforementioned hypotheses were partially or completely confirmed in a quantitative analysis of the pretonic vowel variable rule carried out by Bisol (1981). The study concerned the fluctuation of these vowels in four different sociolinguistic groups in southern Brazil. The author argues that until the middle of the eighteenth century there occurred two vowels in pretonic position both in the front and in the back series in European Portuguese. The high and mid vowels would merge only in specific contexts. The results of the research also support the hypothesis that variation of pretonic vowels is a natural rule of the language that originated in Latin in the fourth century AD. Moreover, the similarities between the rule in the cinquentist language and in contemporary Brazilian Portuguese allow for the conclusion that the same contextual factors that conditioned the rule in the past are operating presently. The rule has in fact maintained the same characteristics.

According to Bisol, the process of pretonic vowel variation, known as vowel harmony, is a phenomenon of regressive assimilation conditioned by multiple factors, the most powerful of which is the presence of a high vowel in the following syllable. The rule affects, in particular, those vowels that remain unstressed throughout the derivational process. As **regards** pretonic $|e|$, factors favouring the rule application are the occurrence of the homorganic high vowel $|i|$ in the following syllable (the nonhomorganic $|u|$ has a weaker influence), a preceding velar consonant and a following palatal consonant.[11] A preceding alveolar consonant and a contiguous labial consonant inhibit the rule. In the case of pretonic $|o|$, both high vowels ($|i|$ and $|u|$) in the following syllable favour equally the rule application. The favourable consonantal environments are a contiguous alveolar segment and a preceding palatal segment. The nasality of the stressed vowel favours the raising of $|e|$ and inhibits the raising of $|u|$ for acoustic reasons (for details see Bisol, 1981:89 *passim*).

The study has also shown that constraints affecting narrowing of initial $|\tilde{e}|$ or $|es|$ are different from those affecting the internal vowel. In the former case the frequency of the rule application was 90 per cent whereas in the latter it did not exceed 30 per cent. As mentioned above, the narrowing of initial |es| and |ẽ| may have resulted from the contamination of several layers of prefixes, which occurred from the earliest times of the language through the mid-seventeenth century (Naro, 1971). The following are examples of the case:

(viii) |es'kɔla| : |is'kɔla| escola   (school)

|es'mɔla| : |is'mɔla| esmola   (alms)

|es'tomagu| : |is'tomagu| estômago   (stomach)

|es'tadu| : |is'tadu| estado   (state)

|ẽ'kargu| : |ĩ'kargu| encargo   (charge)

|ẽ'šētši| : |ĩ'šētši| enchente   (flood)

|ẽ'kõtru| : |ĩ'kõtru| encontro   (meeting)

Bisol's study has not found any definite social significance associated with the mid and high variants of the variable, but recognizes that an assessment of subjective reactions towards the variable, which was not included in the study, would possibly shed light on the issue (1981:86). It has been pointed out by several grammarians (Houaiss, 1958; Révah, 1958) that the mid vowels |e| and |o| are regarded as more correct than the high variants |i| and |u|. What seems to be happening is an irregular correction of the changed form in the sense used by Labov (1972a:179), which 'recovers' the mid vowels in careful styles. The phenomenon is also the source of hypercorrection that changes initial |i| and |u| into |e| and |o|, respectively, as in the following examples:

(ix) |privi'lɛžju| : |previ'lɛžju| privilégio (privilege)

|u'rina| : |o'rina| urina   (urine)

Finally, another important aspect of the variable rule which remains unresolved concerns its evolutionary trend. Is there a drift towards consolidation of the high variants, as has already happened in Portugal? Bisol cautiously suggests, when she compares the data from two age groups, that in the dialect surveyed the raising rule of pretonic vowels may be following a regressive course. But empirical evidence is still very scarce and does not allow for broad generalizations. At most, the available studies lead to the hypothesis that whereas the rule has completed its evolutionary course in Portugal, in Brazil it seems to be a feature in the process of change.

3.1.2 *The consonants*

There are 19 consonant phonemes in Portuguese, as shown in figure 3.5.

	Stops	Fricatives	Liquids Lateral Flap		Nasals
Bilabial	p b				m
Labiodental		f v			
Dental	t d				
Alveolar		s z	l	r	n
Alveopalatal		š ž	λ		ñ
Velar	k g	x			

Figure 3.5 *The consonants*

In order to analyse briefly the positionally conditioned and free variants of consonants, the distribution of the phonemes in the syllable will be taken into account. The basic syllabic patterns in the language can be summarized by the following formula:

$$(C_1) \quad (C_2) \quad V \quad (C_3) \quad (C_4)$$

in which C = Consonant, V = Vowel and the parentheses indicate that the element may occur or not. In the following paragraphs, each syllabic pattern is briefly analysed.

a. $C_1 \, V$

Every consonant can occur in position C_1 in this syllable type, except for the alveolar flap |r| which does not occur in word-initial position.

The dental stops |t| and |d| have alveopalatal affricate variants whenever they occur preceding |i|:

(i) |t| ∿ |tš| |'tšipu| tipo   (type)
      |d| ∿ |dž| |'džia| dia   (day)

The alveopalatal lateral |λ| is very often pronounced as a sequence |lj| in any phonetic environment:

(ii) |'oλu| : |'olju| olho   (eye)
       |žu'eλu| : |žu'elju| joelho (knee)

|ka'oλa| : |ka'olja| caolha (cross-eyed, fem.)

The alveopalatal |ñ| has a variant |ʝ| which occurs following
|i|:

(iii) |ka'riñu| : |ka'rĩʝu| carinho (affection)

The variant |ʝ| seems to be spreading to other phonetic
environments:

(iv) |'bãñu| : |'bãʝu| banho (bath)

The velar fricative |x| varies freely with a glottal fricative
|h| and with a multiple uvular vibrant |r̃|.

(v) |'xatu| ∿ |'hatu| ∿ |'r̃atu| rato (mouse, rat)

b. $C_1 C_2$ V

The consonant cluster in this syllable type is formed by a
stop or a slit fricative in position C_1 (|p|, |b|, |t|, |k|,
|g|, |f|, |v|) followed by an alveolar liquid (|r|, |l|) in po-
sition C_2.

c. (C_1) (C_2) V C_3

The liquids |r| and |l| and the alveolar fricatives |s| and
|z| are the only consonants that occur in position C_3. The non-
syllabic vowels |j| and |w| also occur in this position forming
the diphthongs (see 3.1.3).

The alveolar lateral |l| in position C_3 merges with |w|, but
it can also be velarized |ɫ|

(vi) |bra'zil| : |bra'ziw| ∿ |bra'ziɫ| Brasil (Brazil)

In position C_3 the liquid |r| has several variants, namely the
alveopalatal flap |r|, the retroflex |ɽ|, the multiple vibrant
|r̃|, the velar fricative |x| and the glottal fricative |h|. Very
often it is deleted in informal styles and in non-standard
varieties (see 3.2.1.3). It is therefore convenient to refer to
the sound as the archiphoneme |R| (Mattoso Câmara, 1970).

The voiceless alveolar fricative |s| occurs before pauses and
voiceless consonants. The voiced alveolar fricative |z| occurs
before vowels and voiced consonants. Here again a sibilant
archiphoneme |S|, which is assimilated in voicing to the fol-
lowing segment, is considered.

After the nasal vowels and the nasalized allophones of the oral vowels there occur consonantal segments, considered as allophones of the nasal consonants. According to Almeida (1976: 350-1) they are 'a prolonged nasalized closing phase of the following plosives and are consequently homorganic with them'.

d. (C_1) (C_2) V C_3 C_4

This syllable type is very rare in the language. The only possible sequence is with the liquid $|r|$ in position C_3 and the archiphoneme $|s|$ in position C_4.

Figure 3.6 summarizes the distribution of the consonant phonemes in the syllable structure.

Syllable structure = (C_1) (C_2) V (C_3) (C_4)

C_1 = *All consonants except* $|r|$

$C_1 C_2$ = *Stop*   + *Alveolar liquid*
            Labial fricative

C_3 = *Alveolar fricative*
            Alveolar liquid

C_4 = $|s|$ / v $|r|$ ___

Figure 3.6 *The distribution of consonant
phonemes in the syllable*

3.1.3 Diphthongs

A diphthong is a sequence of two vowels pronounced within the same syllable (Mattoso Câmara, 1956/1978:101). **Diphthongs are** commonly classified as falling diphthongs and rising diphthongs.

A falling diphthong will be defined as starting with a base vowel which will be stressed if the syllable is stressed, followed by a non-syllabic vowel (or semi-vowel) necessarily unstressed. A rising diphthong, on the other hand, starts with the non-syllabic necessarily unstressed vowel followed by the syllabic base which will be stressed if the syllable is stressed.

There are eleven falling oral diphthongs in Portuguese formed
with the non-syllabic allophones of the high vowels: |aj|, |aw|,
|ɛj|, |ɛw|, |ej|, |ew|, |ɔj|, |oj|, |ow|, |uj| and |iw|. As a
result of the final |ʎ| and |w| merger, one more diphthong,
|ɔw|, can be added to this inventory. It occurs in words like
|sɔʎ| : |sɔw|, *sol* (sun).

There are five falling nasal diphthongs, namely: |ãj|, |õj|,
|ãw̃|, |ũj̃| and |ẽj̃|.

The traditional literature in Brazil (Mattoso Câmara, 1956/
1978; Said Ali, 1964) classifies as rising diphthongs only those
formed by |w| following the velar stops |k| and |g|. But there
are indeed other occurrences of rising diphthongs that result
from a process of synaeresis, i.e., the pronunciation in one
syllable of two contiguous vowels that can also be pronounced in
two separate syllables. The choice between the two pronunciations is governed by a variable rule in which the formality of
the style, and consequently the speed of speech, is a relevant
factor.

The synaeresis can operate either on sequences of vowels
within the word (e.g. *piedade* (piety); *suave* (suave)) or in
word-final sequences (e.g. *glória* (glory); *série* (series); *cópia*
(copy)). In the latter case the resulting diphthongs are undergoing, both in Brazil and in Southern Portugal (Vasconcelos,
1901/1970), a process of reduction which will be analysed in
section 3.2.2.1 and chapter 8.

Another occurrence of rising diphthong is the one that results from a glide insertion before the second vowel of a hiatus
or before a vowel following a falling diphthong:

(i) |'fiu| : |'fi^{j}u| fio   (wire)

     |'boa| : |'bo^{w}a| boa   (good, fem.)

     |'tua| : |'tu^{w}a| tua   (yours, fem.)

     |'meju| : |'mej^{j}u| meio   (half)

     |i'dɛja| : |i'dɛj^{j}a| idéia   (idea)

3.2 Aspects of the phonology of the Caipira dialect

As discussed in section 2.3, Caipira is, in a narrow sense, related to the rustic culture of the State of São Paulo. Amaral

(1920/1976) referred to the variety spoken by the *Paulista* rural population as *Dialeto Caipira*. In a broad sense, Caipira is presently an adjective that describes the rustic and backward way of life of rural dwellers regardless of geographical region. In the present work, the expression 'Caipira dialect' is being used rather loosely as a synonym for 'rural dialect'. In the analysis of the linguistic data, however, Caipira dialect refers specifically to the variety spoken in the rural setting where the migrants were born and spent part of their lives, namely, the region of the high Paraíba River in Minas Gerais.

In this section, the phonological rules of the dialect will be discussed. Among these rules, some are specific to the dialect but most of them are shared by Caipira and nonstandard urban varieties. A few of the basic phonological patterns discussed here intersect with grammar, even though no comprehensive morphosyntactic analysis is included within the scope of this work.

The dialect description is based upon the Brazlândia dataset and therefore does not include reference to Caipira features that have been mentioned in the literature but did not show up consistently in the database.

The speech of the migrants does not represent a genuine manifestation of Caipira since it has been exposed to urban influences.[12] The information gathered from the data was therefore compared to six dialectological studies of Caipira. Three of them surveyed larger regions and are now considered as classic pioneer   studies despite some methodological shortcomings; the others were carried out more recently and are restricted to geographically limited areas. Amaral (1920/1976) provided the first dialect survey in Brazil. He studied the dialect in São Paulo, the birth-place of Caipira. From there the dialect spread, together with the westward colonization, to Minas Gerais and Goiás. Teixeira (1938, 1944) surveyed Caipira in Minas Gerais and Goiás, respectively. Chediak (1958) and Penha (1974) analysed Caipira in two villages in the southern area of Minas Gerais. Couto (1974) studied the dialect in a village in the central area of Minas Gerais, the very region from which most of the informants come.

In the analysis carried out in this section, the urban standard variety of the language is used as a frame of reference. In
order to justify this position, the viewpoint of William Labov
(1980:371) has been used:

> At one time it was proper to say that each variety of lan-
> guage should be described as a system in itself, without
> reference to any other. This is possible and sometimes il-
> luminating for phonology and the closed systems of morphol-
> ogy. But now that we have come to recognize the complexity
> of syntax and semantics, it is clear that it is a Quixotic
> enterprise to begin every description from scratch.

Moreover this study is dealing with an ongoing process of linguistic change from a rural, extremely stigmatized variety to
less stigmatized urban varieties, closer to the ideal standard.

Throughout the description every Caipira form will be given
along with the standard variant in this conventionalized
fashion:

Standard	Caipira	Portuguese orthographic form	English translation
$|$żu'eλu$|$:	$|$żu'ej$|$	joelho	(knee)

There is no implication that the dialectal form derives from
its standard counterpart. The symbol (∿) is used to indicate
alternative forms in Caipira.

Most of the phonological processes that are rather productive
in Brazilian Portuguese in general, and in Caipira in particular, are related to the preference for the canonical CV syllable
structure. It should be noted also that deletion of post-vocalic
consonants, a process that produces open syllables, facilitates
the phenomenon of syllable isochrony and, as such, is typical of
syllable-timed languages (Abaurre-Gnerre, 1981). It has been
claimed that the Caipira dialect is spoken with a rhythm even
slower than that of the urban varieties, a characteristic which
is said to be the preservation of an archaic feature of Portuguese (Amaral, 1920/1976:45; Teixeira, 1938:12, 1944:33). If one
accepts such premises, it could then be argued that those processes rooted in the isochrony tendency are further evolved in
Caipira than in urban varieties. That could be presented as a
possible explanation for the large gap between Caipira and the

standard language.

The argument begs a lot of questions however. In the first place, to assume that Caipira has a particularly slow rhythm seems to be a broad generalization, because there is indeed much regional or even local variation as far as speech rhythm is concerned in the rural dialects. Secondly, both rural and urban varieties seem to present a large range of variation in this respect and there is no experimental phonetic evidence, to the best of our knowledge, to suggest that the former are spoken at a slower rate than the latter. On the other hand, however, the Caipira varieties show a surprisingly high level of uniformity in their phonological and morphophonemic characteristics; this is attested by the comprehensive comparison of published rural dialect descriptions provided by Elia (1975).

The phonological processes that are productive in Brazilian Portuguese and, to a larger extent, in Caipira, seem indeed to be related to two phonological universals, namely, the preference for the canonical syllable form and the little resistance that unstressed syllables offer to reduction and change. The basic processes that operate in the language to open closed syllables (denasalization of final unstressed vowels, deletion of consonantal segments and reduction of falling diphthongs) and to reduce consonant clusters, show a gradient stratification in the dialect continuum, but their occurrence in Caipira seems to be considerably higher than in urban varieties.

The *locus* of these reduction phenomena is mainly word-final syllables. In fact, final unstressed syllables can also be completely deleted in the fast speech characteristic of colloquial styles. The following are examples collected in a Caipira-speaking community in Minas Gerais, but final syllable deletion seems to be a gradient feature of the language.

(i) |tra'baλa na'xɔsa| : |tra'bana'xɔs|
trabalha na roça (works on a farm)

|'dƶisi 'keli bri'go| : |'dƶis'keλbri'go|
disse que ele brigou (said that he fought)

|'pɛrtu dƶi'sãw̃'pawlu| : |'pɛrdƶi'sãw̃'pawlu|
perto de São Paulo (near São Paulo)

The frequency of unstressed syllable dropping will vary according to several linguistic and non-linguistic factors. Among the former are probably the phonetic nature of both the deleted and the following syllables, as well as the characteristics of the sentence intonation contour. As for the non-linguistic factors, idiolectal differences (some speakers talk faster than others), regional background, and, most importantly, stylistic constraints seem to play a relevant role in the application of the rule. Actually, deletion of final unstressed syllables, operating at the word level, could be considered as parallel to the process of final consonantal segment deletion operating at the syllable level.

Another phenomenon associated with the weakness of final unstressed syllables is the tendency to reduce the proparoxytone words (words in which the stress is placed on the ante-penultimate syllable), a process very productive both in Caipira and in the urban varieties. Most words in Portuguese are paroxytones, i.e. the stress is placed on the penultimate syllable. The same trend holds for the organization of rhythmic feet, which most often exhibit a paroxytone stress pattern. In contrast to European Portuguese, in Brazilian Portuguese the clitics are more likely to precede the verbal form than to follow it. When they are placed before the verb, they have within the rhythmic unit the same status as a pretonic syllable within the word (Mattoso Câmara, 1970:ch.7).[13] One possible reason for such a tendency can be found in the fact that decrease in articulatory energy after the stressed syllable makes it difficult to keep the same time-spacing of the initial syllables in the utterance of the post-tonic syllables. The pronunciation of words, or of rhythmic units, with two post-tonic syllables requires, therefore, more effort than the pronunciation of words with one post-tonic syllable. The problem, of course, does not obtain in Metropolitan Portuguese, due to its stress-timed character.

One could state in conclusion that most of the processes that operate in Caipira have natural articulatory explanations. Yet a main problem remains: can they be viewed as natural change processes of Portuguese or should they be considered as vestiges of the abrupt rephonologizing phenomena typical of pidgins and creoles?

It should be noted that deletion of post-vocalic consonants in word-end position implies in some cases the loss of number inflection. In the verbal forms, for example, number inflection is affected by the rule of denasalization of final vowels (see 3.2.1.2); as for the agreement rule within the noun phrase, it is directly affected by deletion of final -s (see 3.2.1.3). In fact, in present-day nonstandard Brazilian Portuguese in both verbs and nouns the singular morphemes tend to be substituted for their plural equivalents whenever the notion of plural is redundantly marked. This tendency is considerably more noticeable in Caipira than in the urban varieties, and is completely absent from European varieties. It seems, therefore, reasonable to admit that the extreme morphological simplification of Caipira as well as some specific features of its phonology result from the pidginization process that took place in earlier stages of the language history of the country, as discussed in the previous chapter.

Guy (1981:ch.7) argues very cogently that the hypothesis of a creole-like origin for nonstandard Brazilian Portuguese can provide a unified account for all the descriptions of 'seemingly very creolized rural dialects' in Brazil, a task that, as we have suggested, cannot be convincingly done in terms of natural change processes of the language based on acoustic-articulatory actuating forces only. Guy's arguments lead to the following conclusion: 'under the creole hypothesis these (the rural dialects) can be accounted for as simply scattered remnants of a more highly creolized stage of the popular language which was originally much more widespread. People in the isolated rural areas have less contact with the standard and have decreolized less than the urban masses' (Guy, 1981:322).

In any case, since no pidgins or creoles, such as those existing in other former Portuguese colonies, have been preserved in Brazil, and the empirical evidence for an earlier pidginization is scarce, any search for the actuation and implementation of many features of Caipira must rely upon conjecture. In the analysis that follows, an attempt is made to distinguish between the gradient features, which are also present in urban varie-

ties, and the sharp features, which seem specific to Caipira
and rurban dialects (see 2.1).

3.2.1 *The tendency towards open syllables*

3.2.1.1 *Falling diphthongs*
Some falling diphthongs in Brazilian Portuguese are undergoing
a process of monophthongization. The feature shows a gradient
stratification, i.e. some diphthongs in some linguistic environments are almost categorically reduced even in formal styles of
the standard language. In other environments, however, the reduction is stigmatized and functions as an indicator of both
lower-class speech and rural vernaculars.

The reduction of falling diphthongs is embodied in the general tendency towards open syllables in the language. Diachronic
evidence for this is found in the process of vocalization of
consonants in post-vocalic position in the syllable. Compare:

Latin	Standard Portuguese	Nonstandard Portuguese
Alterum	Outro	Otro

The monophthongization of |ow| and |ej| is not a recent phe-
nomenon in the language. Vasconcelos (1901/1970) observes that
the reduction of |ow| > |o| may have started before the eight-
eenth century. Révah (1958) argues that until that century the
sequence |ow| was a 'real diphthong' both in Portugal and in
Brazil. As for the reduction |ej| > |e|, the former philologist
suggests that it may have started in Portugal in the eighteenth
century.

Vasconcelos has shrewdly observed that the occurrence of the
reduction in the southern regions of Portugal was conditioned
by the following phonetic environment, i.e. the consonants fa-
vouring the reduction and the vowels and pause inhibiting it
(Vasconcelos, 1901/1970:93).

The current processes of falling diphthong reduction in Brazilian Portuguese are of two types. In the first, the semi-vowel
is deleted and the vowel is consequently lengthened. In the
second, the semi-vowel is deleted and the vowel quality changes.

The processes of the first type are:

(i) |aj| : |a|

      |'kajṡa| : |'kaṡa| caixa   (box)

This diphthong in Caipira can also change into |ɛj| or |ej| in the word *raiva*:

      |'xajva| : |'xɛjva| ∿ |'xejva| raiva   (rage)

(ii) |ej| : |e|

      |'pejṡi| : |'peṡi| peixe   (fish)

(iii) |ow| : |o|

      |'owru| : |'oru| ouro   (gold)

In the word *muito* |'mũȷ̃tu| the nasal diphthong is sometimes reduced. The occurrence of |mũtu| is rather frequent in the speech of some informants.

The reduction processes of the second type are:

(iv) |aw| : |o| ∿ |ɔ|

      |aw'mẽtu| : |o'mẽtu| aumento   (increase)

      |awto'mɔvɛw| : |ɔto'mɔvi| automóvel   (automobile)

      |paw'lista| : |po'lista| paulista   (a person born in the state of São Paulo)

(v) |ew| : |o|

      |prew'kupa| : |pro'kupa| preocupa   (worries)

      |ews'takju| : |os'taki| Eustáquio

Whereas the cases of reduction (iv) and (v) seem to show a sharp stratification in the dialect continuum (i.e. they are characteristic of Caipira and contiguous nonstandard varieties)[14] the reductions of the first type, (i), (ii), (iii), are typical gradient features in a process of evolution.

As Lemle (1978) has pointed out, monophthongization of falling diphthongs seems to be conditioned by the following consonantal segment. The author suggests that the reduction is more likely to occur whenever the phenomenon of crasis between the semi-vowel and a homorganic following consonant obtains. According to such a view, the diphthongs ending in |j| are more likely to be reduced when followed by palatal consonants. By the same token, the most favourable environment for the reduction of

diphthongs ending in |w| would be a following labial consonant.
But as the evolutionary course of reduction of the diphthong |ow|
is more advanced, the rule seems to apply almost categorically to
all phonetic environments. This diphthong is indeed the only one
that reduces in final stressed syllables.

In addition to this hypothesis, analysis of the Brazlândia
dataset allows us to advance two more general hypotheses:

1. Falling diphthongs are more likely to reduce in unstressed
syllables.

2. The nature of the following consonantal segment affects
reduction through a phenomenon of homorganic assimilation. The
most favourable environment is that of a following consonant
which is homorganic with the semi-vowel. The next two favourable
environments are a following flap |r| and the nasals.

In a study recently carried out by Santos (1982) at the
University of Brasília, using thirty hours of recordings of the
dataset collected in Brazlândia, the influence of two groups of
structural factors on the reduction of diphthongs |aj|, |ej| and
|ow| was examined. These factors were the following segment and
stress.

Analysis of the linguistic factors was limited to assessing
the frequency of occurrence of reduced diphthongs in each phonetic environment in relation to the number of cases of diphthongs (reduced or not) in each environment. Table 3.1 shows the
overall frequency of reduction in percentage.

Table 3.1. *Reduction of falling diphthongs*

Diphthongs	Total occurrences	Frequency of reduction
|aj|	830	9%
|ej|	1966	36%
|ow|	1843	97%

The diphthong |aj| reduces only when followed by homorganic
consonants. In this case the rule is practically categorical in
stressed syllables and occurs at a frequency of 83 per cent in
unstressed syllables.

The reduction of |ej| is almost categorical when the diph-

thong is followed by homorganic consonant or |r| and the differ-
ence between stressed and unstressed syllables is not relevant.
There were no occurrences of this diphthong followed by a nasal
sonorant. When followed by other consonants, the frequency of
reduction in stressed syllables was 28 per cent, whereas in unstressed syllables it was 54 per cent. In the other environments
the reduction did not occur.

As for the diphthong |ow|, the reduction rule is practically
categorical in the **dataset** in all environments.

The |j| diphthongs followed by a vowel represent a peculiar
case of reduction. In the standard pronunciation a glide is inserted before the vowel (see 3.1.3), resulting in a sequence of
two diphthongs:

(vi) |i'dɛja| : |i'dɛjʲa| idẽia (idea)

In our dataset this diphthong follows two different patterns of
reduction. It is sometimes monophthongized, and the application
of this rule therefore blocks the application of glide insertion:

(vii) |i'dɛja| : |i'dɛa| idẽia (idea)

But very often the rising diphthong that obtains with the glide
insertion is deleted:

(viii) |'šejʲu| : |'šej| cheio (full)

In Caipira the rule is rather productive as a consequence of
the rule of vocalization of the lateral palatal |λ| (see 3.2.3)
and of the nasal palatal |ñ|. In the former case, the following
sequence of rules obtains:

(ix)   vocalization   glide   diphthong
                            insertion   deletion
       |żu'eλu| : |żu'eju| : |żu'ejʲu| : |żuej| joelho
                                                  (knee)

In the case of the nasal consonant, the sequence is the following:

(x)   vocalization   glide   diphthong
                            insertion   deletion
       |'bãñu| : |'bãju| : |'bãjʲu| : |bãj| banho (bath)

In modern Brazilian Portuguese, post-vocalic |ɤ| has merged

with |w| (see 3.2.3) in most accents. Such a merger seems to be in a process of evolution and the feature functions as an indicator of generation differences in most accents: the older generations still keep the |ʎ|, whereas the younger ones have already adopted the |w| (Camacho, 1978). In Caipira, although this merger can also be noted, most often the lateral changes into the flap |r| or into retroflex |ɽ| (see 3.2.3):

(xi) |sɔʎ| : |sɔɽ| sol   (sun)
      |'kaʎdu| : |'kaɽdu| caldo   (soup, juice)

This rule is probably much older than the |ʎ|, |w| merger. It has indeed been noted in the pidgin spoken by Brazilian aborigines in 1620 (Silva Neto, 1950/1977:34-5):

Interestingly, the diphthongs resulting from the vocalization of the |ʎ| have not yet been influenced by the reduction trend, although a few sporadic cases have been registered in Brazlândia. In Caipira, however, the reduction occurs in word-end position:

(xii) |ĩ'kriviw| : |ĩ'krivi| incrível   (incredible)
       |xespõ'saviw| : |xespõ'savi| responsável (responsible)
       |pesu'aw| : |pesu'a:| pessoal   (personal)

Such a phenomenon, nevertheless, can also be interpreted as deletion of post-vocalic |ʎ|, considering that deletion of final consonants is a common rule in the dialect (see 3.2.1.3). In the case of a few words two patterns of reduction were observed:

(xiii) |dʑi'fisiw| : |dʑi'fisi| ∿ |dʑi'fisu| difícil
                                                (difficult)
        |'fasiw| : |'fasi| ∿ |'fasu| fácil (easy)

A final word about falling diphthongs refers to the tendency observed in the speech of some informants to add a rising diphthong to verbal forms ending in |ej|:

(xiv) |fi'kej| : |fi'kejʲu| fiquei ((I) remained)
       |'sej| : |'sejʲu| sei   ((I) know)
       |a'ʂej| : |a'ʂejʲu| achei   ((I) found)

A similar phenomenon also registered is the insertion of a glide before the morpheme *eu* (I), especially when it follows a word ending in a vowel:

(xv) |'pɛgaew| : |'pɛga^{j}ew| pega eu   (catch I)

3.2.1.2 Denasalization

The nasal vowels in modern Portuguese result in general from
earlier sequences of an oral vowel and a nasal consonant. The
vowel assimilated the nasality and the consonantal segment disappeared, thus forming an open syllable (Ali, 1931/1964). In the
nonstandard speech both of Portugal (Vasconcelos, 1901/1970) and
of Brazil the rule of denasalization of final unstressed vowels
is rather productive. In Brazilian Portuguese it is a gradient
feature. In Head's (1981) attitudinal study, briefly discussed
in section 2.1, denasalization and monophthongization of nasal
diphthongs (|ãw̃| : |u|; |ẽj̃| : |i|) were rated with a 'medium'
stigmatization.

Votre (1982) examined retention of nasalization in final position in the speech of eight illiterate speakers from Rio de
Janeiro, divided into two age groups. The cases of nasal vowel
in word-end position were classified into four morphological
classes (A, B, C and D). Three of them embodied verb forms and
the fourth one contained nouns and pronouns. In class A the final nasal was the agreement marker (e.g. *falava, falavam* : (he)
spoke, (they) spoke). In class B, denasalization did not result
in the merger of the singular and plural forms (e.g. *faz, fazem*:
(he) does, (they) do). Class C contained verb forms in which the
nasal had only a negligible effect in marking the plural form
(e.g. *falou, falaram* ∿ *falaru*: (he) spoke, (they)spoke). In
class D, the nasal had no syntactic function at all.

In connection with morphological classes, the joint effect of
the height and of the stress of the vowel was contemplated in
the analysis. The variable rule analysis showed that high vowels
are considerably more likely to denasalize than non-high vowels
(probability of .40 and .60, respectively in the older group).
The influence of stress was even more remarkable. In the older
group, retention of nasality in final stressed vowels occurred
at a frequency of 97.7 per cent (probability of .95), whereas in
final unstressed vowels the frequency dropped to 26.8 per cent
(probability of .05).

The comparison of the two age groups' results allowed for the conclusion that the younger speakers have a different set of constraints and are more advanced than the older group in the process of nasal loss in class A, in which the nasal is the mark of the singular/plural opposition, as well as in class C, which for the older informants is favourable to nasalization. Votre (1982:102) concludes that 'we are dealing with a two-component diachronic drift that operates at different rates, and for different reasons, in the two age groups'. The first component of this drift is supported by historical evidence from the fourteenth century onwards, and mostly affects the nouns. This is very clear for the older group which showed the least retention of nasality in class D. The second component was made evident by change in apparent time, as pointed out above. As a general conclusion, the author adduces that, in spite of the differences between the two age groups, there is an overall and fundamental drift towards denasalization and regularization of Portuguese syllable structure.

Guy's (1981) analysis of denasalization in Portuguese pointed, however, to slightly different conclusions. Both Votre's and Guy's data were drawn from the same *corpus*, i.e. the interviews collected by the research project *Competências Básicas do Português* with illiterate people in Rio de Janeiro (Lemle and Naro, 1977). Guy excluded both diphthongs and stressed vowels from the corpus because they were considered as nearly categorical inhibitors of denasalization and, furthermore, included in the analysis the preceding and the following contexts as a variable constraint. His conclusions can be summarized as follows: denasalization is a rather simple phonetic rule which applies, without reference to abstract morphological categories, to unstressed final monophthongs, with high vowels being most susceptible to the loss of nasality. The absence of nasality in a preceding and following segment and high preceding segments and following vowels all favour the application of the **denasalization rule** (Guy, 1981:226).

No quantitative assessment of denasalization was made in the Brazlândia database, since the rule seems to be almost categorical with both single vowels and diphthongs in final unstressed

syllables and to affect both the nouns and the verb forms
equally. Further details will be presented in the discussion of
the subject-verb agreement rule in chapter 8. The following are
examples from the dataset:

(i) |'bẽsãw̃| : |'bẽsa| ~ |'bẽsu| bênção   (blessing)
      |vi'aʒẽɟ| : |vi'aʒi| viagem   (voyage)
      |'miwtõ| : |'miwtu| Milton

3.2.1.3 Final consonant deletion

The deletion of post-vocalic consonants in word-end position is
a general tendency in nonstandard speech. The consonants that
occur in this position are the liquids |l| and |r| and the sibi-
lant fricatives |s| and |z| (see 3.1.2). Deletion of the sibi-
lant consonant, which is usually the plural marker, reflects a
general trend in modern Brazilian Portuguese to privilege the
singular form at the expense of its plural counterpart. Redundant markers of plurality in the noun phrase tend to be deleted
and the plural morpheme preserved in the first determiner only
(Braga, 1977; Scherre, 1978; Guy, 1981). Loss of concord in the
noun phrase is a gradient feature in Brazilian Portuguese. It
was evaluated with a degree of stigmatization 'medium to high'
in Head's (1981) study (see 2.1.).

Deletion of the final sibilant in the first person plural
verbal morpheme '-mos' seems also to be a gradient feature in
Brazilian Portuguese (see 8.3.2):

(i) |fa'zemus| : |fa'zemu| fazemos   ((we) make, do)

Non-morphemic final sibilant segments, as found in singular
nouns and adverbs, are less likely to be deleted. Deletion in
such cases seems to be a sharp feature, distinctive of Caipira
and rurban varieties. Examples in the speech of the Brazlândia
migrants are as follows. It should be noted that in all of them
deletion occurred in final unstressed syllables:

(ii) |'õnibus| : |'õnibu| ônibus   (bus)
      |'arku'iris| : |'arku'iri| arco-íris   (rainbow)
      |'ãtʃis| : |'ãtʃi| antes   (before)
      |'mẽnus| : |'mẽnu| menos   (less)
      |'sĩplis| : |'sĩpli| simples   (simple)

In final stressed syllables the sibilant is usually pronounced and very often implies the diphthongization of the preceding vowel (see also examples (vi)):

(iii) |xa'pas| : |xa'pajs| rapaz (fellow, guy)
|ves| : |vejs| vez (time, occasion)

The deletion of the liquid |r| in word-end position is a var-
iable rule which also shows a gradient stratification in Brazilian Portuguese. Using the variable rule paradigm, Votre (1978)
studied retention of final |r| in the speech of nine lower-class
illiterate adults and four college students in Rio de Janeiro.
As was expected, the results showed that the probability of the
consonant retention among the latter group (.64) was considerable higher than among the illiterate group (.36).

Analysis of the structural constraints indicated that the fi-
nal |r| is deleted more easily in verbal infinitives (probabili-
ty of retention = .23) than in nouns (.84) despite the fact that
in the former the |r| constitutes a complete morpheme unit.[15]
Deletion is also more likely to occur when the following segment
is a vowel. As pointed out in section 2.1, deletion of |r| in
verbal infinitives was associated with the weakest degree of
stigmatization in Head's (1981) subjective reaction analysis.

In Caipira deletion of |r| in word-end position is productive
in both verbal infinitives and nouns, even though it may be more
frequent in the former class. It also seems to apply irrespective of syllable stress. The following examples were selected
from the database:

(iv) |lu'gar| : |lu'ga:| lugar (place)
|kwaʎ'kɛr| : |kwaʎ'kɛ:| qualquer (any)
|mu'ʎɛr| : |mu'ʎɛ:| mulher (woman)
|se'tor| : |se'to:| setor (sector)
|governa'dor| : |governa'do:| governador (governor)
|xe'pɔrter| : |xe'pɔrtši| repórter (reporter)
|ka'daver| : |ka'davi| cadáver (corpse)

The lateral |ʎ| in word-end position follows a similar dele-
tion trend, but in contrast to the final |r| spirantization or
complete deletion, the |ʎ| deletion is rather stigmatized and

indicates a sharp distinction between rural (or rurban) and more prestigious varieties. Whereas in urban speech final |χ| is usually labialized (see 3.2.1.1), in Caipira it is more often deleted or it merges with |r| when the final syllable is stressed. The merger of the liquids will be further discussed in section 3.2.3. In final unstressed syllables the merger does not seem to occur:

(v)	|karna'vaχ|	:	|karna'va:|	∿	|karna'var|	carnaval (carnival)
	|ã'nɛχ|	:	|ã'nɛ:|	∿	|ã'nɛr|	anel (ring)
	|ã'zɔχ|	:	|ã'zɔ:|	∿	|ã'zɔr|	anzol (hook)
	|bãnãnaχ|	:	|bãnãna:|	∿	|bãnãnar|	bananal (banana plantation)

Another productive phonological process in Caipira that contributes to the formation of open syllables is the epenthesis of a vowel that changes a syllable of type CVC into two open syllables, CV CV. The final segments |s|, |r| and |χ| are sometimes followed by an |i|, as in the examples below:

(vi)	|'majs|	:	|'majzi|	mais	(more)
	|xa'pajs|	:	|xa'pajzi|	rapaz	(fellow)
	|sejs|	:	|'sejzi|	seis	(six)
	|lus|	:	|'luzi|	luz	(light)
	|me'nɔr|	:	|me'nɔri|	menor	(smaller)
	|loku'tor|	:	|loku'tori|	locutor	(broadcaster)
	|popu'lar|	:	|popu'lari|	popular	(popular)
	|ot'ɛχ|	:	|o'tɛli|	hotel	(hotel)
	|ka'zaχ|	:	|ka'zali|	casal	(couple)
	|xu'raχ|	:	|xu'rali|	rural	(rural)
	|'suχ|	:	|'suli|	sul	(south)

3.2.2   *The tendency towards paroxytones*

3.2.2.1   *Rising diphthong reduction*

The sequence of |u| or |i| plus a vowel in word-end position may be pronounced as a hiatus, but more often, as a result of a process of synaeresis, as a rising diphthong (see 3.1.3). In nonstandard Portuguese, both in Portugal and in Brazil, this diphthong is frequently reduced.[16]

Lemle (1978) has observed in the speech of **lower-class** illiterate adults in Rio de Janeiro that the nature of the preceding consonant is a relevant factor in the application of the reduction rule. Diphthongs preceded by |s| and |r| are more likely to be reduced. The influence of this and other factors in the speech of the rural **migrants** in Brazlândia will be discussed in chapter 8.

In contrast to the reduction of falling diphthongs (see 3.2.1. 1), which shows a gradient stratification, the reduction of final rising diphthongs is rather stigmatized and can be considered as a feature that defines a sharp distinction between rural and rurban dialects on the one hand and urban varieties on the other.

3.2.2.2 The reduction of the proparoxytones
The reduction of proparoxytone words in Caipira and adjacent varieties can follow different patterns. The most common is the deletion of the vowel of the penultimate syllable, as in lists (i), (ii) and (iii), below:

(i)	|'šakara| :	|'šakra|	chácara	(small farm)
	|'arvori| :	|'arvri|	árvore	(tree)
	|'šikara| :	|'šikra|	xícara	(cup)
(ii)	|'nũmeru| :	|'nũmru|	número	(number)
	|'bebadu| :	|'bebdu|	bêbado	(drunk)
	|'lãpada| :	|'lãpda|	lâmpada	(lamp)
(iii)	|'kɔsega| :	|'kɔska|	cócega	(tickling)
	|'kɔxegu| :	|'kɔrgu|	córrego	(brook)
	|'muzika| :	|'muzga|	música	(music)
	|'folegu| :	|'foɣgu|	fôlego	(breath)

In (i) the structure C_1V C_1V C_1V changes into C_1V C_1C_2V. In (ii) and (iii) the structure C_1V C_1V C_1V is changed into C_1VC_2 C_1V, but whereas in (iii) the resulting C_1VC_2 syllable conforms to the syllable patterns of the language (see 3.1.3), in (ii) it does not, because stop and nasal consonants cannot occur in position C_2. To avoid such difficulty, words in (ii) are sometimes subject to a further stage of reduction (iv):

(iv) |'nữmeru| : |'nữmru| : |'nữru| nữmero   (number)
       |'bebadu| : |'bebdu| : |'bebu| bêbado   (drunk)
       |'lãpada| : |'lãpda| : |'lãpa| lâmpada   (lamp)

Another pattern of reduction consists of the deletion of an internal vowel and the consonant of the following syllable:

(v) |ispe'sifiku| : |ispe'sifu| especĩfico   (specific)
      |de'pɔzitu| : |de'pɔzu| depốsito   (warehouse)
      |'vaχvula| : |'vaχva| vãlvula   (valve)

The reduction also obtains with deletion of the full last syllable:

(vi) |'tŝitulu| : |'tŝitu| tĩtulo   (title)
       |'likidu| : |'liki| lĩquido   (liquid)
       |ki'lõmetru| : |ki'lõmi| quilõmetro (kilometre)
       |le'žitimu| : |le'žitŝi| legĩtimo   (legitimate)

A special case is the reduction of:

(vii) |is'piritu| : |is'pritu| espĩrito   (spirit)

in which the stressed vowel is deleted.[17]

Finally, it is also possible for the stress placement to be altered without any change occurring in the segmental phonology of the word:

(viii) |ĩ'kõmodu| : |ĩkõ'modu| incômodo   (nuisance)

Except for a few reduced words, viz. *xĩcara : xicra, chácara: chacra, córrego : corgo* which are generalized in Brazilian Portuguese, the reduction of the proparoxytones can be regarded as a sharp feature, characteristic of Caipira and rurban varieties.

3.2.3 *Processes affecting the liquids*

The liquid consonants |l|, |λ| and |r| are the *locus* of much variation in nonstandard Portuguese. Traditional dialectology has viewed the merger of |l| and |r| as well as the vocalization and deletion of these phonemes as the result of the influence of the substrate aborigine languages and the transplanted African pidgins during the first centuries of colonization. Such an interpretation was challenged by later authors. They claimed that the early dialectologists rashly established a relationship of

cause and effect between a characteristic of the substrates and a
feature of dialectal Portuguese. Their analysis therefore lacked
detailed information on the Indian languages and Portuguese
based creoles on the one hand, and Romance philology on the other
(Silva Neto, 1950/1977; Melo, 1971). Mattoso Câmara (1975:57
footnote), however, referring to these specific sources of in-
formation, firmly suggests that the vocalization of |λ| can be
regarded as a result of the influence on Colonial Portuguese of
both slaves' pidgin and the aborigine languages. He observes
that the opposition |1| - |r| and |1| - |ɤ| did not exist in the
latter.

In any case, the merger of the liquids has been noted in
European Portuguese dialects (Vasconcelos, 1901/1970) and in
African Portuguese creoles (Teixeira,1944; Vázquez Cuesta and
Mendes da Luz, 1971). It is possible that the evolution of the
liquids in these different continents followed parallel but in-
dependent processes (see 8.1).

The merger of |r| and |1| in Caipira occurs both in syllable-
end position and in consonant clusters. In the former case it
seems to define a sharp distinction between rural and rurban
dialects and the more prestigious urban varieties. In Head's
(1981) study, it received the highest degree of negative evalua-
tion. Most often the result of the merger is |r| as in example
(i), but the opposite evolution (|r| > |ɤ|), as in example (ii),
also obtains:

(i) |'paɤma| : |'paɾma| palma   (palm)
      |'vɔɤta| : |'vɔɾta| volta   (return)
      |aɤ'gũ| : |aɾ'gũ| algum   (some)
      |aɤ'mosu| : |aɾ'mosu| almoço   (lunch)
      |a'vẽtaɤ| : |a'vẽtaɾ| avental (apron)

(ii) |tʃi'ar| : |tʃi'aɤ| tear   (weaver's loom)
      |su'ɔr| : | su'ɔɤ| suor   (sweat)
      |'garfu| : |'gaɤfu| garfo   (fork)
      |kar'vãw̃| : |kaɤ'vãw̃| carvão   (coal)

In consonant clusters of a stop or a slit fricative plus a
lateral, there may occur the merger of |r| and |1| at the ex-
pense of the latter (iii), or else the liquid may be simply

deleted (iv):

(iii)	|ĩklu'zivi|	:	|ĩkru'zivi|	inclusive	(including)
	|kõ'plɛtu|	:	|kõ'prɛtu|	completo	(complete)
	|plã'tar|	:	|prã'ta:|	plantar	(to plant)
	|'dupla|	:	|'dupra|	dupla	(duo)
(iv)	|'padri|	:	|'padƶi|	padre	(priest)
	|'owtru|	:	|'otu|	outro	(other)
	|pro'grɛsu|	:	|po'grɛsu|	progresso	(progress)
	|sẽtraw|	:	|sẽ'taw|	central	(central)

These processes affecting consonant clusters also seem to be
sharp features in the continuum, but this interpretation must
take into account two facts. Firstly, the merger sometimes
occurs in the repertoire of standard language speakers who have
articulatory problems. Secondly, cluster reduction can be a
productive rule, especially in final unstressed syllables in the
fast styles of the colloquial standard. It received, however,
the highest degree of negative evaluation in the study carried
out by Head (1981) (see 2.1).

The palatal lateral $|\lambda|$ is vocalized in Caipira and rurban
varieties, and this rule functions as a typical sharp feature.
As reported in section 2.1, it was severely stigmatized in the
attitudinal study. Examples from the database are:

(v)	|'miλu|	:	|'miʲu|	milho	(corn)
	|mu'λɛr|	:	|mujʲɛ:|	mulher	(woman)
	|va'ziλas|	:	|va'ziʲas|	vasilhas	(kitchen utensils)
	|'vɛλu|	:	|'vɛjʲu|	velho	(old man)
	|ĩko'λew|	:	|ĩkojʲew|	encolheu	(shrank)

Vocalization of $|\lambda|$ has become a clear Caipira stereotype in
the sense used by Labov (1972a:180). In the process of the urbanization of their speech, rural migrants seem to become soon
aware of the stigma associated with the variable and quite often
resort to hypercorrections such as the following:

(vi)	|majʲɔr|	:	|ma'λɔr|	maior	(larger)
	|'fiʲa|	:	|'fiλa|	fia	((she) spins)
	|pi'ɔr|	:	|pi'λɔr|	pior	(worse)
	|'fejʲu|	:	|'feλu|	feio	(ugly)

A quantitative treatment of this variable is given in section 8.1.

The alveolar lateral |l| in intervocalic position can be vocalized or simply deleted in Caipira. The rule, however, seems to be restricted to the plural forms of a few morphemes of high frequency, i.e. personal pronouns and determiners:

(vii)	|elis|	:	|ejs|~ |es|~ |ezi|	eles	(they-masc)
	|'ɛlas|	:	|'ɛas|	elas	(they-fem)
	|'delis|	:	|deys|~|des|~|'dezi|	deles	(of them)
	|a'kɛlas|	:	|a'kɛas|	aquelas	(those-fem)
	|kũ'elis|	:	|'kwejs|	com eles	(with them)

3.2.4 Sporadic changes of vowels

The *locus* of variation of vowels in Caipira is mainly the pretonic syllables. The cases of variation can be grouped into two types: those that occur within the scope of the front or of the back series of vowels and conform to the patterns of fluctuation of the pretonic vowels in Brazilian Portuguese (see 3.1.1); and more sporadic alternations between front and back vowels which do not seem to follow any systematic trend.

As in other varieties of the language, pretonic vowels in Caipira are subject to a raising process which in most cases is the result of a rule of vowel harmony:

(i)	|ẽtẽ'dẑidu|	:	|ĩtŝĩ'dẑidu|	entendido	(understood)
	|fres'kiɲu|	:	|fris'kĩĵ|	fresquinho	(fresh-diminutive)
	|pelɔ'tŝiɲa|	:	|pilu'tŝiɲa|	pelotinha	(a small quantity)
	|sɔ'ziɲu|	:	|su'zĩĵ|	sozinho	(alone-diminutive)

In regard to this trend, a remarkable feature of the dialect is the occurrence of hypercorrections that change |i| into |e| and |u| into |o|:

(ii)	|u'zina|	:	|o'zina|	usina	(mill)
	|proi'bidu|	:	|proe'bidu|	proibido	(prohibited)
	|ĩtere'sãtŝi|	:	|ẽtere'sãtŝi|	interessante	(interesting)

|xeliɹi'ozu| : |xeleɹi'ozu| religioso (religious)

The rule is very productive in the speech of the Brazlândia informants but in many cases its interpretation is rather complex because the change of vowel quality is not necessarily explicable in terms of hypercorrection but, rather, seems to be a preservation of archaic forms of the language. The following are examples of such cases:

(iii)	|dɹi'rejtu|	:	|de'rejtu|	direito	(right)
	|pri'mejru|	:	|pre'mejru|	primeiro	(first)
	|xibej'rãw̃|	:	|xebe'rãw̃|	ribeirão	(creek)
	|fũ'sãw̃|	:	|fõ'sãw̃|	função	(function)
	|dɹispozi'sãw̃|	:	|despozi'sãw̃|	disposição	(disposition)
	|u'miɣdɹi|	:	|o'miɾdɹi|	humilde	(humble)
	|kuj'dadu|	:	|koj'dadu|	cuidado	(care)
	|vir'tudɹi|	:	|ver'tudɹi|	virtude	(virtue)

Some of these examples can, of course, be accounted for by the rule of vowel harmony. (On the issue of preservation of archaic forms in Caipira, see Amaral, 1920/1976; Silva Neto, 1950/1977.)

Some sporadic vowel changes which are not related to the language trend of pretonic vowel raising or to the opposite hypercorrected phenomenon do not seem to follow a systematic pattern and the most plausible explanation for them seems to be the preservation of sixteenth-century Portuguese dialectal forms inherited from the colonizers and preserved in the insulated Caipira communities. Some of these vowel changes still show up in the speech of the older informants, whose language displays a high degree of dialect focusing (see 5.2):

(iv)	|ba'tʃismu|	:	|bo'tʃismu|	batismo	(baptism)
	|doku'mẽtu|	:	|dɹiku'mẽtu|	documento	(document)
	|dolo'ridu|	:	|dɹilu'ridu|	dolorido	(painful)
	|ĩ'tãw̃|	:	|ĩ'tõsis|∿|ã'tãw̃|	então	(then)
	|proku'rar|	:	|priku'ra:|	procurar	(to look for)
	|posu'ir|	:	|pisu'i:|	possuir	(to own)

Changes in stressed vowels seem to be restricted to verb

forms and probably result from differences in the verb system
morphophonemic rules of Caipira as compared to those of the
standard language:

(v)	|'vivi|	:	|'vɛvi|	vive	((he/she) lives)
	|a'sistṡi|	:	|a'sɛstṡi|	assiste	((he/she) watches)
	|de'zistṡi|	:	|de'zɛstṡi|	desiste	((he/she) gives up)
	|e'zistṡi|	:	|e'zɛstṡi|	existe	((he/she) exists)
	|abi'tua|	:	|abi'toa|	habitua	((he/she) has the habit)
	|de'xuba|	:	|de'xɔba|	derruba	((he/she) casts down)
	|'trowsi|	:	|'trusi|	trouxe	((he/she) brought)

3.2.5 Other phonological processes characteristic of Caipira
There are a number of other phonological processes which are reported to be very productive in Caipira. Some of them represent
typical sharp features and have reached the stage of stereotypes
in the mainstream culture, and therefore are not as frequent in
the variety spoken by most migrants as they probably were (and
may still be) in isolated Caipira communities.

In the speech of the migrants in Brazlândia the following
cases were registered: prothesis, nasalization, metathesis,
aphaeresis and epenthesis.

The prothesis of an |a| to words beginning with a consonant
is rather productive in nonstandard Portuguese in Portugal and
in Brazil. In the latter, most cases of prothesis, including the
following, are typical of Caipira:

(i)	|lẽ'brar|	:	|alẽ'bra:|	lembrar	(to remember)
	|dżiver'tṡir|	:	|adżiver'tṡi:|	divertir	(to amuse)
	|prepa'rar|	:	|aprepa'ra:|	preparar	(to prepare)
	|dõ'mar|	:	|adõ'ma:|	domar	(to domesti- cate, to tame)
	|xeu'nir|	:	|axeu'ni:|	reunir	(reunite)
	|sis'madu|	:	|asis'madu|	sismado	(worried)

The nasalization of oral vowels in initial syllables in Caipira can be regarded as a phenomenon of assimilation in some
cases (ii) or as the result of the alternation between |i| and

|ǐ| (iii), which probably stemmed from the contamination of pre-
fixes in earlier stages of the language (Naro, 1971):

(ii) |ku'ziña| : |kũ'ziña| cozinha   (kitchen)

      |vizǐ'ñãsa| : |vǐzǐj'ãsa| vizinhança   (neighbourhood)

      |a'sǐ| : |ã'sǐ| assim   (so)

      |e'zẽplu| : |ǐ'zẽpru| exemplo   (example)

(iii) |iduka'sãw̃| : |ǐduka'sãw̃| educação   (education)

      |itali'ãnu| : |ǐtali'ãnu| italiano   (Italian)

      |i'gwaχ| : |ǐ'gwaχ| igual   (equal)

Cases of metathesis of |r| and, more rarely, of |s| are very
common in Caipira:

(iv) |prew'kupa| : |po'krupa| preocupa   ((he/she)
                                                        worries)

      |pur'ke| : |pru'ke| porque   (because)

      |ǐter'valu| : |ǐtre'valu| intervalo   (interval)

      |prosi'sãw̃| : |porsi'sãw̃| procissão   (proces-
                                                     sion)

      |perma'nẽtśi| : |prema'nẽtśi| permanente (perma-
                                                     nent)

      |fer'vẽndu| : |fre'vẽnu| fervendo   (boiling)

      |persis'tśir| : |presis'tśi:| persistir   (to per-
                                                     sist)

      |'dɔrmi| : |'drɔmi| dorme   ((he/she)
                                                     sleeps)

      |tor'ser| : |tro'se:| torcer   (to twist)

      |akredži'tar| : |akerdži'tar| acreditar   (to be-
                                                     lieve)

      |presi'zar| : |persi'zar| precisar   (to need)

      |satśis'fejtu| : |sastśi'fejtu| satisfeito (satis-
                                                     fied)

Cases of epenthesis are also found in Caipira:

(v) |aniver'sarju| : |anisver'saru| aniversário (birthday)

     |'dži'pojs| : |džis'pojs| depois   (after)

As **regards** the cases of aphaeresis, many of them are, in
fact, gradual features in the dialect continuum, as they are not
restricted to Caipira or rurban varieties. Mattoso Câmara (1957/

1972:51) observes that the initial consonant of a word receives a special emphasis and indicates a division in the spoken chain. Whenever the word starts with a vowel, the vowel tends to be deleted, since it is the following consonant that exerts the demarcative function. Examples of aphaeresis in the *corpus* of the present study are:

(vi)	|a'ʐuda|	:	|'ʐuda|	ajuda	((he/she) helps)
	|akumu'low|	:	|kumu'lo|	acumulou	(accumulated)
	|aprovej'tar|	:	|provej'ta:|	aproveitar	(to take advantage)
	|adʐiki'rir|	:	|dʐiki'ri:|	adquirir	(to acquire)
	|aka'bow|	:	|ka'bo:|	acabou	(finished)
	|a'xãka|	:	|'xãka|	arranca	((he/she) pulls up, starts off)
	|obi'sɛrva|	:	|bi'sɛrva|	observa	((he/she) observes)
	|inawgu'radu|	:	|nigu'radu|	inaugurado	(inaugurated)
	|igno'rãtʂi|	:	|gino'rãtʂi|	ignorante	(ignorant)
	|edʐi'sãw̃|	:	|dʐi'sãw̃|	edição	(edition)

Another gradual rule of nonstandard Portuguese which is productive in Caipira is the assimilation of |d| in the sequence |nd| when the following sequence of rules obtains: |nd| : |nn| : |n|; and of |b| in the sequence |mb| : |mm| : |m|. The former occurs almost categorically in the gerund forms (vii) and the latter more sporadically, as in example (viii):

(vii)	|fa'lã^{n}du|	:	|fa'lanu|	falando	(speaking)
	|ke'rẽ^{n}du|	:	|ke'rẽnu|	querendo	(wanting)
	|ʐo'gã^{n}du|	:	|ʐo'gãnu|	jogando	(playing)
(viii)	|tã^m'bẽỹ|	:	|tã'mẽỹ|	também	(also)

Notes

1 The International Phonetic Association symbols are used with some adaptation for typing convenience. The alveopalatal fricatives are represented by |ʂ| and |ʐ|; the alveopalatal affricate allophones of |t| and |d| are represented by |tʂ| and |dʐ|, respectively; |r| is used for the alveolar flap,

$|\underset{\cdot}{r}|$ for the retroflex flap and $|\tilde{r}|$ for the uvular trill; the alveopalatal nasal is represented by $|\tilde{n}|$.

2   Referring to a series of arguments against the 'write as you speak' principle which prevailed in Portugal from the six-teenth to the early eighteenth century, by which time, as a consequence of many phonetic changes, it became no longer feasible, Naro (1971:623) observes in a footnote: 'it is in-structive to compare these eighteenth century statements with the common notion that only Portuguese, of all the languages of Europe, was written exactly as pronounced'.

3   Abaurre-Gnerre (1981) argues that this typology should be further refined to include a stylistic criterion, and pro-poses the following 'rhythmic-stylistic continuum' to accom-modate the different styles of several languages:

Style: formal/slow	colloquial/fast
Rhythm: syllable-timed	stress-timed

She says:

English, as a predominantly stress-timed rhythm,would be placed on the right end of the scale, with its slower styles a little to the left, considering that they present occasional prosodic characteristics of a syllable-timed rhythm. Spanish would be placed on the left end, with its faster styles probably on a point relatively more to the right. Brazilian Portuguese, as the phonological processes characteristic of several styles seem to indicate, would occupy a more central position on the scale, but always to the left of the Portuguese of Portugal, which already approaches, even in slower styles, the rhythmic patterns that are pre-dominantly stress-timed. (Abaurre-Gnerre, 1981:31; translated from Portuguese)

4   This assertion should not be taken in absolute, but in rela-tive terms only. Cagliari (1980) compares Brazilian Portu-guese with French, considered as a typical syllable-timed language, and classifies the former as stress-timed. The more appropriate approach seems indeed to be the rhythmic continu-um (see note 3). The claim that Brazilian Portuguese is a syllable-timed language is always made in this work *vis-à-vis* European Portuguese.

5   The distinction between the stressed $|a|$ and the reduced $|e|$ was noted by grammarians of the sixteenth century (Révah, 1958; Naro, 1971). Matta Machado (1981:12-3) thus describes the reduced vowel:'cette voyelle au Portugal est devenue une voyelle beaucoup plus fermée que le $|a|$ tonique... D'après le triangle acoustique des voyelles portugaises, elle serait aussi moins grave que $|a|$ et $|\partial|$. Au Brésil, la voyelle inaccentuée finale 'a' est plus fermée que le $|a|$ tonique, mais elle est moins fermée que $|\alpha|$ de Lisbonne.'

6   'On ne saurait nier que cet e est souvent nul, surtout devant r, et quelquefois après: ainsi le mot 'm e r e c e r' se prononce les deux e e. Je prononce le substantif commun 'pereira' (poirier) comme 'p e r â i r a', et le nom propre

'Pereira' comme 'p r ã i r a' (Vianna, 1883/1973:86).
7 The occurrence of final |e|˚ and |o|, varying with |i| and
 |u|, respectively, in word-end position, in Caipira spoken in
 the state of São Paulo, can either represent an independent
 evolution of unstressed vowels or else a vestige of an old
 feature of sixteenth-century Portuguese. In the latter case
 it can be **considered** as evidence in favour of the analyses
 that do not accept the |i|, |u| pronunciation in cinquentist
 Portuguese.
8 The region of Minas Gerais, where the informants of the present research come from, is not included in such an area.
9 Analysing the examples of pretonic vowel raising given by the
 first Portuguese grammarian, Fernão de Oliveira, in 1536,
 Herculano de Carvalho (1969:95) points out that in all of
 them the rule is conditioned by the nature of the following
 syllable vowel, e.g. *dormir* : *durmir* (to sleep); *recebido* :
 recibido (received); *menino* : *minino* (boy).
10 Abaurre-Gnerre (1981) claims that the lowering of pretonic
 |e| and |o| preceding syllables with either |ɛ| or |ɔ| is
 also to be regarded as a phenomenon of vowel harmony.
 Examples of these are:

|e| - |ɛ| : |ɛ| - |ɛ|
|pe'lɛ| : |pɛ'lɛ| Pelé

|o| - |ɛ| : |ɔ| - |ɛ|
|xo'bɛrtu| : |xɔ'bɛrtu| Roberto

|o| - |ɔ| : |ɔ| - |ɔ|
|oxo'rɔza| : |oxɔ'rɔza| horrorosa (horrible)

11 The consonants were classified as follows:

Labial: p, b, m, f, v

Alveolar: t, d, s, z, n, l, r

Palatal: t, d, tš, dž, ĺ, ñ, š, ž

Velar: k, g, x

A discussion of the dynamics of a variable rule analysis
like the one carried out by Bisol (1981) is presented in
section 7.1.
12 A more appropriate way of referring to such a state of affairs is to distinguish between the 'focused' dialect of the
 original setting and the 'diffused' dialect of the migrants'
 community. These concepts will be introduced and discussed in
 section 5.2.
13 'Rhythmic unit' is being used in a sense equivalent to Mattoso Câmara's (1970:34) *vocábulo fonológico*, i.e. a spontaneous
 division in the chain of speech, which embodies one or more
 free morphemes but contains just one primary stress. It is
 usually composed of an unstressed particle (a preposition, an
 article, etc.) plus another word. Still, according to Câmara,
 vocábulo fonológico should not be confused with the notion of
 'strength groups' (*grupos de força*) which are the divisions
 in the speech chain separated by natural pauses.

14 The use of 'contiguous' is based on the assumption of the dialect continuum described in chapter 2.

15 In verbal infinitives the final |r| is a morphemic unit and yet is more susceptible to deletion than in the monomorphemic nouns. This seems strange considering that morphemic units have semantic value. The explanation for the phenomenon is that the infinitive morpheme -r is redundant: the infinitive form always co-occurs with a preceding modal or auxiliary element. This evidence corroborates Naro's (1980:166) argument that 'deletion of a morphemic segment is more likely than deletion of the corresponding non-morphemic segment if the morpheme is redundant; otherwise the opposite is true'.

16 Describing southern dialects in Portugal, Vasconcelos (1901/1970:76) observes:

> La langue populaire a une tendence générale, du moins, apparente, à éviter les oxytons et les proparoxytons, par l'effet de certaines lois auxquelles obéissent les sons: ainsi sal devient sale (sali, sala); pátio devient paito dans le Sud; des noms en -ência deviennent des noms en -ença (dans le Sud).

17 It should be noted that 'esprito' is an archaic form often encountered in sixteenth century Portuguese texts.

4.0 Introduction

This chapter reviews different traditions in the application of network analysis. The first section discusses the use of the sociometric technique in community studies and the anthropological approach to the social function of network structure. The second section deals with the application of the network paradigm in sociolinguistic research. Qualitative and quantitative approaches to the language network relationship are discussed. The last section is concerned with the function of language as a symbol of personal identity. The effects of network characteristics in shaping people's orientation towards different social categories are examined. The conflict between the 'status' and 'identity' orientations and its linguistic consequences are analysed in the light of social-psychological theories concerned with the motivation which underlies language behaviour. The multi-disciplinary characteristics of the present chapter represent an effort to introduce the network paradigm as an effective analytical tool to tackle the issue of variation, especially in fluid settings undergoing rapid change.

4.1 The network paradigm

Network analysis, in a broad sense, is the study of the relations that exist in an ongoing system. When applied to social systems, network analysis is a structural strategy which is primarily concerned with relations among the individuals in any group. Guimarães (1970) defines it 'as a research strategy in which each individual in the system is perceived by the investigator, and perceives or is led to perceive himself, as an element in a complex set of social relations' (Guimarães, 1970:7).

For Mitchell (1973:22) a social network is 'basically thought
of as the actual set of links of all kinds among a set of individuals'.

The recognition of the network paradigm as an effective analytical tool seems to be related to a shift of scientific emphasis from a monadic view of the individual in isolation to the
focus upon the relationship among individuals (Guimarães, 1970).
The emphasis on human relationships as the preferred subject
matter of analysis parallels, in a broader sense, the linguistic
tradition which is mainly concerned with the functional rather
than the formal aspects of language (Hymes, 1974: ch.3). In a
narrower sense, it can be related to the linguistic approach to
language variation which recognizes the patterns and density of
human communication as a mediating variable between language and
the socio-ecological characteristics of the speech community. An
early instance of this trend can be found in Leonard Bloom-
field's argument that linguistic diversity is directly related
to density of communication, commented upon by Gumperz (1972):

> Bloomfield here postulates an intervening level of human
> communication which mediates between linguistic and non-
> linguistic phenomena. Political, economic, or even geo-
> graphical factors are no longer seen as directly reflected
> in speech. They affect language only to the extent that
> they can be shown to channel verbal communication among
> speakers, causing certain individuals to have more verbal
> contact with some than with others and thereby influencing
> the rate at which innovations diffuse. (Gumperz, 1972:3)

The basic issue of 'who communicates with whom' seems to have
been a constant concern in twentieth century linguistics. Yet no
systematic way of assessing such relations was developed within
the scope of linguistic science.[1]

Although the concept of network in social sciences was
initially only used in a metaphorical sense (Mitchell, 1969),
from the 1930s early investigators connected with different
disciplines started to elaborate a network paradigm for analytical purposes.

There are two main traditions in the history of network
studies related to psychology and sociology (and/or social anthropology). The former stemmed from the area of small group
research and worked with artificially constructed groups under

experimental conditions (Guimarães, 1970). The latter followed
mainly the method of participant-observation in real communities.
Whereas the principal concern of the psychological approach was
the dyadic relationship as a means of analysing leadership,
friendship choices, flow of information etc, the sociological
studies were especially concerned with the explanatory force of
interaction analysis, as it is explained by Mitchell (1969):'The
interest of these focuses not on the attributes of the people in
the network but rather on the characteristics of the linkages in
their relationships to one another, as a means of explaining the
behaviour of the people involved in them'(Mitchell, 1969:4).

Network characteristics were classified by Mitchell (1969:12)
as 'morphological', referring to the patterning of the links in
the network, and 'interactional', related to the nature and content of the links. Guimarães (1970) makes a distinction between
'structural' or topological properties and 'functional' or
operational properties of the network. The former are related to
the number of individuals, the physical, social and organi-
zational distance among them etc. The latter include information
flow, content of communication, social roles and norms etc.

Amongst the several experimental avenues that sprang from the
concept of network and were explored in different disciplines
with a number of purposes, two are especially relevant for the
present work, namely, the use of sociometric data for the analysis of communication networks in communities, and the social
anthropological strand that investigates the normative content
of the links of social networks in relation to their characteristics.[2] These two approaches are briefly discussed in the following subsections.

4.1.1 *The study of communication networks in communities*
Sociometry can be defined as a quantitative treatment of preferential inter-human relations (Guimarães, 1970), and is sometimes
referred to as the 'naming technique' serving basically as a
device for the measurement of interpersonal contacts. In a broad
sense, sociometry embodies several techniques of measurement,
data-gathering and analysis of interactional patterns and of
communication structures in social systems.[3]

Sociometry was first employed in studies of small groups by Jacob Moreno and his associates in 1953. Small group research was mostly conducted by psychologists under experimental conditions and dealt with conceptual and operational measures of face-to-face interaction.

The concept of 'communication network' was put forward by Bavelas (1948) and, as Bell (1976) explains, within the framework of the social psychological small group tradition, 'network' can be understood as 'the pattern of channel usage between individual members of a group. It is to be expected that the patterns of communication within a group will vary in a stateable way which correlates with group structure, function and so forth' (Bell, 1976:106-7).

Laboratory exercises were designed to investigate the relationship between different network configurations, i.e. different communication structures in artificially organized small groups and group effectiveness. (For a review on these configurations and on theoretical findings in this area, see Guimarães (1972, esp. ch.2) and Bell (1976:106-9).)

Sociometric techniques have been employed in a number of situations that range from a small group (e.g. choice or rejection of pupils in a classroom) to a complex system such as a large community. The testing may be restricted to a single naming question of the type: 'who are your three best friends in group X?', or may include a battery of questions regarding topic and frequency of interaction or other aspects of the interpersonal contact.

Sociometric questions are often used to supplement the technique of direct observation. Riley (1963) argues that the data derived from observation usually reflect overt activities of the members of the system and may not uncover certain aspects which are not acted out while the observer watches. Answers to questions, on the other hand, may reveal the underlying structure of orientation, the subjective patterns of attitudes, feelings etc, which is not easily accessible to observation.

Sociometric data can be analysed by means of simple representational devices such as the sociogram and the sociometric matrix or sociomatrix (for instances of these devices, see 7.2).[4] But the analyst must remember, as Mitchell (1973:23) ob-

serves, that these are symbolic representations of an abstract
set of relationships. In order to use them meaningfully, the
analyst must know 'what the lines actually represent and in what
way they are deemed to be isomorphic with reality'.

Sociometric data in matrix form are amenable to manipulation
by mathematical techniques, such as binary matrices, matrix
multiplication and graph theory.[5] Such techniques can provide
the means for the statement of the properties of the network in
formal terms and allow for more rigorous testing.

As mentioned above, sociometric data have been used in the
study of complex systems, like, for instance, a large community.
One of these studies that set up a descriptive model to compare
empirically several social systems in terms of their interpersonal communication structure was carried out by Guimarães
(1972) and has been especially influential in the present work.

The focus of his study was 'communication integration' measured through sociometric choices given by respondents from
twenty rural communities in the state of Minas Gerais, Brazil.
The respondents were major farm decision-makers for their respective households and owned at least part of the land they
worked. The sociometric choices represented informal friendship
ties. Each person indicated the three best friends with whom he
talked most frequently. Friendship ties were considered to be
valid indicators of active communication channels. Thus a system
characterized by a relatively large number of informal friendship relations would also be considered to have a large number
of available communication channels.

Communication integration was defined as 'the degree to which
the subsystems, subgroups, or individuals in a communication
system were structurally interlinked, via interpersonal channels' (Guimarães, 1972:4). This communication integration is
high or low depending on whether a large proportion of members
maintain a relatively high level of interpersonal contact or not.

It was hypothesized that communication integration and modernization, defined as the impact of exogenous inputs upon relatively traditional social systems, were positively related.
The assumption was that a system in which the contacts were
spread over a wider area and people would talk freely among

themselves irrespective of socioeconomic differences would be
more receptive to exogenous influences and less likely to exert
a boundary control upon the in-flow of information. This assumption is summarized in figure 4.1.

Salient characteristics	Social system	
	Modern	Traditional
Communication integration	High	Low
Degree of openness	High	Low
Boundary control (structural limitations upon in-flow of environmental inputs)	High	Low
Encoding mechanism (degree of reception, or search for, environmental inputs)	High	Low

Source: Guimarães (1972:91)

Figure 4.1   *Modern and traditional social systems and some
of their salient characteristics*

Drawing on sociometric techniques, matrix algebra and graph
theory a computerized routine - THE NETWORK ROUTINE (see 7.2) -
was designed and used to process the sociometric data and provide an index of communication integration for each community.
Each index was examined in connection with selected variables
which in past studies had been shown to correlate positively
with modernization. The results of the study showed that most of
the extra system variables (e.g., mass media exposure, external
contacts, contacts with change agents) are strongly related to
communication. The author concluded that:'Communication, as the
information processing subsystem of the social system, would
function as a mediating factor in the process of social change.
When this mediating factor is "integrated", and the receiving
system is open and capable of reorganization, it is more likely
that the system will tend towards modernization'(Guimarães,
1972:iii).
The most important contribution of this study, from a sociolinguistic point of view, is that it provides a reliable quanti-

tative experimental technique for the assessment of the amount
of communication, as well as of the characteristics of communication channels, within a given community. Moreover, it has
demonstrated that the indices obtained in this way tend to be
good indicators of dynamic social processes taking place in a
community. Such processes can, of course, be reinterpreted in
sociolinguistic terms.

In the present study, part of this analytical procedure has
been adapted in order to be replicated, not for the analysis and
comparison of communities - as was the case in the original
study - but for the analysis and comparison of the individual's
network within a migrant community.

*4.1.2 The study of the normative content of the links in social
networks*

Mitchell (1969) defines the content of the links in a social
network as the meanings that the members of the network attribute to their relationship, such as kinship obligation, religious cooperation etc.; and in later work (1973) he elaborates
on the normative aspect of this content, which is associated
with the expectations that two individuals have of each other
according to their social characteristics and attributes. This
is in accord with his earlier definition of role in terms of
social network, conceived as the behaviour between two people in
the light of 'the normative framework of the role-relationship
encompassing the expectations of ego and alter of each other'
(Mitchell, 1969:46).

The first systematic study of the relation between morphological features of a network and social behaviour was Barnes'
study of social class in a Norwegian parish as a 'network of
relations according each other approximately equal status'
(Barnes, 1954:45). 'Network' is used in this context as an image
of a social field, with individuals represented by the points
and their interaction with each other by the lines.

Barnes' study set the basis for distinguishing rural or small
scale societies from urban or mass societies in terms of density
of network. In fact, he used the expression 'small mesh' and
'large mesh' of social networks to describe small and mass

societies respectively. But the concept of density is implicit
in his analysis and is equivalent to the notion of completeness
in graph theory, i.e. the number of links that actually exist as
a proportion of the maximum number of links that could possibly
exist (Mitchell, 1969; Milroy, 1980, ch.3).

The following measure of density is proposed by Barnes (1969:
63):

$$D = \frac{200a}{n\ (n-1)}$$

where 200 is a fixed number; a refers to the actual number of
links and n to the total number of people in the network.

The notion of network density can be easily   understood by
comparing the two sociograms below (figures 4.2 and 4.3).

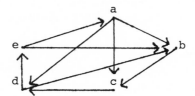

Figure 4.2   *High-density network structure*

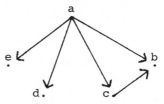

Figure 4.3   *Low-density network structure*

In figure 4.2 the density is: $\dfrac{200\ .\ 9}{20} = 90\%$

In figure 4.3 the density is: $\dfrac{200\ .\ 5}{20} = 50\%$

Another relevant notion implied in Barnes' concept of 'small
and large mesh' relates to the degree of redundancy in the net-

work links. A link between two persons will be single-stranded
or uniplex if they are related in one capacity only, e.g. as
employer/employee. It will be multi-stranded or multiplex if
they are bound in many ways, e.g. as kin, as co-workers, as
neighbours etc. (Milroy, 1980:51).

Density and multiplexity tend to co-occur and are likely to
be found in traditional, closed social systems. Urban, open
systems, on the other hand, tend towards sparseness and uni-
plexity of network.

The basic distinction between high and low density networks
was further explored in Elizabeth Bott's (1957) classic study of
allocation of marital roles in twenty families in London, in
which she examined the relation between the degree of segregation in role-relationship of husband and wife and the 'con-
nectedness' of the family's social network. Her concept of 'con-
nectedness' was described as the extent to which the people
known by a family knew and met one another, independently of the
family. A major finding that emerged from Bott's study related
to the capacity of certain types of networks to function as a
mechanism of norm reinforcement.

> When many of the people a person knows interact with one
> another, that is, when the person's network is close-
> knit, the members of his network tend to reach consensus
> on norms and they exert consistent informal pressure on
> one another to conform to the norms ... But when most
> of the people a person knows do not interact with one
> another, that is, when his network is loose-knit, more
> variation of norms is likely to develop in the network.
> (Bott, 1957:60)

The degree to which a network can exercise the norm reinforcement function is related to the extent to which an individual can use his relationship to contact people either directly or by using others as intermediaries, and conversely, to the
extent to which other people can contact him back. As Mitchell
(1969) puts it:'where the relationships among a set of persons
are dense, that is, where a large proportion know one another,
then the network as a whole is relatively compact and relatively few links between the persons need to be used to reach the
majority'(Mitchell, 1969:18).

The links are regarded as channels for the flow of the normative consensus which brings pressure to bear on the members of the network. If the network is rather closed and homogeneous, all the links are channels for the flow of the same messages and therefore the power of the system to reach a **consensus is very great.**

As was stated at the outset of this subsection, such normative pressure must be interpreted in the light of the nature of social role-relationships enacted by the individuals in the course of their interaction. A high level of moral density is associated with a small repertoire of undifferentiated roles, whereas a diffuse and complex pattern of social roles co-occurs with a low level of moral density (Banton, 1973).

The characteristics of social role-relationships have in fact provided a further criterion for the distinction between small village societies and urban societies. As Banton (1973:47) explains, in the former, people interact with one another as individuals on the basis of several different role-relationships. This gives rise to a 'tightly interlocking network of social ties' in which people are dependent on one another for social reputation. The urbanites, on the other hand, choose their associates from a larger range and are able to carry out many kinds of social relationships through separate compartments.

The concept of moral or consensus density stems from the Barnes/Bott tradition. Southall (1973) prefers to use the term 'density', however, with a different meaning, related to the degree of role-relationship complexity. While the urban milieu is characterized by a high level of role-relationship density, the village milieu shows a low level of role-relationship density (see 5.3). He explains:'Complexity refers to high density of role-relationships and simplicity to low. On the other hand, multiplexity refers to low density of role-relationships and the playing of most available roles with the same set of persons, a situation characterized as high moral density by Banton with reference to role and by Barnes with reference to network' (Southall, 1973:81).

Figure 4.4. summarizes the discussion of these concepts and helps to make clear how they are being used in the present work.

Salient characteristics	Societies	
	Modern	Traditional
Multiplexity	Low	High
Moral density	Low	High
Role-relationship density	High	Low

Figure 4.4 *Modern and traditional societies and some of their network characteristics*

4.2 *Network analysis applied to sociolinguistics*

As happened in other disciplines, the idea of social networks was first employed in sociolinguistics at a conceptual level, as an ancillary theoretical unit in elaborating the definition of the speech community. The sociolinguistic tradition rejected the definition of speech community in terms of linguistic features alone and postulated, as definitional criteria, together with the mastering of at least one form of speech, the communality of rules of conduct, such as those related to social interpretation and evaluation, appropriateness of codes or styles, norms of address and patterns of speech usage in general (Gumperz, 1968; Labov, 1972a; Hymes, 1974). The usefulness of the network concept in the sociolinguistic theory stems from the fact that it stands at a lower level of abstraction *vis à vis* the concept of speech community.

4.2.1 *Network as a theoretical construct*

Drawing on the classical distinction between language and speech, Hymes (1974:50) postulated the concepts of 'language field' and 'speech field'. While the former is defined as 'the range of languages within which a person's knowledge of forms of speech enables him to move', the latter is 'the range of communities within which a person's knowledge of ways of speaking enables him to move communicatively'. Uniting the two, Hymes argues, is the individual's 'speech network', 'a specific linkage of persons through shared knowledge of forms of speech and ways of speaking'.

Fishman (1972:22-3) asserts that within any speech community

'functionally differentiated linguistic repertoires' are associated with 'behaviourally differentiated interaction networks',
actualized within different domains, such as the family, friendship circle, interest or occupational groups. The author recognizes further that in complex societies some networks are 'experiential', whereas others are 'referential'. The verbal repertoires in experiential networks are acquired by 'dint of actual
verbal interaction'. The referential networks, on the other
hand, may not exist in a physical sense and the verbal repertoires referentially acquired are implemented by force of symbolic integration. This is the case of the standard variety of a
language, which, as a supra-regional code, serves the purpose of
integrating the citizens into a symbolic national speech community. Sankoff and Labov's (1979:202) claim that 'every speaker
is a member of many nested and intersecting speech communities'
could possibly be understood in terms of this variety of interactional as well as attitudinal, symbolically integrated networks.

Speech or communication networks are therefore an important
construct in the methods for delineating a speech community,
which should be viewed as a large-scale category, especially in
the sense put forward by Labov (1972a). According to him a
speech community is a group of people who share a given set of
norms of language, irrespective of differences in their speech.
His criterion for this definition is the isomorphism of attitudes towards language manifested by speakers from several
social classes (see 4.3).

But the concept of network is also crucial for the establishment of smaller-scale categories such as a community. Milroy
(1980:14) argues that the notion of community, defined according
to Hymes (1974:51) on the grounds of 'common locality' and
'primary interaction', can be very useful in sociolinguistic
analysis in so far as territorially-based communities are less
abstract social units to which people feel they belong. And network analysis can provide the means for assessing both common
locality and primary interaction.

4.2.2   The social function of close-knit networks

The discussion so far has focused on the conceptual use of the idea of networks in sociolinguistic theory, but will proceed now to examine the actual employment of the network paradigm for analytical purposes in empirical sociolinguistic research.

The majority of these sociolinguistic studies explore the assumption that the anthropologists' analysis of social constraints governing interpersonal relationships may be utilized in the interpretation of verbal performances (Blom and Gumperz, 1972:209). As Gal (1979:15) puts it, the use of the network paradigm for the analysis of language diversity is based on the fact that norms of language usage are partly social, and therefore differences in people's social networks can account for the process by which differences arise in their norms and expectations concerning linguistic behaviour.

More specifically, sociolinguistic network studies draw on the social anthropological view that densely interrelated networks (in the sense of moral density and multiplexity) exert a function of norm reinforcement which results in the development of resistance to the forces of innovation. As a consequence of this, inter-group distinctiveness is emphasized and the members of close-knit networks are insulated from outside influences, including mainstream linguistic values. This state of affairs is illustrated in figure 4.5:

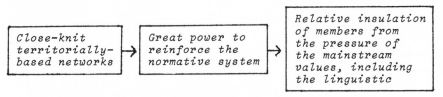

Figure 4.5 *The social function of close-knit networks*

The relations displayed in figure 4.5 can indeed be interpreted in more than one way. Milroy and Margrain (1980) argue that researchers connected with both the anthropological and the sociolinguistic tradition of network studies have made use of the concept as an explanatory device, i.e., they believe that 'it has a powerful capacity to <u>explain</u> social behaviour, rather than simply <u>describe</u> correlations between network type and

behaviour' (Milroy and Margrain, 1980:47; emphasis in original).
Therefore, these authors suggest, sociolinguistic network
studies do not simply correlate extralinguistic indices with
linguistic variables, but rather use the former to explain the
latter.

Romaine (1981:112) criticizes this position and argues that
no nomically causal relationship may be established between network index scores and individual linguistic variation within the
group because 'there are no antecedently available laws which
guarantee the effects'.[6] The relation is therefore pseudo-
causal, she observes, for:'phenomena like social networks and
social groups as such are not given to us as definite observable
objects or natural units. They refer to certain structures or
relationships between some of the many things we observe within
spatio-temporal limits... Quantitative analysis in these cases
does not measure empirical constructs but assigns numerical
values to relationships within a model' (Romaine, 1981:112).

Moreover, Romaine claims that Milroy and Margrain have categorically established a causal and necessary relation between
network characteristics and the individual's linguistic behaviour.

In fact it does not seem to us that Milroy and Margrain
advocate any such deterministic relation. On the contrary, when
they discuss the statistical results that showed a positive and
significant relationship between language and network scores on
several variables tested in the Belfast study (Milroy, 1980),
they concede that 'on the whole these results suggest that many
factors work together in controlling linguistic scores, and that
we should be cautious of attributing too much importance to any
single extralinguistic variable'(Milroy and Margrain, 1980:66).

They are indeed extremely cautious when they state their
conclusion about the network influence on speech characteristics. According to them it is plausible to suggest that speakers
tend to be more susceptible to influence from the standard language as their network structures become less dense, probably
because their personal networks then will no longer exert
counter-institutional pressures on their behaviour (Milroy and
Margrain, 1980:67).

The problem raised by Romaine actually broadens the scope of discussion concerning the usefulness of the network concept for sociolinguistic analysis. It pertains to the broader epistemological issue of the theoretical adequacy of any social science such as sociolinguistics. In a discussion of this issue, Bell (1976:197) observes that 'the empirical orientation typical of the human sciences makes the drawing up of such theories particularly problematical'. The problem, according to this sociolinguist, lies in the lack of clear correspondences 'between internally defined constitutive constructs and their equivalent epistemic counterparts derived from external empirical data'. He concludes then that 'relations between the two can be presumed but rarely proved' (emphasis in original).

Such a position is in accord with Nagel's (1961:49) claim that the concept of scientific law is not technically defined in any empirical science, and is often used without a precise import. Therefore, any sharp demarcation between lawlike and non-lawlike statement can be arbitrary. According to this author it is doubtful whether 'any formulation of uniformities in human social behaviour (e.g. those studied in economics and linguistics) can properly be called laws'. The type of 'law' generally formulated in social sciences, as well as in biology and sometimes in physics also, Nagel continues, asserts invariable statistical (or probabilistic) relations between events, but, of course, does not assert that the occurrence of one event is invariably accompanied by the occurrence of the other (our emphasis). In his words: 'such laws are manifestly not causal, though they are not incompatible with a causal account of facts they formulate'. The author adduces, finally, that 'the explanation of many phenomena in terms of strictly universal causal laws is not likely to be feasible practically' (Nagel, 1961:77).

In the present work, we acknowledge the problems inherent in the operational use of the network concept, yet we believe that it is a useful analytic tool capable of providing the sociolinguistic description with, at least, 'observational adequacy' in the sense put forward by Chomsky in the first edition of Aspects of the Theory of Syntax in 1965, and commented upon by Bell (1976:196). In other words, the network construct, defined in

epistemic and operational terms, provides an interpretation of
linguistic behaviour which is 'consistent with observed primary
data'. More importantly, it helps disclose aspects of linguistic
variation that are overlooked by the method of simply correlating linguistic and large-scale sociodemographic variables.

Our interpretation of figure 4.5 is, then, that there are
regularly patterned relations, liable to statistical assessment,
between network characteristics and individual linguistic behaviour. Such behaviour is partially governed by social rules,
which, in part, are conditioned by the characteristics of the
individual's social network. Network features are therefore an
efficient set of variables to predict and interpret language
variation.

4.2.3 Network sociolinguistic studies
Most of the sociolinguistic studies that use the concept of network analytically rely on the binary closure model that stems
from the Barnes/Bott tradition. The conceptual framework owes
much to Gumperz' studies in which he explores the gap in the
quality of in-group and out-group relations (Gumperz, 1976a).

Several sociolinguists have investigated the connection
between network closure and language maintenance, both in small
villages which are being exposed to currents of innovation, and
in areally-defined groups in metropolitan environments, which
show a high level of internal cohesiveness due to the polarization of social, ethnic or religious values. In either case, the
close-knit networks are associated with preservation of the
nonstandard or minority language whereas open networks are
marked by preference for the culturally dominant or nationwide
language.

These studies have made a significant contribution to understanding the complex relation that obtains between socioecologi-
cal and political factors and the maintenance or disruption of
diglossia in multilingual or multidialectal situations. In particular, the approach to language variation and change through
analysis of the speakers' network of relations has shed light on
two complex issues in sociolinguistics, namely, the process
whereby non-monolingual communities will tend either towards

stable diglossia or to the displacement of one variety in favour
of the other (Fishman, 1972, 1980) and the apparent paradox of
the maintenance of nonstandard varieties in the repertoires of
urban communities in spite of the overwhelming normative influence of the standard language (Ryan, 1979; Milroy, 1980).

Studies of code-switching and language shifting (Blom and
Gumperz, 1972; Gumperz, 1976a; Gal, 1978, 1979) illustrate the
first issue, whereas the second is dealt with through small-
scale studies of nonstandard varieties in metropolitan environments (Labov, 1972b; Milroy, 1980). These studies are briefly
discussed below.

In a classical study of code-switching in Hemnesberget, a
town of 1,300 inhabitants in northern Norway which remains as
'an island of tradition in a sea of change', Blom and Gumperz
(1972) have shown that the speakers' selection between the local
variety and the standard is differently patterned in the closed
networks of the locally employed artisans compared to the more
dispersed network of the section of the population which is
associated with outsiders. The two codes are almost isomorphic
in syntax and phonetics, differing in morphophonemics only, but
they are kept separate in the speech community due to the cultural identities with which they are associated and the social
values that they imply. The local variety is the language of
home and neighbourhood and functions as an important marker of
the local culture and identity. The standard, on the other hand,
is learned in school and in church and is associated with pan-
Norwegian values.

Code-switching among the members of the close-knit networks
is constrained by a direct relationship between language and
social situation; using the authors' term, among the locals the
switching is 'situational'. These residents view the vernacular
as a symbol of 'local team' values and have it as a preferential
code for in-group interaction irrespective of the topic of conversation. Switching to the standard will occur only when the
social situation or the social event must be redefined, as when
outsiders step up to a group engaged in conversation.

Those residents whose social connections include both local
and supralocal ties follow a different switching pattern related

to kinds of topics or subject matters and not to a change in the social situation. The authors have labelled the phenomenon 'metaphorical switching'. Whenever phrases of the local vernacular are metaphorically inserted in a conversation carried out in the standard, they add a special meaning of confidentiality to the conversation.

As a conclusion the authors suggest that the most reasonable explanation for the differences in the speech behaviour of the two groups 'seems to be that the dual system of local values, differences in individual background, and the various social situations in which members find themselves operate to affect their interpretation of the social meaning of the variables they employ'(Blom and Gumperz, 1972:432).

The preservation of the diglossic situation in the community seems assured as long as the local dialect maintains its value as a symbol of distinctness and of the speakers' identification with their peers.

Two studies of code-switching in bilingual communities, carried out by Gumperz (1976a) and Gal (1978,1979) respectively, have identified an analogous correlation between types of network and language choice.

Gumperz (1976a) studied a peasant community in the Gail Valley, Kärnten, Austria, which is undergoing the impact of modernization, and found that the process of language shift from the traditional Slovenian into the more prestigious German 'reflects basic changes in the structure of interpersonal relations rather than alterations in the extra-linguistic environment' (Gumperz 1976a:19). The analysis focused on the communicative routines of the residents and on the conventions which govern their interaction with interlocutors of varying social categories.

For many decades the Gail Valley has preserved Slovenian, while elsewhere in Kärnten this language has disappeared almost completely. The explanation for its maintenance in Gail Valley, Gumperz argues, lies in the fact that, until recently at least, social changes had not destroyed the local system of overlapping close-knit networks.

Despite the long period of relatively stable bilingualism,

during which code-switching strategies have taken on specific
pragmatic meanings, as a result of recent economic developments,
Slovenian is beginning to give way. However, as this minority
language is gradually displaced by the dominant code, the function of group loyalty, which was played by the former, is taken
over by a local variety of German. The differences between in-
group and out-group interaction are thus preserved.

A closer look at the process of language shift under very
similar sociological conditions was carried out by Susan Gal
(1978, 1979) in Oberwärt, Austria, a German- and Hungarian-
speaking village. The gradual process of German hegemony in the
community's repertoire was approached in the light of two processes, namely linguistic presentation of self and the constraints placed on it by the social networks of speakers. The
economic prosperity and the consequent modernization that has
taken place in the village since the last century have drawn the
young population from peasant agriculture into industrial work
and German has become a symbol of the Oberwärters' claim to
worker rather than to peasant status. This change in the
speakers' presentation of self occurred as their social networks
changed. In view of that Gal argues that 'it is through their
effects on the shape of social networks, on the statuses
speakers want to claim, and on the cultural association between
linguistic varieties and social groups that macrosociological
factors can influence the language choices of speakers in every-
day interactions'(Gal, 1979:17).

As regards Gal's methodology, language switching in Oberwärt
was analysed in terms of the speakers' choice of code according
to different interlocutors in different situations. Implica-
tional scales were built up and the main factors determining the
position of the speaker on the scales were found to be age and
degree of peasantness. Each speaker was ranked along a peasant-
to-urbanite continuum according to different indicators of his
commitment to peasant activities as opposed to wage labour -
for instance , the ownership of pigs and cows. Information on the
peasant or worker statuses of the people with whom the speaker
most often interacted for a period of time provided a measure
of the peasantness of the individual's network. This measure was

a better predictor of language choice than was the speaker's own peasantness. This led to the conclusion that whatever a speaker's social status, his linguistic presentation of self is constrained by his social network.

Two studies of metropolitan areally-defined groups are especially relevant in illuminating the intriguing issue of the preservation of low-prestige varieties in the cities: Labov's (1972b) study of four pre-adolescent street gangs in Harlem and Milroy's (1980) research on three working-class communities in Belfast.

Labov used the sociometric technique and, on the basis of the number of names given as preferential friends, of names received and of reciprocal namings, classified the youngsters as core, secondary and peripheral members of the gangs. He could also identify the 'lames', i.e. the isolated boys who did not keep a close contact with the gang members. The study showed a positive correlation between the degree of each youngster's integration in the peer group and his adherence to the Black English Vernacular grammar, and concluded that the highly cohesive structure of the groups exerted strong control over the so-called vernacular culture.

A basic assumption in the Belfast study was that the content and structure of individual network ties can be observed and quantified. A scale was devised to measure the degree of density and multiplexity in the personal networks of residents, on the basis of the following indicators of network attributes (Milroy, 1980:141-2):

1. Membership of a high-density, territorially-based cluster, in other words, of a sector or compartment of the network associated with a specific type of activities of leisure, work etc;[7]

2.The condition of having substantial ties of kinship in the neighbourhood;

3.The condition of working at the same place with at least two others from the area;

4. The condition of sharing the same place of work with at least two others of the same sex from the area;

5. Voluntary association with workmates in leisure hours, whenever conditions 3 and 4 were satisfied.

A high level of integration in the network, assessed through
this scale, can be interpreted as a situation in which a limited
number of people interacted in a limited territory as kin, workmates and friends.

Five phonological variables were chosen as indicators of the
local vernacular and correlation tests demonstrated that there
is a reliable relationship between a speaker's linguistic habits
and the characteristics of his network. Moreover, they indicated
that the relation between the individual language and the structure of his network may vary according to sociodemographic factors such as age, sex, rate of unemployment, geographic mobility
etc.

Milroy reaches the following conclusion:'Personal network
structure is in these communities of very great importance in
predicting language use: a dense multiplex network structure
predicts relative closeness to vernacular norms. However, the
constraints on the capacity of network structure to influence
language use are equally important, for the relationship between language and network is not absolute'(Milroy, 1980:160).

One significant contribution of Milroy's work is that dense
and multiplex personal networks that are likely to characterize
old-established working-class areas in industrial countries,
in the same way as those networks of rural areas, may exert
counter-institutional pressures, insulating their members from
mainstream linguistic values. In view of that, she has convincingly argued that close-knit networks such as the street
gangs in Harlem and the neighbourhood groups in Belfast can be
regarded as a source of motivation for the maintenance of low-
prestige varieties in the repertoire of city dwellers, despite
the ubiquitous influence of the standard language.

4.3 The function of language as a symbol of personal identity
A fertile aspect of the application of the network paradigm in
sociolinguistics comes from the possibility of it being supplemented by the social-psychological accommodation theory put
forward by Giles and Powesland (Giles and Powesland, 1975; Giles
and Smith, 1979; Giles, 1980). The basic postulates of the
accommodation theory are implicit in all sociolinguistic studies

discussed in this chapter, but in view of their importance for
the present study, they will be more closely analysed in this
section.

Gal (1979) has acutely observed that social networks do not
influence language directly. Their influence is exerted to the
extent that network characteristics are likely to shape people's
predisposition to identify themselves with a certain social
group:

> Particularly relevant here are the effects of networks on
> the social categories with which speakers aim to identify
> themselves. Social networks influence people's communica-
> tive strategies when such identification is expressed
> through speech. In turn, the power of social networks to
> constrain linguistic presentation of self depends on the
> fact that social contacts associate certain linguistic
> choices with particular social categories. (Gal, 1979:15-16)

The investigation of the attitudes, motives, feelings, as
well as of the strategies involved in the use of language as a
means of achieving social integration and implementing group
identification (which Gal is referring to here) pertains mostly
to the domain of social psychology. An influential theory, still
in development, which deals with these phenomena is accommodation theory. Its main postulate is that people are motivated to
adjust their speech - or to 'accommodate' - in order to express
values, attitudes and intentions towards others (Giles, 1980:
105). The theory highlights the negotiative character of any
interaction. Such a negotiative process aims at providing the
participants with a common set of interpretive procedures which
allow the speaker's intentions to be properly encoded by him and
correctly decoded by the listeners (Giles and Smith, 1979:46).

The accommodation model draws on four psychological theories,
concerned, respectively, with the processes of similarity-
support-attraction, social exchange, causal attribution and
inter-group distinctiveness, which are briefly discussed below;
and it has developed three basic concepts: convergence, divergence and complementarity.

According to the similarity-support-attraction principle, the
more similar a person's attitudes, beliefs and behaviour to
certain others, the more likely it is he will be attracted to
them. Speech convergence is one device used in this search for

attraction and support. The term was coined to refer to the
process of speech shift, whereby speakers endeavour to become
more like those with whom they are interacting. It is basically
a process of adaptation, extreme examples of which are language
simplification strategies such as 'baby-talk' and 'foreign-
talk' in the sense put forward by Ferguson (cf. Ferguson and De
Bose, 1977).

Speech convergence involves reduction of linguistic dissimilarities and can be manifested in several dimensions. It may
occur by a shift of language, dialect or accent, or be restricted to the paralinguistic level, which includes shift of
speech rate, pause and utterance lengths, vocal intensities etc.
It may include also adaptation of non-verbal behaviour and of
message content, the latter taking into account the listener's
familiarity with the topic being discussed. As convergence decreases the perceived discrepancies between the participants, it
encourages further interaction and generally results in a favourable appraisal of the speaker who is trying to accommodate
to the listeners. In fact, a person adjusts his speech to the
way he believes his interlocutors will best receive it.

Speech convergence, as a strategy to achieve similarity, indicates that people are striving to cooperate and it usually
leads to increase of intelligibility, predictability and sup-
portiveness in the interaction and, ultimately, to social integration.

The opposite process is that of linguistic divergence, a
shift away from the interlocutors' speech characteristics. It is
usually a tactic of social dissociation, used by ethnic groups
as a strategy for maintaining their identity, in so far as it
represents a means of emphasizing in-group similarity and out-
group distinctiveness. It should be viewed then, just like convergence, as a strategy of conformity and identification. Speech
divergence is part of a broader process of inter-group distinctiveness, by means of which, in inter-group encounters, individuals may search for or create a positively-valued distinctiveness from an out-group member on several dimensions they
value highly, including the linguistic (Giles, 1980:119).

As was suggested above, the engagement in a convergence

process may entail social reward represented by increase of
attraction and approval. In fact, the multitude of language
attitudinal studies, e.g. **the matched-guise researches** (Giles and
Powesland, 1975, among others), have shown that prestigious dialects and accents are considered more persuasive and of a better
quality than their less prestigious counterparts. By the same
token, the speakers of the former receive higher evaluative
ratings on most dimensions than those of the latter. Taking
these results into consideration, it seems clear that the initiative of an upward convergence taken by the inferior in an
asymmetrical interaction can be a source of potential reward.
But the convergence may, however, represent a loss of the
speaker's perceived integrity and personal or group identity,
being deleterious to his self-esteem. Convergence and divergence
should therefore be viewed in the light of the social exchange
theory, according to which, 'prior to acting we attempt to
assess the rewards and costs of alternate courses of action'
(Giles and Smith, 1979:48).

Another important notion for an understanding of the accommodation phenomenon stems from causal attribution theory. Any individual tends to interpret and evaluate the actions of others
in terms of the motives and intentions he considers as causes of
their behaviour. Accordingly, to engage in a convergent speech
act, for instance, may not be viewed positively if the listener
attributes to the speaker the intention of patronizing, condescending, threatening, ingratiating or even caricaturing.

A third concept developed by the accommodation theory is that
of speech complementarity. In a dyadic interaction, a relation
is referred to as complementary when one participant is acknowl-
edged to hold a subordinate role to the other party. In such
cases both divergence and convergence may be rather integrative
for both participants. Speech complementarity usually involves
divergence, in simple linguistic terms, yet psychologically it
implies acceptance of the situation rather than dissociation. It
is likely to occur when one participant assumes the submissive
one-down position (Giles, 1980).

Although speech convergence, divergence and complementarity
are probably universal phenomena, their linguistic manifesta-

tions are culturally bound.

The social psychology tradition concerned with linguistic phenomena - from which the accommodation model sprang - represents a relevant contribution for a closer understanding of the causes and motivations of language variation. Answers for the still unanswered question: 'Why do people speak the way they do in different social situation?' are looked for in the dynamics of attitudes and motivations, and, especially, in the processes of identity signalling.

Concern with the individual's motivation underlying language variation and change has also been present among sociolinguists. At least two important efforts in this direction were undertaken by Labov (1966) and Le Page (1975/1980). Although the approaches of these two scholars follow different traditions and conflict in some aspects - the latter as a creolist, and the former as an urban dialectologist - they are both imbued with some basic notions that underlie the accommodation model, such as similarity-attraction and rewards and costs of identity switch. Both of them also seem to draw on the concept of reference group, which was defined by Berreman (1964:232) as follows: 'Basically, the reference group concept is this: when a person's attitudes and behaviour are influenced by a set of norms which he assumes are held by others, those others constitute for him a reference group.'

According to Le Page, linguistic behaviour is permanently subject to multiple and co-occurring sources of influences related to different aspects of social identity, such as sex, age, regional background, occupational, religious and ethnic groups. Each utterance produced by any speaker is an act of identity. As the speakers move through a multidimensional sociolinguistic space, they use the resources of language variability to express this great complex of different identities (Milroy, 1980:115).

Le Page advanced a hypothesis to account for the general motivation for individual linguistic behaviour. According to this hypothesis speakers create their rules so as to resemble as closely as possible the members of the group with which they wish to identify themselves from time to time. Their performance is constrained, however, by one or another of the following four riders to the general hypothesis (Le Page, 1980):

1. the extent to which people can identify the model groups;
2. the extent to which they have access to such groups, and the ability to work out the rules of the model group's repertoire;
3. the weight of various (possibly conflicting) motivations towards one or another model group and towards retention of their own identity;
4. the ability to modify their linguistic behaviour.

Labov (1966) has explored the hypothesis of the conflict between what he calls prestige and identity orientation. The complexities of distribution of linguistic variables in an urban community cannot be understood, Labov claims, without the analysis of patterns of social mobility.

Using socioeconomic indicators, Labov divided the sample of his Lower East Side (New York City) survey, carried out in 1963-4 (Labov, 1972a) into three main types according to social mobility: 'upward', 'steady' and 'downward'. The sample comprised people of four socioeconomic classes: lower-class, working-class, lower middle-class and upper middle-class. Labov argues that, except for the lowest stratum, the other class groups actively participate in a system of dual sociolinguistic norms. The duality of the system is made evident by the fact that 'those who have the highest incidence of a stigmatized feature are more sensitive to its use by others' (Labov, 1966:196). In fact, despite the social and stylistic stratification in the actual performance of the speakers, most of them showed a high degree of uniformity in their subjective reactions to nonstandard features; a phenomenon which seems to be rooted in a prestige-based ideology.

The highest degree of endorsement of the publicly accepted middle-class norms appears in the second highest status group, in which the upwardly mobile individuals show the archetypal pattern of hypercorrection. Conversely, the least recognition of middle-class values occurs in the lowest status group; hence the author's claim that this group does not participate actively in the system of dual sociolinguistic norms.

Statistical analysis of the data also revealed further relations between social mobility types and adherence to prestige
linguistic norms. Upwardly mobile persons are likely to borrow
the norms of an exterior reference group, usually the next
higher group with which they are in contact; a group with a history of social stability shows a consistent performance without
a wide range of style shifting; the downward mobile category is
characterized by the nonacceptance of the normative patterns
that govern the behaviour of the **segments**.

The most important conclusion of the study comes with the
statement that most New Yorkers are able to decide on the type
of speech appropriate for high-ranking occupations. When they
use a highly stigmatized form, it is not because they are unaware of the social significance of this variable. Yet the recognition of the prestige conferred on some variants does not imply
the same range of behaviour for all: 'For many New Yorkers the
application of such middle-class values appears limited by conflict with other values - namely, the value system symbolized by
their group's vernacular from early adolescence onward. Upwardly
mobile individuals show the maximum tendency to apply the values
of an external reference group to their behavior' (Labov, 1966:
203).

Loyalty to the group's vernacular is more closely investigated in his later study of the Harlem adolescent groups (Labov,
1972b) briefly discussed above (see 4.2.3), and in his investigation of sound change in Martha's Vineyard (Labov, 1972a).

It has been suggested throughout the chapter that dense and
multiplex network ties contracted within a limited territory are
likely to be associated with low-status groups. Upwardly mobile
individuals, on the other hand, tend to contract uniplex and
more sparse network ties. Milroy (1980:185) suggests in addition
that the processes of urbanization and industrialization may
contribute to the dispersal of traditional close-knit networks
and consequently can accelerate linguistic standardization.

Drawing on the analyses put forward by the sociolinguists,
anthropologists, and social psychologists, and discussed in this
chapter, it seems plausible to establish co-occurrence relations
between the social psychological motivation for vernacular main-

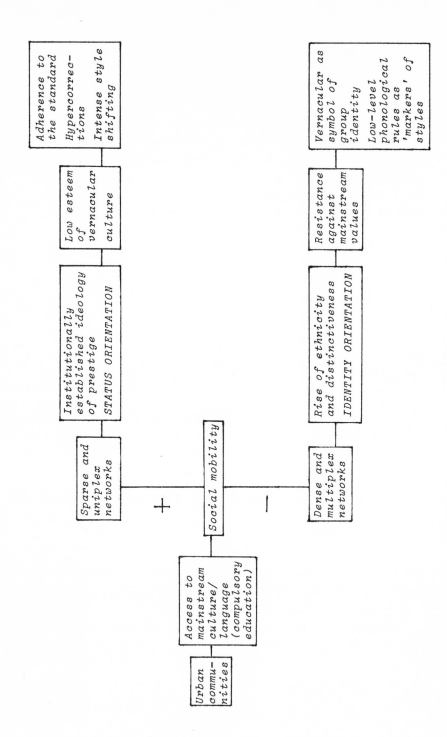

Figure 4.6   The relation between network patterns and vernacular maintenance

tenance and the structure of networks in urban settings. The role of social mobility is deemed crucial in establishing such relations, which also take into consideration the conflict between prestige and identity orientation. The issue is summarized in figure 4.6. It is important to note, however, that network structure alone does not seem to be a sufficient condition for adherence to either an identity orientation or a prestige orientation. As Milroy (1980:196) points out, the correct generalization appears to be that persons with sparse and uniplex networks are relatively more exposed to the influence of the prestige norms and, consequently, more liable to change their speech habits in the direction of the standard code.

Notes

1 Hockett (1958:326) seems to come very close to an operational use of networks when he makes use of graphs in order to highlight the concepts of 'idiolect', 'dialect' and 'language'.
2 For details on research conducted by social anthropologists, see the collections of articles edited by Mitchell (1969), Aronson (1970), Boissevant and Mitchell (1973).
3 The definitions of concepts as well as description of methodological techniques advanced in this sub-section, unless otherwise indicated, draw on two works by Guimarães (1970, 1972).
4 A sociogram is a chart made of points and lines with arrows in which the points indicate the persons in a network and the lines with arrows the direction of the relationship. A sociomatrix is a matrix of N by N dimensions corresponding to a system of N persons. The procedure is simply to list the persons in the system along the rows and the columns in the same order. The rows correspond to the communication sources, and the columns to the receivers. Plus and minus signs are used for positive and negative choices and blanks for no contacts. (For further details, see Guimarães, 1970.)
5 Definitions and descriptions of these concepts are provided in section 7.2.
6 Romaine (1981:110) defines causal explanation according to the principle of the philosophy of science, namely: 'q because p' i.e. p is nomically sufficient to determine the event to be explained: q. (See on the issue Nagel, 1961, especially ch. 4.)
7 Milroy (1980:142) defines cluster 'as a portion of a network where relationships are denser internally than externally'.

5.0 *Introduction*

This chapter is concerned with the process of rural to urban
migration and its linguistic consequences. In the first section,
the adjustment of the migrant to the municipal setting is discussed and a small number of studies that deal with the migration issue in Brazil are briefly surveyed. In the second section
the concepts of dialect focusing and diffuseness are defined and
a description of the migrants' vernacular diffuseness process is
proposed. In the third section a methodological scheme designed
to assess the differences in the migrants' rural-to-urban transition process, by means of network analysis, is provided.
Throughout the chapter, excerpts of the Brazlândia migrants'
discourse which are particularly representative of their opinions and attitudes are transcribed.

5.1 *The rural migrant in the urban environment*

In chapter 2 the issue of rural-urban migration was discussed
within a broader framework of social changes and of the national
trend towards urbanization. In the present section the migration
process is focused upon more closely with emphasis on the assimilation to an urban way of life by the migrants and its linguistic consequences. The discussion is supported by the information
provided by a few sociological studies carried out in Brazil and
in other Latin American countries as well as by the data
gathered from the migrants in Brazlândia, which for the most
part corroborate the results of other investigations.

Gonzales and Bastos (1975:4) in a study of low-income migrants in Brasília define the process of migration of those
individuals whose decision to migrate results from their own

initiative, as the 'change of residence from one socio-spatial area to another brought about by economic opportunities'. The places of origin and destination (i.e. the expulsion and the attraction areas) are therefore opposite poles as far as the economic opportunities are concerned. In fact, the main motivation for the migration is the search for better living conditions: steady work, health treatment and schooling for the children, which are not available in most rural areas.[1]

The following passages of discourse of adult migrants that live in Brazlândia are very enlightening for an understanding of their decision to leave the countryside. The excerpts are given in Portuguese and the transcription keeps most of the nonstandard features of their speech. An English translation is provided but in many cases this translation is merely an approximate gloss of what was said, due to the impossibility of recovering in English many dialectal characteristics present in the texts. FM, a 54-year-old carpenter, says:

(1) For some time now, no one wants to live in rural areas anymore. In some way I agree with them; I was one of those who left the countryside because of that, right? I had no land of my own, I lived dependent on another, on a farmer. Farmers are not helpful are they? You have to plant, and if you plant you have to divide the crop in two, sometimes in three parts, don't you?

(1) De um tempo pra cá, ninguém qué roça mais. Num certo ponto eu dô razão; eu mesmo fui um desses que saí da roça por causa disso, né? Que eu não tinha terreno de meu, morava dependente de oto, de fazendero. Fazenderos não dão cuié de chá mesmo, né? Tem que plantá, planta, tem que parti à meia, ota hora à terça, né?

JM, a 43-year-old father of six children, by the time of the fieldwork had been living in Brazlândia for ten months and was trying to find a steady job. His words corroborate the previous information:

(2) I think that living in the city is better, because as for myself I have already had a lot of difficulties with my family in the countryside, no health services and, like we say, not enough to eat because

(2) Eu penso que morá na cidade seja melhor, pu que eu pelo menu já passei muita dificuldade com a minha famia lá pus matu, falta de tratamento, e como diz, falta do que a gente comê, pu que a gente morava nas

we lived on the farms, the farmers only want ... only want to look after themselves, they don't care about helping the poor peasant to do anything, because if they get their profits, the peasant's problem isn't their business. And, at the end of the harvest they want their share. If the peasant has enough to pay his expenses, ok, if not, they (the farmers) take the lot down to the last grain.

fazenda, fazendero só qué ... só qué fazê pra eles num qué sabê de dá assim um apoio pu coitado do rocero fazê nada, puque si dando pra eles, o roceiro que se vira pra lá. E no fim da safra eles qué o deles. O sujeito tem pa despesa, muito bem, se não tem, eles toma até o derradero.

The women are also likely to show their preference for the urban life, but their emphasis is mainly on the better conditions for the family. The following are the words of MR, a 59-year-old woman.

(3) But with everything I suffered ... I have no regrets about having left Minas. I left a daughter there, grandchildren, but everything I suffered there ... I thank God for being here. It was a good time for me there, but the difficulties I had ... health condition ... I prefer life in the city because I have led a life which has been very difficult and tiring but I prefer life in the city because life here is better my children can study, because I couldn't afford it and health treatment also, right? Because of my health, I prefer to live in the city, now, my old man didn't like living in the city at all, he was furious about it.

(3) Mas com tudo o que eu passei ... num tenho pesar nenhum de tê saído lá de Minas. Deixei uma filha lá, us neto. Mais o tanto que eu sofri lá ... Dô graças a Deus de tá aqui. Pra mim teve um tempo bom (na roça) mais a dificuldade qu'eu passava ... estado de saúde ... eu adoto mais a vida na cidade assim ... atraveis qu'eu tenho passado munta vida difícil e trabalhosa demais, mais eu adoto mais a vida na cidade pelos melhoramento de vida, meus filho estudá, qu'eu num tinha essa condição e o tratamento de saúde também, né? Pelo estado de saúde, eu tenho mais torcida pa morá na cidade, agora o meu véio num torcia pa morá na cidade de jeito nenhum, morria de raiva.

Whereas the adults' appraisal of their former and present condition is very realistic, their children's view of the rural life complies with the current ecologically oriented ideology.

JS is a 25-year-old marine who was born on a farm but was

raised in the Federal District. He has a high school degree and his opinion clearly reflects publicly accepted ideas:

(4) Look, from my point of view, people are happier in the countryside. Because a person in contact with nature, with everything that is good, I think that he has a better life than in the town. Because here there are a lot of things that make it so that we don't live well: there's the sound pollution, air pollution and other things, right? These all stop you from being able to live well. But there, quietness, tranquillity, this makes you live longer.

(4) Olha, do meu ponto de vista as pessoas vivem mais felizes na roça. Porque a pessoa em contato com a natureza, com tudo aquilo que é bom ali eu acho que tem mais condição de vida do que no centro urbano. Porque aqui são vários fatores que influi pra que a gente não viva bem: é poluição sonora, é poluição do ar e várias coisas, né, que influi pra que a gente não viva bem. Lá não, sossego, tranqüilidade, isso faz com que a pessoa viva mais.

This same informant, however, claims that in the city one has more comfort, and better chances of improving one's lot.

In his study of urbanization in Mexico City, Lewis (1973:129) found that 'peasants adapted to city life with far greater ease than one would have expected, judging from comparable studies in the United States and from urban-folk theory'. Cândido (1964: 174) comes to a similar conclusion as regards the incorporation of rural dwellers in the urban culture in Brazil. He observes that their adjustment is usually easier than it might appear because the transition is facilitated by the gradual introduction of urban traits into the countryside. This means that even before the migration, the Caipira is already familiar with some features of the urban *modus vivendi*.

In view of this, Cândido claims that quite often the Caipiras manage, over a period of a few years, if not to assimilate, at least to accommodate themselves to the patterns of city civilization. But this author distinguishes between 'imposed' and 'proposed' patterns of such civilization. Amongst the features imposed on the migrant, he adduces the new rhythm of work, new ecological relations, the consumption of manufactured goods, etc. The proposed traits, on the other hand are, among others, the rationalization of the family's budget, the abandonment of traditional beliefs and the individualization of work.

As regards the adjustment in the migrants' linguistic repertoire, one might, taking advantage of Cândido's fertile dichotomy, observe that the contact with the oral (and sometimes the
written) urban standard language, in varying degrees, is a cir-
cumstance imposed on the migrant while the assimilation and the
gradual acquisition of the standard variety should be viewed as
a proposed pattern.

The problem of urbanization of the migrants' Caipira dialect
is inextricably entangled with the broader issue of a trend towards homogenization in urban society in Brazil. This phenomenon
was studied by Oliven (1982) who investigated patterns of behaviour and value orientations of different social classes in a
large southern city.[2] The assumption was that, despite the
tendency towards uniformity, implemented by the mass media, by
education and the institutional structure, there exists an
opposing tendency towards differentiation, not only in economic
terms but also in those areas in which the lower classes can
offer a more effective resistance to the diffusion of the
mainstream cultural orientations.

The results have shown that the lower classes share cultural
orientations with the upper classes in those areas related to
practical and instrumental dimensions of life, such as the
importance of formal education and generic political issues, but
have different practices and orientations in those areas associated with more personal dimensions, such as family and religion.

The author suggests, in conclusion, that:

> Specifically in relation to the lower classes, we might
> suggest that there exists a dialectical process through
> which they simultaneously share features of the dominant
> culture and present elements that do not belong to that
> culture. So, while the upper classes of the Brazilian
> cities identify themselves more promptly with the domi-
> nant values and customs, the lower classes develop adap-
> tive mechanisms that allow them to deal with the capi-
> talist relations of production and at the same time keep
> their identity. (Oliven, 1982:124; translated from Portu-
> guese)

Oliven concedes, however, that even though the category of

social class is a basic variable in the analysis of such differences, it is impossible 'to postulate a linear relation between socio-economic position and adherence to cultural orientations, a process that   is more complex and permeated by contradictions' (Oliven, 1982:79).

How can these social-anthropological insights help to clarify the process of the migrants' linguistic adjustment which is being studied here?

Firstly the phenomenon of the merger of rural dialects with urban nonstandard varieties and the possible concomitant process of acquisition of the standard variety by the migrants and their children is part of the homogenization trend that Oliven discusses. Consequently it must also be subject to equal pressure from two opposite forces, namely, the standardization pressures on the one hand and the tendency towards maintenance of the nonstandard forms as signs of group identity on the other.

Secondly, the claim that the large scale category of social class may not suffice to explain the complex phenomenon of adherence to different cultural orientations is in accord with the assumption of the present work that network analysis, as a small scale methodological tool, offers an alternative possibility of a refined analysis of such complex phenomena.

These two points will be discussed in the next section. It should be noted beforehand, however, that the analysis of adherence to prestige linguistic forms is by the very nature of linguistic behaviour not liable to be assessed by means of survey techniques which allow for clear-cut distinctions between prestige-oriented and non-prestige-oriented answers. Linguistic variability used as a means of signalling cultural orientation and values is a rather complex phenomenon, affected both by the social structure and by the social processes, as Halliday (1978) explains:

> Variation in language is in a quite direct sense the ex-
> pression of fundamental attributes of the social system;
> dialect variation expresses the diversity of social struc-
> tures (social hierarchies of all kinds), while register
> variation expresses the diversity of social processes. And
> since the two are interconnected - what we do is affected
> by who we are... - dialects become entangled with regis-
> ters. The registers a person has access to are a function

of his place in the social structure; and a switch in regis-
ter may entail a switch of dialect. (Halliday, 1978:2-3)

It is therefore simplistic to assume that values people hold
and valuations that they make in relation to language can be
tapped by the direct questioning techniques typical of survey
methods.

5.2   *Dialect focusing and diffuseness*

As was suggested in the previous section, the complexities of
the urban society process of cultural homogenization may not be
fully explained in terms of social classes because such a categorization overlooks the many differences that may exist among
the members of the same social class. The inhabitants of Brazlândia, for example, according to the large scale social class concept, could all be lumped together in the category of urban
lower-class with rural background. But this classification overlooks much variation as regards income, occupation, degree of
adaptation to the urban environment, and, consequently, degrees
of urbanization of their rural vernacular. As was suggested before, network analysis can shed light on apparently subtle distinctions that would not be otherwise disclosed. The assessment
of an individual's experiential network can probably be a fairly
good indicator of his referential network and consequently may
indicate his degree of adherence to the mainstream culture (see
4.2). Network analysis seems therefore to be a sharp analytical
tool with which to tackle the issue of prestige adherence.

Taking advantage of this analytical device the following description of the rural migrants' vernacular urbanization process
is proposed. The concepts of dialect focusing and diffuseness,
as postulated by Le Page (1975/1980), were especially useful in
this analysis. Milroy (1982), following Le Page's theory,
explains: 'The language patterns of geographically or socially
mobile persons, which cannot be said to be characteristic of any
particular nameable accent, but rather a mixture of various
social and regional accents might be said to be relatively diffuse'(Milroy, 1982:141). On the other hand, language is described as focused when speakers perceive it in some sense as a
distinct entity. Focusing, as Le Page sees it, is related to the

development of the sense of group identity, and by no means implies linguistic homogeneity but rather the emergence of a norm
in which variability follows systematic patterns. It usually
takes some decades for a focusing process to consolidate (Milroy,
1982).

What is happening in Brazlândia seems clearly to be a phenomenon of dialect diffuseness, as people of different regional background and with varied degrees of exposure to the standard language are brought into contact with each other.

For the purpose of the present work, a focused dialect is one
that shows a high incidence of nonstandard variables, which can
be of two types: those that define a sharp distinction between
rural and urban speech (sharp features) and those that show a
progressive increase in frequency in the speech of several social
groups, irrespective of being rural or urban (gradient features;
see 2.1). Dialect diffuseness, on the other hand, represents a
decrease in the frequency of both sharp and gradient nonstandard
variables.

The language spoken in isolated rural communities can be considered as a highly focused form of rural vernacular, which contains virtually the whole set of nonstandard features that define a sharp distinction between rural and urban varieties and
also presents a high incidence of the gradient features of popular Portuguese.

As the speakers of rural vernaculars come into direct or indirect contact with the written and oral standard language, their
dialect tends to become more diffuse; then the occurrence of
typical rural lexical items will decrease and some of the nonstandard rules of their repertoire which were almost categorical
will tend to become variable rules. Diffuseness is not viewed
necessarily as an assimilation of Standard Portuguese but rather
as a movement away from the stigmatized rural dialects. The
process of dialect diffuseness is summarized in figure 5.1.

The geographic mobility of the migrant, who moves from his
rural niche to a new habitat, is the first factor for the diffuseness of his dialect. The transition very often implies an
inter-occupation mobility and, more importantly, the search for
a change from an economy of subsistence to an economy of

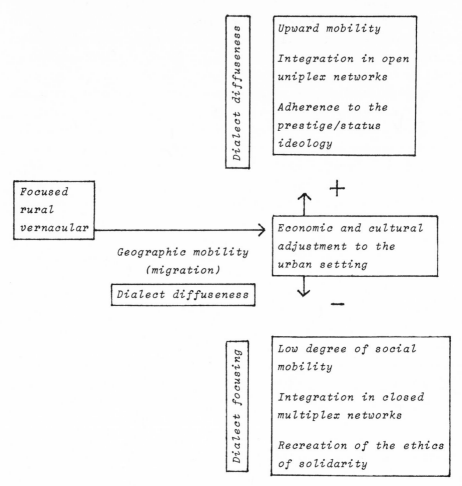

Figure 5.1   *Rural-urban migration and dialect diffuseness and focusing*

accumulation, to use the terms employed by Cardoso de Oliveira
(1983:139).[3]

The evolutionary course of the migrants' language patterns
will largely depend on their economic and cultural adjustment to
urban civilization.[4] Integration in the new system is related to
better chances of social mobility and changes in their socialization process. As the migrants become more integrated in the
urban setting their communication networks are likely to en-

large, and acquire the characteristics of urban social networks, becoming more uniplex and sparse (see 4.1.2). This change is likely to be accompanied by a tendency towards adherence to the orientation of the upper classes. Such a state of affairs will facilitate the process of dialect diffuseness.

The opposite process is also easy to trace. The migrants that do not succeed in this economic and cultural transition, as a survival strategy - which was very well described by Lomnitz (1977) in a Mexican shanty-town - will find shelter in squatter settlements where the ethics of solidarity prevail.

Whenever geographic and social immobility co-occur, after a few decades a focused dialect is likely to emerge. It should be noted however that the focused dialects will be marked by many nonstandard features, but in relation to the dialect continuum, they will be closer to the standard variety than the original isolated rural vernaculars. In Brazlândia these processes of lower-class dialect focusing are still difficult to assess due to the young age of the community, but there they are probably following a gradual evolutionary course.

Analysis of the integration of the migrant in the urban system, which is crucial for an understanding of the parallel phenomenon of dialect diffuseness, is indeed more complex than figure 5.1 may suggest. A positive correlation between upward social mobility and the adoption of the prestige status ideology is a less controversial issue. However, the opposite relation between lack of social mobility and the rejection of such ideology should not be taken as a necessary corollary of the former proposition. It is possible for any individual to present a low level of socioeconomic mobility and still borrow the values of an external reference group. This would seem to be the case which Labov (1966:191) referred to as 'status incongruence'.

It is important to note also that a migrant population may be considered as poor and marginal according to socioeconomic criteria, and still exhibit a high level of satisfaction with their present situation. This is indeed what Schühly (1981) found in his investigation of sociodemographic and socio-psychological characteristics of *favela* (shanty town) dwellers with rural background in a hinterland city of the state of São

Paulo.[5] The author concluded that the migrants considered themselves to be integrated in urban society and when they compared
their present situation with their former condition, the realization of the many improvements that they had experienced was a
source of much satisfaction. Moreover the fact that they had the
middle-class as a reference group in their aspirations for their
children's social mobility (a phenomenon that has been referred
to as 'intergenerational mobility') also contributed to their
social adjustment.

In fact, evidence of this intergenerational mobility is
abundant in the Brazlândia data. The following excerpt of BS's
discourse (a 42-year-old carpenter) is an example of it:

(5) One thing that I'd like to
see is my children in a
life much better than
mine, right; for this
reason I've been living
in Brasília for fourteen
years, to let them study,
as long as they can.

(5) Uma coisa qu'eu mais gostaria de vê meus filho numa
vida assim bem milhó do que
a minha, né; pra isso qu'eu
já tô há catorze anos em
Brasília, pra deixá eles
estudá, enquanto pudé.

The assumption that dialect diffuseness is parallel to the
broader social process of adherence to the mainstream cultural
orientation can also be empirically demonstrated by the data
collected in Brazlândia. What follows are passages of the discourse of two men who are Saint Vincent de Paul Conference (i.e.
group) leaders in the community. Both can be considered as well
integrated in the urban way of life and their speech shows a
high degree of diffuseness, as will be discussed in chapter 8
where the quantitative treatment of the data is presented. Their
discourse depicts a clear alignment with the mainstream ideology.

In this first text, BS, 42 years old, describes the philanthropic ideology of his conference:

(6) When I moved to Brasília,
I had the impression that
in Brasília there wouldn't
be any poverty, because
the *vicentino* work is to
help a person when he is
suffering, when he is
maybe without anything,
right? He's sick and

(6) Quando eu mudei pra Brasília, eu tinha a impressão
que em Brasília não havia
necessidade, pu'que o trabalho vicentino é só pa
ajudá a pessoa quando tá
sofrenu, quando tá talvez
sem nada, né, tá doente,
sem as coisa. Aí eu pensa-

hasn't got anything. Then I thought that in Brasília the money 'runs' and there almost wouldn't be any need for someone to help. Then *Senhor* F. invited me to attend, to visit a conference. I went and he soon scheduled me to visit a poor family. I went to visit the family and began to see that there actually is a lot of poverty. More than there in Minas, in the interior.

va que em Brasília corre dinheiro e quase nem tinha necessidade de arguém ajudã. Aí então o senhor F. me convidô p'assisti, pa visitá uma conferença. Fui visitá e ele me escalô logo pa visitá uma família pobre. Fui visitá a família e comecei a vê que há muita necessidade. Mais do que lá em Minas, no interiô.

In this second passage, the same informant comments on the national economic situation:

(7) I see then Brazil in a situation which is very difficult and I think that no one in Brazil has the answers for solving it. This business of this external debt, right? Brazil dominated by the countries that have oil. Actually I don't know if I am right to say it, but I think that Brazil has almost no freedom anymore, as they say, that is, independence I mean, I almost don't see Brazil as an independent country. I'm even ashamed to see the celebrations of the independence week. A captive Brazil celebrating independence!

(7) Eu enxergo assim o Brasil numa situação meio difícil e acho que quase ninguém no Brasil tem condição de resorvê isso. Esse negoçu dessa dívida externa, né? O Brasil dominado pelos país que tem petrolhu. Incrusive eu num sei ... s'eu tô errado em falá isso, mais acho que o Brasil não tem quase mais é liberdade como eles fala, é independença, qué dizê, eu quase não encaro o Brasil como país independente, eu tenho até vergonha de vê as comemorações da semana da independença. Um Brasil cativo e comemoranu independença, né!

In the following passage, 54-year-old FM advances his opinion about the Indians' situation.

(8) Yes indeed, the Indians also have their place, also, don't they? Then it can't be so ... they are true Brazilians, the Indians are, and they are being expelled, they are being expelled. I mean, no one is worrying about them, right?

(8) Pois é, os índio também têm o lugarzinho deles, também, né. Então num pode ... eles são os verdadeiro brasileiro, são os índio, e tão senu expulso, tão senu expulso. Qué dizê que ninguém pensa neles né?

Throughout this chapter it has been suggested that several

factors seem to facilitate the migrants' adjustment in the new environment. Three main sets of such factors will be briefly discussed in the following paragraphs: the necessity of coping with the urban social structure as a survival strategy, the influence of many institutional channels, which serve the function of recruiting the population into an urban referential network, and finally, the migrants' psychological motivation to assimilate a new set of values.

Adult migrants arriving in a city have to learn how to cope with basic practical matters such as the use of public transportation and the handling of the bureaucracy related to social security which gives them access to medical care and legal employment. In these matters they receive much help from more experienced kin-folk or fellow migrants.[6]

Access of the rural migrants to the urban culture is also fostered through many institutional vehicles, among which formal education plays a relevant role. Almost all adults interviewed in Brazlândia stated that one of their main motivations for migration was to provide their children with schooling. Indeed almost all children there attend school regularly and a few adults go to night school. Even so, most of those people who migrated as adults are still illiterate or semi-literate.

The importance given to formal education is well manifested in the discourse excerpts below. All the people who were interviewed appear to be aware of the fact that education is necessary for upward social mobility. They make a clear categorization between 'schooled' and 'unschooled' people.[7] MM, a 40-year-old garbage collector, points to a handicap of being illiterate:

(9) You know, for someone who can't read, it's even difficult (to find a way) to travel, right. I can't read at all.

(9) Ocê sabe, quem num sabe lê é até de ruim jeito de viajá, né? Eu num sei de jeito nenhum.

NS, a 43-year-old tailor, clearly relates education to a chance to improve one's lot.

(10) Let's say, if I had studied ... If I was a man that had at least one course ... then I might

(10) Vamos dizê, se eu tivesse estudado ... fosse um homi que tivesse pelo menos uma formatura ... aí vinha a

have a chance.

chance, né?

JM, male, 43-year-old, no regular employment, has a similar opinion:

(11) I mean, there are other ways (of improving your lot) someone who's good at reading can get a good job and manage to deal with life itself, someone like that gradually improves (his life) and may reach a better culture, right?

(11) Qué dizê que tem otos meios, né, quem tem uma boa leitura pode pegá um bom emprego e sabeno mexê com a vida memo a pessoa vai meioranu divagarzim, ainda panha uma cultura mió, né?

The most touching assessment of the illiterates' disadvantages, however, was provided by TS, a 40-year-old woman. Illiteracy is, of course, the source of much linguistic insecurity. What follows is part of her dialogue with the fieldworker.

(12) FW: What is the major desire that you have in your life, *dona* T?

TS: You know, what I'd like would be to study.

FW: You'd like to study, right?

TS: Oh, yes very much! (To be) a person ... so that I could stand in the front, like that and talk and read like that without being ashamed, without trembling, without ...

(12) FW: Qual o maior desejo que a senhora tem na vida, dona T?

TS: A senhora sabe, o que eu tenho muito desejo é de tê estudo.

FW: É estudo, né?

TS: Oh, mais como! Uma pessoa assim ... que eu podia chegá assim na frente assim e conversá e lê assim sem ter acanho, sem tremê, sem ...

Other vehicles which promote the migrants' urbanization are media exposure, participation in urban events, spatial mobility within the city limits, the social and technical setting of work, and especially participation in voluntary religious associations.[8] Membership of organized religious groups seems indeed to be a crucial instrument in the migrants' adjustment and welfare in Brazlândia. MP, 24 years old, young mother of two children, makes it clear that the participation in a Mothers' Club, directed by Catholic nuns, is very relevant in her socializing process.

(13) (In the Mothers' Club) we

(13) (No Clube de Mães) a gente

make a lot of friends, right? Take me for instance, I've been living here for three years and I don't know many people. And in the Mothers' Club I made a lot of friends, lots of friends, because the sister puts all of us together there.

ranja tanta amizade, né? Igual eu mesmo, moro aqui há três anos e num conheço muita gente não. E lá no Crube da Mãe ranjei tantas amiga, tanta colega, que a irmã reúne todas nóis ali.

The third set of motives that help explain the migrants' adjustment is the psychological predisposition towards assimilation. Such predisposition should be understood in relation to a common feeling shared by all the migrants, namely, the aspiration for an easier and more comfortable life than the one they led in the country.

In view of the widespread phenomenon of the resistance of minority ethnic groups to assimilation, which can be witnessed to a varying degree in Western society, the claim of the migrants' willingness to accept the mainstream culture may sound superficial or unrealistic. Yet it must be noted, firstly, that Caipira is not a clear and definite mark of identity, but, on the contrary, a rather vague and ambiguous one. The migrants will more easily identify themselves with their geographic background, e.g. as *mineiros* (from the state of Minas Gerais), as *goianos* (from the state of Goiás) etc, than with a more abstract category on the grounds of a rural culture. Their situation is very different from that of a Brazilian Indian ethnic group, for example, who, in contact with the inclusive culture, may keep a clearly defined ethnic identity (see on this issue, Cardoso de Oliveira, 1968).[9]

Secondly, the transition for the migrants is not primarily a move from a rural to an urban culture, but a move from a situation of marginality to integration in a system of production, a condition which not all of them are likely to achieve. Many of the migrants interviewed, when comparing the rural and the urban ways of life, did not praise the latter for its own sake. They clearly stated that both have their advantages and disadvantages but 'for someone who does not own a piece of land the city is the only alternative'. A few of them would like to go back, but not to their former condition of poverty. They would return only if they could afford to buy a small farm.

Thirdly, it should be emphasized that the assimilation trend is for them a rather gradual and selective process, as Cândido (1964) and Oliven (1982) have pointed out.

The migrants are likely to become nostalgic when they recall good memories, as in the description of religious festivals, weddings and the like, but once in a while negative evaluations of the Caipiras, which reflect commonly accepted stereotypes, can emerge, as in the passage below, uttered by FM, the 54-year-old carpenter.

(14)There is a disadvantage (as far as parties are concerned) in the country-side if there is a fight, then knives come out, and pistols and guns,every-thing. It seems that people there don't under-stand many things, they think that a gun or a knife can solve the problem.

(14)Na roça tem uma desvanta-gem (nas festas), é que se sai uma briga aí sai faca, sai garrucha, sai revolvi, sai de tudo. Parece que o povo lá não entende muito das coisa, achu que u re-volvi ou a faca é que re-solve o problema...

Notice that the informant refers to the rural dwellers as they and criticizes the men's demonstration of courage, asso-ciating it with ignorance. In summary, no social advantages seem to accrue to the migrants if they maintain a Caipira outlook and behaviour. On the contrary, the assimilation of the new cultural patterns is very much imposed on them by pragmatic considera-tions.

The existence of this psychological predisposition towards assimilation is a crucial point in the present study. Most of the sociolinguistic network studies previously mentioned (ch.4) were conducted in social settings where two relevant character-istics obtain. Firstly, literacy has already been a universal commodity for those populations for many decades. Secondly, much significance has been vested in the division of the population into categories based on a variety of criteria, such as local vs. nonlocal descent, or ethnic, religious or status differentia-tion. Such a situation usually leads to an overt recognition of group distinctiveness.

In Belfast, as in Hemnes, the vernacular speakers have access
to the standard variety of the language and to the referential
national network that it subsumes. In both cases the choice of
the vernacular for in-group interaction is mainly motivated by
loyalty to the 'local team'. The dialect has become the most
powerful symbol of group identity and represents an attitude of
resistance against the culturally dominant language. Both
Gumperz' and Milroy's approaches to the social function of the network were basically concerned with its consequences for dialect
maintenance and not for dialect change. The Network Strength
Scale used in Belfast was designed to assess the speakers' commitment to neighbourhood links. A high density and multiplexity
score was regarded as an indicator of their adherence to local
values and consequently to their degree of resistance to mainstream cultural values, including the linguistic (see 4.2).

The present study is not orientated towards the focusing of
dialect but rather towards diffuseness. The network approach
used here does not aim primarily at assessing the degree of
insulation in the speakers' networks but rather their degree of
integration within a broader experiential and referential network. Whereas Milroy's main concern was with network multiplexity as a factor in implementing differentiation, the main
concern here is with network patterns as a means of assessing
the degree of assimilation of the standard/urban language by the
rural migrants.

In the next section the characteristics of these insulated
and integrated networks are discussed.

5.3   *Insulated vs. integrated networks*

The social networks in Brazlândia show the characteristics of
many low-status 'rurban' communities, that is, their members are
tightly linked by ties of kinship, by pre-migration relations
and by the interaction at the neighbourhood level, which is
based on the exchange of goods and favours (see 6.1). This statement
is, however, a generalization which overlooks important internal
differentiation. There are indeed many structural and interactional differences from one individual's network to another's.
The methodological scheme discussed in this section was designed

in order to capture these distinctions.

Network analysis is a specially useful research tool in the study of fluid social systems undergoing rapid change (Afendras, 1974). This is exactly the case of the rural-urban transition in Brazlândia. Banton (1973:47) has argued that 'a sociological interpretation of urbanization must attempt to identify and explain the differences in the quality of social relations in urban and rural surroundings'. He proceeds to explain that 'rural-urban continuity' will largely depend on whether or not the migrants are tightly interrelated by pre-migration ties of kinship or neighbourhood. And concludes:

> Where rural-urban continuity is high the migrant will maintain something of the same outlook, <u>taking his</u> <u>relatives and former neighbours as a positive reference</u> <u>group</u>. But the general effect of migration is to remove individuals from the controls exerted by their old peer groups and to give them new scope for choice. Where rural-urban continuity is low, a worker is more likely to live entirely within the city, both physically and psychologically. <u>He has continually to deal with</u> <u>strangers, and their standards have in many cases</u> to be <u>taken as models.</u>He cannot rely upon peer group sanctions but must develop interpersonal controls on a new basis. (Banton, 1973:59-60; emphasis mine)

Kemper (1975) accordingly observed in Mexico City that the migrants:

> shift from a restricted view of the urban social system to a broadly based participation in social alliances related to occupational and eventually neighbourhood commitments. Thus the 'urbanization' of migrant social relations - i.e. the shift from dependence on fellow migrants to a search for ties with other often more powerful, urban allies - is crucial to their strategy for upward socioeconomic mobility. (Kemper, 1975:234-5)

The experience of 51-year-old RC, a night watchman in Brazlândia, who works as a gardener for middle-class families outside the town in his spare time, corroborates the point. He said:

(15) Through this job (gardener) I made many acquaintances ... And people of all classes, doctors, lawyers, people like that, and in all of

Através desse serviço (de jardineiro) eu fiz tanta amizade ... E pessoas de toda classe, sabe. De classe média até classe alta, médico, advogado,

them, I have friends   dessa gente dessa classe
there.   toda, tenho amizade.

Hogan and Berlinck (1976), in a study of rural migrants in
the state of São Paulo, observed that the longer they lived in
complex urban settings, the more opportunity they had of becoming enmeshed in more elaborate communication networks. Their
access to different channels of information was crucial for
access to urban resources and, ultimately, for their adjustment.

Southall (1973:83) envisages such a process as a rise in the
density of social role texture. He states: 'It is assumed that
increasing density of role-relationships accompanies any transition, temporal or spatial, from rural to urban structure.'[10]

A note of explanation is in order here. Southall associates
a high density of role-relationships (also referred to as interactional density) with the complexity and heterogeneity of the
urban milieu. He observes that the concept is analogous to demographic density and directly connected with the acquisition and
maintenance of status and power. It should be kept distinct,
then, from the concept of the consensus or moral density which
obtains in close-knit multiplex networks (see 4.1.2). It was in
the latter sense that 'density' was used by Milroy (1980).

The general assumption is that a complex and heterogeneous
urban environment calls for a larger number of culturally differentiated roles than a traditional and relatively homogeneous
community does. A person integrated in an urban culture will
therefore tend to enter a number of varied relationships on the
basis of these differentiated roles.

Network analysis seems to represent an effective analytic
tool for tackling the issue of the transition of the migrants
from a simpler to a more complex situation of role-relationships. It can provide the criteria for the **establishment** of a
basic distinction between <u>insulated</u> and <u>integrated</u> networks.
The former represents an early stage in the transition process,
a high level of rural-urban continuity, in Banton's terms. In a
physical sense, it tends to be territorially bounded, i.e. the
links are actuated and implemented by virtue of the physical
proximity and contiguity of the households. In a social sense,
it tends to be restricted to the extended family, pre-migration

acquaintances and neighbours and to be associated with a low
level of role-relationship density.

An integrated network is territorially unbounded and more
heterogeneous as far as the recruitment framework is concerned.
The links are recruited and implemented in a larger range of
social contexts. According to Banton's methodology, it represents a low level of rural-urban continuity and is associated
with a more complex system of role-relationships.

An insulated network seems to favour the maintenance of the
rural culture and therefore the focusing of the vernacular. It
is likely to exhibit a high level of the consensus or moral
density which functions as a mechanism of resistance to change.
Such a resistance does not necessarily operate at the level of
consciousness, i.e., the resistance may not be a conscious attitude motivated by the kind of sharp and conflictive inter-group
opposition frequently found in industrial Western countries,
but rather a consequence of the very state of isolation.

The function of mutual reinforcement is likely to be less
influential in an integrated network as the migrant is exposed
to a larger range of outside influences. The linguistic consequence of such a state of affairs seems to be a higher level of
vernacular diffuseness (see figure 5.2). Moreover, as the migrant establishes a larger number of links in his new environment he is faced with the necessity of enacting new social roles
in new situations. This represents an enlargement of both his
referential and his experiential networks and ultimately may
lead to changes in his linguistic behaviour.

The relation that obtains between social roles and linguistic
behaviour is described thus by Bell (1976):

> We assume that each individual is a member of several dif-
> ferent types of groups, within each of which he has a
> status - an institutionalised or merely tacitly accepted
> place in the hierarchy of the group ... We further assume
> that each status will have assigned to it particular roles
> - structural and rule-governed ways of participating in
> the activities of the group - that for each role there
> will be norms of behaviour, to which the individual actor
> will be, to a greater or lesser extent, expected to conform
> and that some of these norms will be norms of linguistic
> behaviour - appropriate language-codes. (Bell, 1976:102;
> emphasis in original)

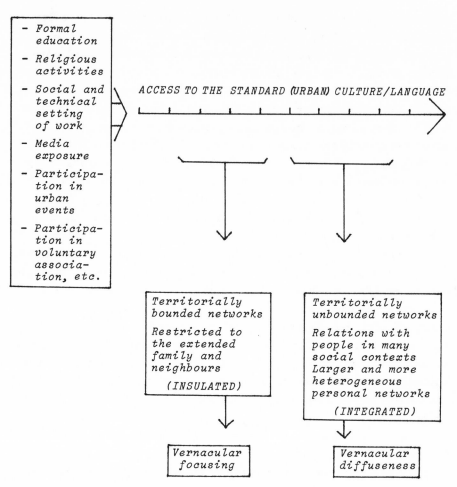

- *Formal education*
- *Religious activities*
- *Social and technical setting of work*
- *Media exposure*
- *Participation in urban events*
- *Participation in voluntary association, etc.*

ACCESS TO THE STANDARD (URBAN) CULTURE/LANGUAGE

Territorially bounded networks

Restricted to the extended family and neighbours

(INSULATED)

Territorially unbounded networks

Relations with people in many social contexts Larger and more heterogeneous personal networks

(INTEGRATED)

Vernacular focusing

Vernacular diffuseness

Figure 5.2   *Network patterns and vernacular change in Brazlândia*

The assumption underlying the present study is that a high level of complexity in an individual's role-relationship implies a high degree of flexibility in his verbal repertoire regarding appropriateness of code and style.

As Gumperz (1976b) points out, whenever interaction is carried out with speakers of different background, the situations are marked by a diversity of norms and attitudes which implies diversity of communicative conventions. He says:'To be effective here speakers must be aware of differences in inter-

pretation process. They cannot expect that their unspoken communicative conventions, characteristic of their own peer group,
are understood by others and must be flexible with respect to
speech style' (Gumperz, 1976b:13).

Dialect diffuseness in the speech of those migrants who interact in integrated networks can also be explained in terms of Le
Page's (1980) hypothesis of language variation as a function of
group membership (see 4.3). According to his hypothesis, the
speaker creates his system of verbal behaviour so as to resemble
those common to the group with which he wishes from time to time
to be identified.

If the migrant switches from an insulated network of kin-folk
and fellow-migrants into a larger network of new acquaintances,
some of whom are more advanced in the process of urban culture
acquisition, he will tend to take the latter as models for his
verbal and nonverbal behaviour. He will then commit himself to
an effort towards the assimilation of more prestigious ways of
speaking, which represents a movement away from the vernacular.
His language is then likely to present many instances of hypercorrection especially in asymmetrical speech interactions, as he
endeavours to master a code with which he is still not familiar.
Figure 5.3 gives an outline of the analysis carried out so far.

The distinction between insulated vs. integrated networks
should not be taken as bi-polar, correlating with the traditional folk/urban dichotomy. It must be borne in mind that neither
one of the two types is typically of the urban middle-class
kind. The 'urban' characteristics of an integrated network have
to be understood in a relative rather than an absolute sense.
What we have been referring to as the migrants' urbanization is
a complex process during which the migrant will be permanently
faced with the ambivalence between an out-group identification,
motivated mainly by pragmatic reasons, and need for the in-group
psychological and social support.[11] The suggested typology is
merely an analytic artifact designed to deal with the gradient
process of rural-urban transition and the two types of networks
should not be considered as clear-cut entities. The distinction,
however, seems to be very helpful in the context of this study.
The methodology which was designed in order to operationalize

Types of networks	Analytical criteria			Characteristics of verbal repertoire
	Norm reinforcement	Density of role-relationships	Group membership	
Insulated networks	Group sanction/ consensus: resistance to change	Low density of role-relationships: interaction within a limited number of people	Original peer group as a reference group	Dialect focusing Limited access to the prestigious code
Integrated networks	Larger exposure to out-group influences	Higher density of role-relationships: interaction with people with dif-ferent background in many social contexts	Identifica-tion with more prestigious groups	Dialect diffuseness More flexibility concerning control of prestige code and styles Hypercorrections

Figure 5.3 Types of networks and the rural–urban transition

the criteria used to establish this basic distinction is discussed in chapter 7.

Notes

1 Charles Wagley (1971) describes thus the situation of the
   rural migrants in Brazilian cities:

   It is obvious that the members of this enormously swollen
   urban lower-class, who work in industry and in the booming
   building trade, do not make up an 'urban proletariat' in
   the European sense, holding urban values and 'born and
   bred' to the city. The vast majority of them are, in a
   sense, peasants living in the city ... They are paid poorly
   by U.S. or even by European standards, but still they earn
   three or four times more than in the rural areas. Furthermore, they have steady work rather than the intermittent
   employment which is all they can find at home. Their real
   wages increase, yet slowly, they acquire new necessities
   and are beset with a whole new set of problems. (Wagley,
   1960/1971:211)

   Except for the employment opportunities that are now more
   scarce than in the fifties, Wagley's description is still a
   very accurate picture of the present-day migrant situation.
2 The research is fully described in Oliven's Ph.D. thesis
   'Urbanization and Social Changes in Brazil: a case study of
   Porto Alegre', University of London, 1977.
3 The author uses the terms in the context of the Mexican
   official policy of the Indians' integration in the inclusive
   society.
4 Halpern claims:

   The degree of continuity implied in the rural to urban
   transition has led some observers to postulate that in
   some ways the most difficult transition occurs not in the
   rural-to-urban move but in the movement from the working-
   class into the middle and professional groups, and that
   the working-class community is a huge processing mechanism
   providing for entry into urban society. (Halpern, 1967:39)

5 Schühly's research was carried out in Campos de Jordão, one
   of the 572 counties in the state of São Paulo.
6 For a detailed account of this solidarity ethic, as well as
   on the exchange of information among the migrants, see
   Lomnitz, 1977 and Berlink, 1977, among others.
7 A closer translation would be 'a person with study' or 'a
   studied person' as opposed to 'a person without study' or
   'a non-studied person'.
8 Some of these factors are treated in the methodology as
   independent variables and are discussed in section 7.1.2.
9 Michael Banton's (1973) analysis of the extent and strength
   of opposition between social groupings - which he calls
   'structural opposition' - seems very enlightening for a
   better understanding of the migrants' situation *vis-à-vis* the
   middle-class culture. He says:

   Where a population is divided into social categories based

upon stable and relatively visible criteria like race,
caste, and ethnic group (especially when the latter is
associated with linguistic, religious, and customary
differences), this makes for a rigidity in the structure
and for the allocation of many important roles by ascription. Such distinctions lend themselves to categoric
interaction across group lines, to a high level of group
opposition ... Where the major social cleavages are based
upon unstable characteristics, notably economic class or
social status reckoning, the position is otherwise. Inter-
group relations occur mostly within the context of work
institutions organized on a formal basis, which distracts
attention from social features belonging to other realms
of activity.

Banton concludes, then,that:

Unless class differences are tied tightly to economic
opportunities and the underprivileged groups become
sharply conscious of their subordination, class or status
cleavages do not constitute so pervasive an organizing
principle of interpersonal relations as racial or ethnic
divisions. (Banton, 1973:60-2)

10 Building on a tradition laid by Linton and Goodenough,
Southall (1973) describes 'role' and 'role-relationship' as
follows:

Role is understood as a differentiated and named structural position in a particular social system. Such a position involves a collection of rights and duties ... We
have to distinguish not only the presence of the idea of a
particular role in a culture, but also the number of times
that it is played ... It is the conceptual idea of the
particular, defined, structural position which I call
role, and every instance in which it is played, whether by
different persons, or by the same person to a number of
others, I call a role-relationship. (Southall, 1973:75)

11 A detailed discussion of a situation of ambivalence between
out-group identification and in-group support is provided by
Cardoso de Oliveira (1968: ch.9).

6.0 Introduction

This chapter focuses upon fieldwork strategies and sampling
methods, as well as on the characteristics of the research site
and of the sample population. The first section is dedicated to
a description of the research site and includes demographic and
ethnographic information on the community. The second section
deals with the sampling procedures and the third with the relationship between the fieldworker and the informants. Finally, in
the last section, detailed sociodemographic data on the sample
population is presented.

The synthesis of the quantitative sociological data and of
the ethnographic information may, hopefully, contribute to provide a clear picture of the migrants' way of life and social
relations in Brazlândia.

6.1 The research site

Field research was conducted in Brazlândia, a satellite city
located 43 kilometres from Brasília. According to the 1980
census, Brazlândia has a population of 22,486 people in the
urban area and 3,342 in the surrounding rural area. The latter
is divided into small farms which cater to the Federal District
population.

Brazlândia, which originated from a village - Povoado da Cha-
padinha - received its present name when it became a district in
1933, according to the official version, or in 1932 if one
accepts the information of the oldest residents. In any case, it
antedated the foundation of Brasília by almost thirty years. It
is today divided into two sections: the 'traditional' sector,
which is the original settlement, and the new sector - Brazlân-

dia Nova - where the study was carried out.

The new sector was built in the 1960s to receive people driven out of shanty towns around the capital. The former residents reacted strongly against the transference of the squatter population to the area, and the newcomers were severely discriminated against. At present, people refer to these segregating attitudes as something of the past and, at least amongst the surveyed population, no vestiges of the earlier resentment seem to have been preserved. Actually the new sector is much larger in area and in population and most of the city facilities, such as the bus station, the streetmarket, the football field, the largest Catholic church, the hospital and the cemetery are located there (see the map on page 125).

The traditional sector has kept the outlook of old hinterland cities, except for a few large new buildings and the public swimming pool. The new sector, on the other hand, exhibits features of designed cities with the streets - not all of them paved - dividing equally-sized blocks. The streets and blocks are identified by a system of letters (N standing for *norte*, north and S for *sul*, south) and numbers (those on the east side of the main avenue are even, and those on the west side are odd). People interviewed in the city, however, do not seem to be aware of the rationale underlying the numbering system.[1]

Brazlândia has the second lowest per capita income of all satellite cities in the Federal District. Very few local jobs are available and people must commute to Taguatinga - the largest satellite city - or to Brasília to work. Those who are locally employed hold low-paying jobs in public institutions or are engaged in agricultural activities on the neighbouring farms.

The city is regarded as quiet and peaceful as compared to the other satellite cities of Brasília, due to its relatively low level of population turn-over and low rate of criminality. The community studied presents that peculiar situation that has been sometimes described as 'rurban' in anthropology (Southall, 1973): it is neither a typically urban nor a traditional closed community. Except for the children who were born after the immigration took place, the majority of the population has a

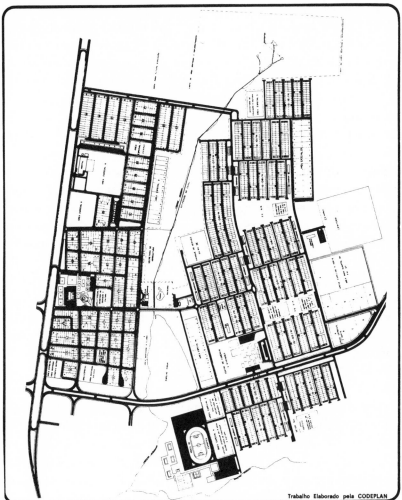

Trabalho Elaborado pela CODEPLAN

rural background (see table 6.1, section 6.4). Despite that, it
cannot be considered as a so-called 'peasant-island' in which
most of the original cultural conditions are recreated. It does
not represent a typically marginal population either, in the
sense of being segregated from the mainstream of the economy, as
defined by Lomnitz (1977). Although most of the people hold very
low-status jobs and many are in fact unemployed, they nevertheless have access to social security benefits, free medical care
and schooling and a number of other public amenities. In this
sense, they are better off than most rural people in the interior
of Brazil, where such benefits are rarely available (see 5.1).
Furthermore, most long-term established migrants have succeeded
in considerably improving their conditions of life.[2] The many
brick houses built in the city to replace the original shacks are
evidence of this mobility (see table 6.3, section 6.4). It usually takes five to ten years of hard work and much saving at the
expense of some basic consumption needs to have the house built
and it represents therefore an important fulfilment.

On the other hand, Brazlândia exhibits features of traditional
and self-contained communities. Some families still raise pigs
and chickens in their backyards, as they used to do in the
countryside. One can also observe there a sense of common territoriality and dense patterns of social networks. Such characteristics are not usually found in middle-class residential areas in
Brasília, where , as tends to happen in newly-built residential
areas, networks are likely to be rather sparse and uniplex (see
4.1.2).

Social networks in Brazlândia tend to comply with the regular
pattern found in lower-class communities where the ethics of
solidarity and reciprocity prevail. This fact might be somewhat
unexpected, considering that the new sector is a reasonably
recent settlement formed with a re-located population. In a
study conducted in another satellite city of Brasília, some
migrant women who were not integrated in extended families reported being isolated in their neighbourhood (Ridley, 1979). It
was observed in Brazlândia, however, that the extensive kinship
links, the intensive exchange of information at the neighbourhood level, the physical contiguity and proximity of the house-

holds and participation in **voluntary religious associations, all**
seem to contribute to form close-knit networks (see 5.3). As the
literature has extensively shown (see ch. 4), such types of networks are usually encountered both in lower-class, long-term
established urban districts and in self-contained peasant communities.

In Brazlândia, neighbourhood ties are very strong. The front
doors are usually open all day long and neighbours visit one
another regularly.[3] The men gather in the streets to chat, the
women stand in small groups next to the front gates to talk to
passers-by and the children use the streets as a common play-
ground. People tend to think of themselves as a friendly community where everyone knows everyone else, even though it is not
literally true. On this issue, it is enlightening to compare con-
trasting opinions of some informants.

In the following excerpt, RC, a 51-year-old watchman and gardener, asserts emphatically the community's friendliness:

(1) You notice that here in
Brazlândia it is a place
where people are more
closely linked to each
other, and this is due to
two things: that the city
is small and the way
people are, one can say
that it is a population
that, in Brazlândia, they
are very much tied one to
another, I mean, that
almost everyone knows
everyone or is known
by everyone . In the
other cities a person very
seldom talks to his next-
door neighbour. Very often
they are next-door neigh-
bours and do not even say
good-morning to each other
all year long, that way,
the chap minds his own
business and doesn't pay
any attention to the
others: here it is different, people wander about
very freely, visiting each
other's homes.

(1) A gente observa que em
Brazlândia é um lugá que
o pessoal tem mais aproxi-
mação uns dos oto, que é
devido duas coisas: que a
cidade é pequena e o sis-
tema do pessoal po' dizê
que é um povo que em Brazlândia são muito ligado
uns aos otro, qué dizê que
quase todo mundo conhece
ou são conhecido, sabe?
Nas otra cidade raramente
a pessoa conversa com o
vizim de porta. Munta vez
é vizinho de muro e não
fala nem bom-dia pro otro,
o ano intero daquele jei-
to, né, então o cara fica
só com sua e sem dá aten-
ção aos otro; aqui em
Brazlândia é diferente, o
pessoal passeia munto à
vontade, vai visitá as casa uns dos otro.

VM, a 16-year-old girl, however, provides a different account

of neighbourly relationships. The fieldworker asked her whether
she was acquainted with the neighbours and knew which state they
came from. She admitted that she did not know them well and
added:

<table>
<tr>
<td>

(2) Because if I start asking
    them questions, you know,
    they might think that I
    want to be prying. I don't
    like others to be prying
    into my life, then I
    leave them alone.
</td>
<td>

(2) Porque se eu for começar
    a fazê perguntas, né, eles
    pode achá qu'eu tô querenu
    m'involvê. Eu num gosto
    que os otros s'envolvam na
    minha vida, então dexo
    eles lá.
</td>
</tr>
</table>

In fact, neighbourhood ties seem to be stronger for the adults
and the small children. Whereas the adults, especially the women
are likely to pick their friends in the neighbourhood, both the
male and the female young people usually recruit their friends at
school, at work or in the religious associations.

The choice of fellow-migrants as preferential friends also
varies according to the sex and age of the informant. The older
men are more likely to show a clear preference for people coming
from the same state. As for the younger men and women in general,
geographic background is not important in selecting their acquaintances. The following two passages illustrate the two attitudes, respectively. The former informant is a 59-year-old male.
He is the leader of a folk dance club. The latter is a woman
aged forty-seven.

<table>
<tr>
<td>

(3) My friends are from my
    state, if he is *mineru*
    [from Minas Gerais], then
    we can trust him, right?
    Because we know that a guy
    ... that there are bad
    people everywhere, there
    is no doubt about that.
    But the 'system' [customs]
    of our state, the style is
    just one, right? We know
    already, if we go to a
    minero's house then we go
    into the kitchen to eat,
    right from the pots.
</td>
<td>

Meus amigo são conterranu;
falô que é mineru a gente
tem um termo de confiança,
né? Porque a gente sabe
que o sujeito ... que todo
lugá tem gente ruim num
resta dúvida, né? Mas o
sistema do estado da gen-
te, o estilo é um só, né?
A gente já sabe, se chega
na casa dum minero, já
vai cumê na cunzinha, nas
panela.
</td>
</tr>
</table>

A strong preference for the fellow-migrants as friends, however, was manifested by 5 per cent of the informants only. Most
of the people interviewed share the attitudes reported by LS in
the following passage:

(4)FW:(fieldworker): Do you think that because the people, every one coming from a different place, is it more difficult for the people to get along here?

LS:I don't think so. Each one comes from a different place, but once we're here, we are all equal - the same thing.

FW:And don't you think, for example, that you being *baiana* |from Bahia| it would make it easier for you to get along better with *baianos* than with *mineiros*, for example?

LS:No, I don't see anything of that, at all. For me it is all the same thing, it doesn't matter to me whether a person is *baiano*, or *minero* or *paulista*...

(4)FW:(fieldworker): A senhora acha que o fato das pessoas, cada uma vir assim de um lugar, dificulta das pessoas conviverem bem aqui?

LS:Eu acho que não. Vindo cada um dum lugá, mais depois de tudo aqui fica tudo igual, a mesma coisa.

FW:E a senhora não acha, por exemplo, que o fato de a senhora ser baiana facilitaria a senhora se dar melhor com baiano do que com ... mineiro, por exemplo?

LS:Não, não vejo nada disso não. Acho tudo a mesma coisa, pra mim tanto faz, tanto sê baiano, como minero, como goiano, paulista...

The observation in the community and the information gathered there led to the conclusion that Brazlândia shows a high level of social cohesion. Despite the heterogeneity of geographical backgrounds, its population is succeeding in recreating, in a short span of time, the ethos of solidarity which is typical of the small hinterland communities.

6.2 *Sampling procedures*

The fieldwork in Brazlândia was carried out from October 1980 to December 1981, with a three-month gap from January to March 1981. In the first three months, the activities were rather exploratory. A first contact with the city administrator - a position corresponding to the mayor - was made with the help of a common friend. A few visits to the city followed and some pilot recordings were made with a 50-year-old man who works in the city administration office, was born in the region and is resident in the traditional sector of the city, and with a 32-year-old illiterate housewife, with rural background, who lives in the new sector.

Despite the willingness of the administration personnel to help, after a few weeks I decided to change the approach strategy because the association with the city authorities could contribute to increase the social distance between the fieldworker and the informants and make it more difficult for the former to be accepted as a *bona-fide* researcher.

The next step was to pick on a few houses at random, to ask for the housewife and get permission to talk to her. At the second attempt I met a young woman who belongs to a large extended family. She introduced me to her uncle and aunt, a very receptive and gentle couple. The husband volunteered to take me to the houses of some friends who were, like himself, long-term established migrants, holding leadership positions in the community. The approaching technique employed after that was to introduce myself as a friend of X or Y.

In April of 1981 a period of intense participant observation started, during which more than thirty hours of unstructured interviewing, natural group sessions, religious meetings etc. were recorded. A rather close contact was developed with a group of migrants from Minas Gerais, a neighbouring state. This group had recently begun a folk dance club. Meantime I met a family that participated actively in a Saint Vincent de Paul's Society Conference and through this contact I became acquainted with other Conference members. The dance group and the Conference were then used as anchorage groups, in the sense put forward by Barnes (1954).[4]

From October to December of the same year, a team of five people carried out the structural interviews that were recorded and followed a questionnaire designed to collect sociodemographic and sociometric information about the informants.[5] The interviews started with the dance club members and some of the *Vicentinos* (members of the Saint Vincent de Paul's Society Conference). At the end of the interview the following question was posed to them: 'Who are the people to whom you talk most often besides those living in your home?'

For practical reasons the interviews were restricted to the anchorage group members and their 'first-order zone relations' (Barnes, 1969) i.e., the people they monitored. The procedure

yielded a 'sample'of 118 individuals that seem to represent, with
a reasonable degree of confidence, the universe of the anchorage
group members' relations.

The judgment sample thus obtained was made up of 53 men and 65
women with ages ranging from 15 to 74. It was divided according
to age into two groups: the adults and the young people.The latter were
single, below 25 years of age, were attending school - or had
dropped out very recently - and, most importantly, had migrated
from the rural area as children (below 13 years of age).[6]

An important factor to be controlled in the analysis of the
linguistic variables was geographic background.[7] Taking this into
account, three different groups of informants were considered for
analytic purposes, as follows:

1. The anchorage group comprising 33 adults: 16 men and 17
women. These people are rural migrants coming from the same region of Minas Gerais and provided the basic linguistic data for
the study. Their sociometric choices were processed and two network scores, namely, the integration and the urbanization indices, were assessed for each one of them (see 7.2 and 7.3).

2. A youth control group, comprising 7 boys and 6 girls. They
are the children, grandchildren, nephews and nieces of the
anchorage group informants and have the same regional background
as their elders. They were born in the rural area and arrived in
Brazlândia as children. The linguistic data that this group
yielded have been used as a frame of reference for the analysis
of their elders' speech (chapter 8). No network indices have been
assessed for them because the people they nominated during the
interviews were generally school mates scattered around the city.
Locating their nominees would therefore require an enormous effort
and several extra weeks of fieldwork that we could not afford.
As has already been pointed out, while the adults tend to recruit
their friends amongst kin, neighbours and religious association
colleagues, the recruitment framework for the young people is
mainly the school and the church. During the fieldwork no
informally-organized street groups of young people were
identified. For those migrants' children the most important
instrument of group cohesion, besides school, seems to be
membership of religious associations and sports teams.

3. A first-order zone group, comprising 30 men and 42 women
with varied geographic backgrounds and ages ranging from 15 to
74. They are people nominated by the anchorage group members, and
although their interviews were recorded, the linguistic data that
they produced have not been included in the present analysis for
three reasons. Firstly, there was the problem of geographic
heterogeneity; secondly, a few of them do not come originally
from rural areas; thirdly, the data were gathered from them
through interview schedules only, whereas for the two former
groups, besides the structured interviews, there were several
hours of taped unstructured interaction - group sessions, religious meetings, informal talking, etc. Figure 6.1 represents the
distribution of groups 1, 2 and 3 of the sample.

During the 12 months of fieldwork, 127 hours of verbal interaction were recorded. Of these, 85 hours were transcribed and 75
hours provided the *corpus* for the analysis of the linguistic
variables.

6.3   *Fieldwork strategies*

The fieldworker's main concern when entering the community was to
be dissociated from the image of a middle-class Brasília resident
university teacher and to be accepted as a friend. The purpose
was to override - or, at least, to diminish - the social asymmetry between fieldworker and informants. The quality of the linguistic data as well as an accurate apprehension of the social
phenomenon under study would ultimately depend on the establishment of a good rapport with the local people. The task was to a
great extent facilitated by the informants' tremendous cordiality
and disposition to collaborate. They were very affable and concerned with the fieldworker's welfare and the fulfilment of the
research goals. It was explained to them that the data were for
a book about the adaptation of rural migrants in the cities. Such
explanation was sufficient in most case, and only very rarely did
further details on the research project have to be provided. No
explicit reference to linguistic diversity was made because I
was afraid that it might contribute to increase the feelings of
linguistic insecurity that were so clearly manifested in their
behaviour and discourse. I wanted to distract their attention

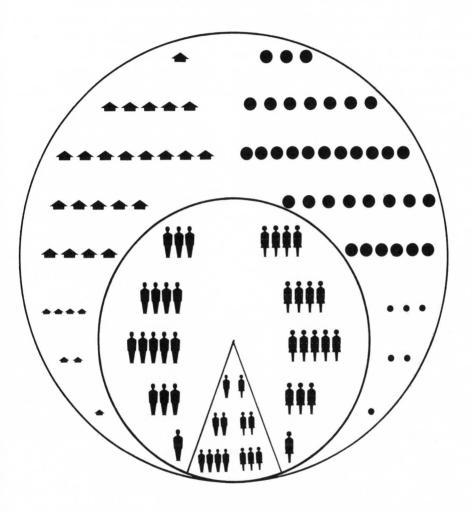

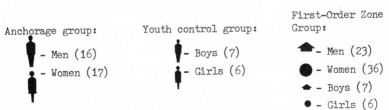

Figure 6.1 *The three groups of the sample*

from the tape recorder and from the act of speaking itself. The tape recorders were placed within a sufficiently close distance but lavalière microphones were not used.

At the beginning the informants appeared to think of the field-worker as a social worker and made extravagant requests, viz. for help in finding a job or for legal advice. Of course, any patronizing attitude could only contribute to mark me as an outsider and therefore every effort was made to emphasize my status as a friend who in fact needed their cooperation. In the course of the fieldwork I had the opportunity of doing them little favours, such as offering a lift, inviting the Caipira duo - two members of the dance club - to give a show at the University, typing letters and the lyrics of songs, etc. but this was always done on an exchange basis. It was also part of the fieldworker's commitments to fulfil some social obligations, such as to visit a newly-born baby or a mourning family, as well as to memorize people's names in every family network so that many references to acquaintances, relatives and friends could be made throughout the conversations. This was an extremely useful device for improving the rapport.

Throughout most of the fieldwork I had the assistance of Braúlio Porto, a student of Sociology who was born and raised in the same region where the anchorage group informants come from. Many of them were acquainted with Braúlio's older relatives and this was in fact the preferred topic of conversation between him and the older informants. Although he was not an insider in that community, he was cognizant of the informants' original region, way of talking, customs and traditional families. Claiming the identity of *mineiros* was indeed for both Braúlio and myself an effective approaching strategy.

The interaction with the informants was carried out in many different circumstances, and almost everything was recorded. Most recordings were made in their houses but some were made in their work-places, in the church - during and after the Conference meetings - and in a community centre where the dance club rehearsals and presentations took place.

As a rule, the informants were very willing to cooperate. Being on tape was considered almost as a **responsibility**. They felt they had to provide as much information as possible, and many of them volunteered accounts and interpretations of facts which they deemed relevant for the research topic, viz. the rural-urban migration. But the basic strategy for obtaining a fluent conversation was to discover and to explore the inform- ants' main interest, which could be football, Caipira music, hunting and fishing, politics, etc. Some informants showed an almost child-like interest in listening to their recorded voices. They were also very interested in recording themselves playing the accordion or the guitar, singing or telling stories.

There was a tacit agreement not to discuss personal mat- ters. Whenever a question or a remark could involve private af- fairs it would elicit generic comments only. However, as the fieldwork progressed and friendship ties were established be- tween the parties, the informants were more likely to volunteer factual private information or to indulge themselves in gossip- ing. Sometimes during group sessions with a family's members and friends, someone would remind the others that they were on tape and therefore should refrain from discussing certain topics, especially when they might be offensive or derogatory to someone. In any case, conversation with the men was often more fluent than with the women. As the women's universe is very much centred on family's relationships, and information of this sort was neither available to the fieldworker nor was supposed to be a topic of conversation, the first interactions with the female informants did not produce spontaneous and copious data. Things improved when I began to have access to self-recruited group sessions of kindred women during which the recurring topics of discussion were pregnancy, child-birth, child-rearing and the like.

As pointed out at the outset, the informants were very cooper- ative and the interaction with them was carried out in a friend- ly atmosphere. There were few cases of negative reactions, and as they had to be handled tactfully, it is worth reporting them. Incidents never happened with the anchorage group members. The visits to these families were always preceded by some contact of the fieldworker with a member of the family, either at a friend's home or in the church and the community centre during the Confer- ence meetings or the dance functions. But when the team of

college students began to carry out interviews with the first-
order zone group, a few informants, not acquainted with the
fieldworker, were very suspicious and refused to receive the
interviewers or to let them record the conversation. In such
cases a more detailed explanation about the research project was
offered to them and that included reference to many local people
with whom the fieldworker was connected. After this explanation
was provided, all the reluctant informants, with a single excep-
tion, agreed to being interviewed.

The interview event carried out under the heaviest strain
occurred, however, during the exploratory stage. I went to visit
a young married couple in the company of the wife's father, a
long-term established migrant. The couple were clearly upwardly
mobile people and they resented being included in a sample of
rural migrants for research purposes, despite their actual rural
background. The young man showed a very low esteem for the rural
culture, including the folk dance club. He did not see any point
in cultivating past folk traditions when there was so much to be
done in the present. People ought not to be concerned with folklore or sociological surveys and should pay more attention to the
basic needs of the starving population, he argued. He also seemed
to avoid close links with his relatives in the community. His
speech showed a high degree of self-monitoring and was marked by
the occurrence of a bookish lexicon, which included many adverbs,
and by a very low incidence of nonstandard features. Even though
the couple were reasonably polite, the situation was rather
embarrassing. My strategy was then to shift the style and carry
out the conversation in a very careful standard Portuguese. Formality in those circumstances was used to convey a deferential
attitude towards the interlocutor and to indicate that the fieldworker had reanalysed the status relationships of the event
participants. The fieldworker remained throughout the interview
at a one-down position, allowing the informant to utter a long
and instructive speech about his field of expertise. The informant's negative attitude towards the event was, of course, motivated by what, in that case, had been a wrong approaching
strategy, i.e. the reference to rural migration. His behaviour,
linguistically and otherwise, was consistent with an intention of

asserting his identity as a middle-class cultivated urbanite.

At his point it is worth saying a few words about the dance club and the *Vicentino* **Conference.** The Society of Saint Vincent de Paul is a world-wide Catholic association with philanthropic purposes. It was introduced in Brazlândia a few years ago by the present parish priest and it soon became the most influential volunteer association in the community. Membership in one of the several local *Vicentino* Conferences is highly valued for several reasons. In the first place, it is connected with the Catholic Church, the religion of the mainstream, and therefore benefits from the Church's prestige. Secondly, the philanthropic ideology of the organization is clearly embedded in the dominant ideology. The *Vicentinos* do not enjoy any special prestige in a middle-class milieu, but in Brazlândia they actually represent an elite oriented towards the welfare of the public. Thirdly, there are material advantages in being a member of the Society. The Conference represents social and psychological - and sometimes, financial - support and offers leisure opportunities which are a precious commodity in the city. In sum, it seems to be a very powerful mechanism of recruitment of the migrants into an urban referential network. As will be discussed in chapter 8, the *Vicentino* leaders are in fact the migrants that present the highest degree of dialect diffuseness in their speech.

The dance club resulted from the initiative of social workers who work with the community but it owes its existence to the interest and persistence of JP, aged fifty-nine, and his wife, JJ, aged fifty-six, who are the leaders of the group. The club was created with the purpose of recovering old folk dances of the state of Minas Gerais. Membership in the group is restricted to the *mineiros* with few exceptions. Differently from the *Vicentino* Conference, which has a highly institutionalized organization with well-defined recruitment procedures, participation in the dance group depends exclusively on an invitation from the leader. When the group started, JP invited a group of fellow-migrants to join but of this original group only a few remain. One of them died, some moved to other cities and others simply quitted. Presently most of the participants of the group are newly-arrived migrants who are connected to JP by kinship or friendship ties.

The rehearsal sessions which are held at the community centre and are open to everyone are an excellent opportunity for leisure. During them people are basically engaged in three activities: listening to the Caipira duo, dancing in pairs and performing the old folk dances, though the last is the exclusive privilege of the group members. The event differs from traditional urban dances in a number of aspects. When dancing in pairs, the man does not hold the woman tightly, even when they are man and wife. That would be considered to show a lack of respect. There is also a constant exchange of partners, irrespective of marital links. Another interesting characteristic is the presence of little children and babies with their mothers. In fact, many features of the rural culture are faithfully recreated in those functions and are a source of much delight for the participants.

It should be noted, however, that the dance meetings are attended mostly by older migrants and newly-arrived families. The members of long-term established families who have experienced some upward mobility do not seem to be interested in such events. Many of them, especially the young people, regard the dance as the manifestation of folklore and some adults appear to have a condescending attitude towards it. In spite of being an enjoyable activity for people that participate in it, the dance club is not prestigious in the community as a whole and is kept alive mainly because of the enthusiasm of JP himself.

Although membership of the *Vicentino* Conference and of the dance club were not formally treated in the present study as variables constraining linguistic behaviour, the brief descriptions above suggest that in fact the participants of the two groups contrast in important aspects. The *Vicentinos* are likely to be oriented towards publicly accepted urban values; people connected with the dance club, on the other hand, seem to maintain a high appraisal for rural cultural traits. As will be discussed in chapter 8, these differences are closely reflected in language use.

6.4 The sociodemographic characteristics of the sample population

In this section some sociodemographic characteristics of the
whole sample population, which includes the three groups referred
to in section 6.2,are presented. The purpose is twofold. Firstly it
aims at providing a more accurate picture of the socioeconomic
situation of the informants and at shedding light on the process
of the difficult transition from an economy of subsistence to an
economy of accumulation, which the migrants endeavour to perform.
Secondly, the assessment of differences in the situation of men
and women in relation to several sociodemographic variables is
relevant for a closer understanding of the co-occurring differences in their linguistic behaviour. The same thing applies to
the differences between the two age groups.

   As table 6.1. shows, the great majority of people interviewed
are rural migrants. Only four individuals were not born in rural
areas. The youth group have migrated to the city as children, most of
them below the age of 10 years. 60 per cent of the informants
lived in the rural area for more than 15 years, and 30 per cent
for more than 30 years.

Table 6.1.   *Time of residence in the rural area*

Years	Youth		Adults		Total	
	N	%	N	%	N	%
None	2	1.5	2	1.5	4	3.0
1 - 5	13	11.0	4	3.0	17	14.0
6 -10	9	8.0	6	5.0	15	13.0
11-15	2	1.0	10	9.0	12	10.0
16-20	-	-	15	13.0	15	13.0
21-25	-	-	9	8.0	9	8.0
26-30	-	-	11	9.0	11	9.0
More than 30	-	-	35	30.0	35	30.0

   Table 6.2 shows the duration of the informants' residence in
the Federal District.[8] 19 per cent are new-comers but 63 per cent
of the informants have been living in the Federal District for
more than 10 years.

Table 6.2.   *Time of residence in the Federal District*

Years	N	%
1 - 5	23	19.0
6 -10	21	18.0
11-15	43	37.0
16-20	21	18.0
21-25	10	8.0
Total	118	100.0

Long-term established migrants are more likely to have improved their living standards, whereas the new-comers usually
live precariously in shacks made of wood, sharing one point of
water supply in the frontyard, one latrine and one shower-bath
with other families that live in the joint households. Table
6.3. gives a picture of the household conditions. The number (N)
and the percentages refer to individuals and not to households.

Table 6.3.   *Household improvements*

Description	N	%
Brick house	61	52.0
Indoors bathroom	75	63.0
Piped water in the kitchen	79	67.0
Radio	98	83.0
TV	79	67.0
Refrigerator	60	50.0

As regards their present occupation, the informants were
classified in five occupational groups (table 6.4.). Category A
of unskilled rural workers embodies the activities of cattleman,
agriculturist, wood-cutter etc. in which most of the migrants
were engaged before migration although now only 13 per cent of the
male informants have continued in this type of activity. Some of
them are new-comers who accept irregular jobs on the neighbouring farms on a temporary basis, as they hope to find steady
urban employment. Others are retired and work as sharecroppers
in order to improve their family budget. Finally, a few of them
own small farms where they spend most of the time, coming to
Brazlândia on week-ends to visit their wives and children. A
rural job is an option open to men only. Although the women were

used to this sort of hard work before migration, they do not seem
to admit it as a job alternative any more, either because they
cannot reconcile it with the child-rearing and house chores or
else because they are starting to reinterpret the allocation of
female and male tasks according to urban standards.[9]

Table 6.4. *Work category*

Description	Men		Women	
	N	%	N	%
A. Unskilled rural worker	7	13.0	–	–
B. Unskilled urban worker	24	45.0	35	54.0
C. Semi-skilled urban worker	12	23.0	8	12.0
D. Worker with tech. train. (8 yrs school)	3	6.0	9	14.0
E. Worker with tech. train. (11 yrs school)	–	–	2	3.0
Do not work	7	13.0	11	17.0
Total	53	100.0	65	100.0

Most of the informants (45 per cent of men and 54 per cent of
women) are unskilled urban workers. This category (B) includes
the jobs of watchman, janitor, porter, gatekeeper, street-market
vendor, bricklayer, cartman, rubbish-collector, street-sweepers
etc. for men and domestic jobs for women. Full time housewives
were also included in this category.

Category C embodies the semi-skilled urban workers, such as
mechanic, shoemaker, tailor, seamstress, barber, electrician,
plumber, soldier, carpenter, waiter etc.

Category D corresponds to jobs that require technical
training. People holding these jobs are expected to have at
least eight years of schooling. The category includes the jobs of
typist, shop-assistant, kindergarten teacher assistant, nurse-
aids, sergeants, etc.

Finally, to category E are allocated those jobs that require
a better technical training, demanding at least eleven years of
school. Only two female elementary school teachers were classified in this category.

An examination of table 6.4 gives the impression that the
work opportunities are equal for both the men and the women. The
study of a brief occupational history of each informant, however,
allowed for the assessment of what we have called work category
mobility and revealed that the male migrant is at a clear advantage as regards integration in the job market. Two types of work
category mobility were established, namely, steady mobility and
upward mobility.   The steady mobility type represents a
stationary experience as regards the acquisition of some professional skill. Those informants that have maintained the same
work category that they had before migration and those that have
only experienced an inter-occupational change from the unskilled
rural work (A) to an unskilled urban work (B) - which is not
considered to be an actual evolution but rather a consequence of
migration - were included in the steady mobility type. The upward
mobility type represents a progression from unskilled to skilled
work, i.e. from categories A or B to C, D or E.

Table 6.5. *Work category mobility*

Type	Men		Women	
	N	*%*	*N*	*%*
Steady mobility	28	53.0	59	91.0
Upward mobility	25	47.0	6	9.0
Total	53	100.0	65	100.0

Table 6.5 shows a striking difference in the performance of
men and women as regards the adjustment to the urban job market. Whereas 47 per cent of men have succeeded in acquiring a
better occupation, only 9 per cent of the women were engaged in
upward occupational mobility. These numbers seem indeed to be
good evidence that the men are in the lead in the process of
integration into the urban *modus vivendi*.

This advantageous position of men is not associated, however,
with any superiority in the level of their formal education. As
table 6.6. reports, the level of schooling of men and women is
equivalent. Most of the adults of both sexes are illiterate (30
per cent of men and 26 per cent of women) or spent less than

four years in school (32 per cent of men and 26 per cent of women).

Table 6.6. *Level of schooling I*

Years	Men		Women	
	N	%	N	%
None	16	30.0	17	26.0
1 - 3 years	17	32.0	17	26.0
4 - 7 years	11	21.0	16	25.0
8 -10 years	6	11.0	11	17.0
11 years	3	6.0	4	6.0
Total	53	100.0	65	100.0

Table 6.7. reveals that there is a negative correlation between age and level of formal education. As the former increases, the latter decreases. The young generation that moved from the rural area at an early age is attending school regularly. 11 per cent of them have already completed the school of *segundo grau*, which represents eleven years of schooling.

Table 6.7. *Level of schooling II*

Age	None		1 - 3		4 - 7		8 -10		11		Total
	N	%	N	%	N	%	N	%	N	%	
15-25	-	-	4	3	2	2	10	8	13	11	29
26-35	4	3	5	4	3	2.5	5	4	2	2	19
36-45	6	5	16	14	3	2.5	2	2	1	1	28
More than 45	23	20	12	10	6	5	1	1	-	-	42
Total	33	28	37	31	14	12	18	15	16	14	118

If one compares tables 6.4 and 6.7 it will be noticed that 14 per cent of the sample population have completed a *segundo grau* course (table 6.7.) and yet only two individuals hold jobs of category E (requiring eleven years of schooling). This mismatch between formal qualification and job opportunities shows in fact that the lower-class youth, in spite of the fact that they go to school, are still not equipped to compete in the job market under fair conditions. Most of the youths in Brazlândia are either unemployed or underemployed.

Table 6.8. *Spatial mobility I*

Type	Men		Women	
	N	%	N	%
Low	33	62.0	48	74.0
High	20	38.0	17	26.0
Total	53	100.0	65	100.0

Table 6.9. *Spatial mobility II*

Type	Adults		Youth	
	N	%	N	%
Low	68	74.0	13	50.0
High	24	26.0	13	50.0
Total	92	100.0	26	100.0

The spatial mobility of the migrants within the city limits
may be considered as an indicator of their adjustment to the new
setting. Tables 6.8. and 6.9. show the degree of mobility of men
as compared to women and of the adults as compared to the youth,
respectively. A low level of spatial mobility means that the
individual is very much confined in Brazlândia, leaving the city
occasionally only for special kinds of health treatment, for
catching the interstate bus, etc. A high level of spatial mobility means that the person travels to other satellite cities and to
Brasília daily or very often.

The women have less spatial mobility than men. Only 26 per
cent of the women, mostly those that have domestic jobs, travel
regularly. The young people, despite the fact that many of them
are unemployed, are more mobile than the adults.

Another indicator of adjustment to the city life is   participation in urban events which take place in Brasília. A battery
of questions was included in the questionnaire to assess such
participation. The questions concerned recurrent events, e.g. the
Independence Day Parade and the monthly change of the national

flag in the parliament square; visits to public places, e.g. the zoo, the city park; and occasional happenings, e.g. the Pope's visit to Brasília in July of 1980, TV shows. Table 6.10. summarizes the results of the participation in urban events scale for men and women. The results follow the same pattern, with the men presenting a better performance.

Table 6.10. *Participation in urban events I*

Type	Men		Women	
	N	%	N	%
Low	43	81.0	58	89.0
High	10	19.0	7	11.0
Total	53	100.0	65	100.0

Table 6.11. compares the results for the two age groups. The amount of participation in urban events is rather small for both groups but the young people scored higher than the adults.

Table 6.11. *Participation in urban events II*

Type	Adults		Youth	
	N	%	N	%
Low	82	90.0	18	70.0
High	10	10.0	8	30.0
Total	92	100.0	26	100.0

Mass media exposure is considered to be a vehicle that fosters modernization of traditional societies as well as homogenization of the urban centres (Guimarães, 1972; Oliven, 1982). The influence of the media on dialect diffuseness will be discussed in chapter 7. A battery of ten questions was included in the questionnaire to assess the migrants' degree of media exposure. Tables 6.12., 6.13. and 6.14. summarize the results obtained.

Women are just as exposed to the media as men, but there is a striking difference in the behaviour of the two age groups, as is shown in table 6.13.

Table 6.12. *Media exposure I*

Type	Men		Women	
	N	%	N	%
Low	34	64.0	43	66.0
High	19	36.0	22	34.0
Total	53	100.0	65	100.0

Table 6.13. *Media exposure II*

Type	Adults		Youth	
	N	%	N	%
Low	73	80.0	5	19.0
High	19	20.0	21	81.0
Total	92	100.0	26	100.0

Table 6.14. *Media exposure III*

Frequency of exposure	Radio		T V		Cinema		Newspapers		Magazines		Books	
	N	%	N	%	N	%	N	%	N	%	N	%
Frequently	79	67.0	49	42.0	15	13.0	18	15.0	17	15.0	22	19.0
Occasionally	35	30.0	59	50.0	81	69.0	41	35.0	24	20.0	40	34.0
Never	4	3.0	10	8.0	22	18.0	59	50.0	77	65.0	56	47.0
Total	118	100.0	118	100.0	118	100.0	118	100.0	118	100.0	118	100.0

The influence of the different communication vehicles is
indicated in table 6.14.

The radio is the most widespread medium, followed closely by
the television. Attendance at the cinema is not a regular habit
for most informants. 18 per cent of them have never seen a movie
in a movie theatre. Many informants complained about the poor
conditions of the local theatre and the bad quality of the films,
but of course the cinema is an expensive item for their budgets.
The same applies to newspapers, magazines and books, which are,
of course, a commodity available to the literate only, hence the

high percentages of people that never read them. The informants' exposure to books is a little higher than to newspapers and magazines because the former category included the Bible and other religious books as well as school books.

Another scale designed to evaluate the migrant's process of adjustment to the city life concerned political awareness, i.e. knowledge of national political events and people. It was assessed by means of six questions covering different types of information such as the date of the next elections, the name of the political parties and the recent resignation of a minister. Tables 6.15. and 6.16. report the results.

Table 6.15. *Political awareness I*

Type	Men		Women	
	N	*%*	*N*	*%*
Low	43	81.0	61	94.0
High	10	19.0	4	6.0
Total	53	100.0	65	100.0

Table 6.16. *Political awareness II*

Type	Adults		Youth	
	N	*%*	*N*	*%*
Low	85	92.0	19	73.0
High	7	8.0	7	27.0
Total	92	100.0	26	100.0

As might be expected, the men performed better than the women, but the most conspicuous differences remain between the two age groups.

The information conveyed by these statistics on several sociodemographic aspects of the sample population, in spite of its limitation, leads to some conclusions that are relevant for a better understanding of the migrants' dialect diffuseness, a process which is, supposedly, concomitant with their assimilation to the urban standards of life. That the men are in the

lead in such assimilation seems to be clear and this phenomenon
has cultural as well as economic explanations. When asked whether
a married woman should have a job, 64 per cent of the informants
answered no. The division of labour and the allocation of rights
and duties to men and women seems still to be very traditional.
Such values seem to be rather resistant to the changes that affect them gradually, mainly as a result of economic pressures.
Long-term established female migrants are more likely to hold
paid jobs and this is indeed a good indicator of the family's
adjustment to urban cultural standards.

Another relevant point that emerges from the data concerns the
differences between the young people and their elders. The former
are to a larger extent subject to the mainstream urban influence
through school, the media etc. Such a state of affairs is clearly
reflected in their behaviour, in particular in their linguistic
behaviour, as will be demonstrated in chapter 8.

Notes

1 The reference to the cardinal points to locate a city region,
   introduced in Brasília and in the satellite cities, is not a
   widespread tradition in the Brazilian culture. Public places
   in the cities and towns are usually named after local or
   national personalities.
2 We are considering as long-term established migrants those who
   have been living in Brazlândia for more than ten years (see
   table 6.2., section 6.4).
3 Interestingly though, when interviewed, the married women
   would not admit having the habit of visiting neighbours very
   often. They reported being at home most of the time and
   visiting relatives and neighbours only in case of illness.
   The attitude is in accord with a traditional belief that
   'lugar de mulher é em casa' (a woman's place is in the home).
   It is also possible that they do not recognize as visiting
   their frequent and quick dropping in on each other and the
   permanent contact with the neighbours in the front yard, which
   is, in many cases, shared by several families.
4 The point of anchorage of a network is usually considered to be
   the specific individual(s) whose behaviour the researcher
   wishes to study (Mitchell, 1969:13).
5 The team included four university students and myself. The
   students were: Márcia Damaso, Bráulio Porto, Roberto Patrocínio and Ricardo Lobato. The following students also participated in a few interviews and group sessions: Tulia Vogensen,
   Alíris dos Santos, Niviene Maciel, Neuza Carvalho and Ilza de
   Borja.
6 Among the young informants only two did not have rural background.
7 The sample population comes from the following Brazilian

states: Minas Gerais:71; Goiás:16; Bahia:13; Ceará:5; Pernam-
buco:3; Piauí:2; Espírito Santo:2; Paraíba:1; Rio Grande do
Norte:1; Maranhão:1; Mato Grosso:1; São Paulo:1; Paraná:1.
Total:118.

8 The Federal District includes the city of Brasília, ten
satellite cities and the surrounding rural area.

9 In other regions of the country, however, it is very common for
both male and female rural migrants to earn their living
working on nearby farms which they commute to every day. They
are called *bóias frias* (cold meals) an allusion to the fact
that they have no facilities to warm up the meal they bring
with them from home.

7.0 Introduction

The purpose of the analysis of linguistic variation in this book
is primarily the assessment of the migrant's dialect diffuseness.
Four variables, namely, the vocalization of $|\lambda|$, the reduction of
final rising diphthongs, subject-verb agreement in third person
plural and subject-verb agreement in first person plural have
been selected as indicators of the phenomenon.

As was explained in detail in chapter 5, dialect diffuseness
is viewed as co-occurring with the speakers' process of transition from a closed insulated network of kin and fellow-migrants
to a more heterogeneous integrated network. The choice of the
quantitative analytic method presented a major problem because
what was required was a method or methods which would be capable
of capturing with a reasonable degree of accuracy the linguistic
complexities of this cultural phenomenon.[1]

Two basic linguistic analyses were carried out. The first one
approaches variation through the Labovian technique of aggrega-
ting scores. The informants are divided into subgroups according
to sex, age, degree of media exposure etc. and the analysis aims
at determining the links between patterns of linguistic variation and these independent variables. The basic assumptions underlying the procedure can be summarized as follows: (1) the
subgroups of the sample population, divided according to these
independent variables, will show different degrees of adjustment
to the urban environment, i.e. some will be in a further stage
of integration than others; (2) the linguistic norms associated
with the subgroups will reflect such differences. The motivation
for the former assumption is found both in the ethnographic data
gathered in the community as well as in the quantitative assess-

ment of the sociodemographic characteristics of the population described in chapter 6. The latter assumption stems from the traditional sociolinguistic correlational approach. The methodology used in the analysis of the aggregated scores is discussed in the next section.

The second type of linguistic analysis does not rely on group scores: the informants are treated individually, and the analysis aims at assessing the extent of individual variation. In order to do this, the individual linguistic scores are correlated with two network scores, namely, the network integration index and the network urbanization index. These indices were devised in such a way as to be reliable indicators of the migrants' transition process from insulated into integrated networks (see 5.3).

The relation between network characteristics and language behaviour was a major concern of the discussion in chapter 4. Still, it is worth repeating here with Milroy (1980:135) that 'the network concept was developed to explain individual behaviour of various kinds which cannot be accounted for in terms of corporate group membership'. The speech of the rural migrants in Brazlândia does indeed show a large range of variation typical of the fluid situations of dialect contact. We hope that the analysis carried out at the individual level can contribute to shed light on aspects of this variation that might be overlooked in the first analysis. The methods for assessing the network indices are described in the two last sections of this chapter. In chapter 8 the quantitative analysis of the linguistic variables is presented and discussed in detail.

7.1 *The variable rule paradigm*

The models and methods of linguistic analysis discussed in this section are cast in the tradition of the Labovian theory of variation. The theoretical framework as well as the methodology of the so-called variable rule paradigm are very well established and have been extensively discussed in the literature. They will therefore only be sketched here.[2]

A major axiom of the theory is that variation is an inherent and rule-governed property of human languages and not a product of irregular dialect mixture (Labov, 1972a:225). A large number

of elements of the linguistic structure are involved in systematic and patterned variation, which is regarded as   synchronic
evidence of change in progress and/or as a reflex of socioecologi-
cal factors on language.

Another major assumption underlying the theory is that the
linguistic analysis should be based upon *corpora* gathered in a
speech community and not by introspection. It therefore recovers
a traditional orientation of data gathering in linguistics.
Furthermore the quantitative treatment of the data thus obtained
is considered the 'major route for resolving theoretical alterna-
tives in a decisive way' (Labov and Sankoff, 1980:xi).

The first challenge to a linguistic theory that acknowledges
an orderly heterogeneity in languages and works with   non-ideal
corpora was to devise heuristic procedures for assessing   the
linguistic and non-linguistic influences on those aspects of language that cannot be dealt with by means of categorical and
optional generative rules. This was made possible with the introduction of the concept of variable rules, that were designed in
order to meet a general principle of accountability, as Labov
(1972b:94) explains:'Any variable form (a member of a set of
alternative ways of "saying the same thing") should be reported
with the proportion of cases in which the form did occur in the
relevant environment, compared to the total number of cases in
which it might have occurred.' It follows from the statement
above that for any area of variation in a given language it is
necessary to identify the categories, or constraints, that are
determinants, in a statistical sense, of the relative proportions of each variant of the variable rule, i.e. of each possible
realization of the variable. The constraints (also referred to as
factors) can be defined 'as forces that operate simultaneously to
make the application of the rule more or less probable' (Naro,
1981:67). Guy (1980:4) defines a factor as 'any constraint on
the rule that can be stated in the environmental description of
the rule'. An environment is then viewed as a string of factors,
each factor representing a potentially constraining force. Finally, the factors are organized in factor groups. If one considers
a factor group as a variable in the context of the rule, then the
factors of the group constitute all the possible realizations

of that variable (Guy, 1981:32-3).

There are two types of constraints on a variable rule: linguistic and social. The former concerns the linguistic item under study, the latter concerns the speaker. The linguistic constraints result from the relation between the item being studied and other linguistic items and operate at different levels of the grammatical system. The social constraints are related both to the social structure of the speech community and to social processes.

These concepts can be more easily understood if an example of a variable rule is presented. Let us examine the rule of denasalization in Portuguese, as studied by Votre (1982), discussed in section 3.2.1.2. A final nasal vowel in Brazilian Portuguese can be realized in two alternative ways, viz. as a nasal or as an oral vowel, e.g. |'ɔmĩ| or |'ɔmi| *homem* (man). Each of these realizations is viewed as a variant of the rule. In order to assess the relative proportion of occurrence of each variant, the influence of phonological and syntactic constraints (i.e. linguistic constraints) as well as of a sociodemographic constraint on the application of the denasalization rule was studied. The following four factor groups were postulated. The first one was morphological class, and it included four different classes (four factors or constraints). The second one was height of the vowel and it included two factors, namely, |+high| and |-high|. The third group also included two factors, viz. stressed and unstressed, and concerned the strength of the syllable. Finally, the fourth factor group concerned the age of the speakers and embodied two factors, namely, old and young informants. Supposing that the word *homem* was uttered by a young speaker, the environment of the rule application, seen as a string of factors, would be described as follows: class D, high vowel, unstressed syllable and young speaker.

The data for the variable rule analysis are presented in the form of observed frequencies of rule application, i.e. we count the total number (T) of occurrences of a given environment where the rule applied or did not apply. In the example above, all the occurrences of words like *homem* would be counted whether the final syllable retained nasalization or not. Next, we count the

number (A) of times that the rule actually applied; in our example, the number of times that words like *homem* were pronounced
with a final oral vowel. Each data element is fed into a computer program in the form of a fraction as follows:

$$\frac{A}{T} = \frac{\text{rule applications}}{\text{eligible environments}}$$

together with a series of symbols representing the features
making up the environment (Rousseau and Sankoff, 1978:58).

The ultimate purpose of the analysis is to establish the effect of each environmental factor on the application of the rule
as well as to determine the way the effects of each constraint
combine to produce the total effect of the environment. This
overall probability of rule application is obtained by multiplying or summing the effects of all the constraints present in
the environment. This procedure is based on the assumption that
the proportions of the different variants which occur in a given
environment will, in the long run, reflect the overall probability (Guy, 1980:3).

7.1.1 *The additive model*
There are two probabilistic models that can be used to compute
the overall probability of rule application, namely, the additive
and the multiplicative models. As the former was used in the
present study it will be discussed in some detail in the following paragraphs, The multiplicative model has a much longer tradition in the field of quantitative sociolinguistics and has been
the object of much mathematical refinement in the last decade.
Several versions of it have been successively developed, the most
adequate of which is the so-called logistic model (Sankoff and
Labov, 1979), which was incorporated by David Sankoff in a computer program known as VARBRUL 2. (For details, see Rousseau and
Sankoff, 1978; Naro, 1980 *inter alia*.) As VARBRUL 2 was not
available for the data analysis of this study, the additive model
was employed.[3]

The additive model was introduced by Labov in 1969 but it was
soon considered to be inappropriate and rejected. The model is

implemented by means of a statistical method called analysis of
variance (ANOVA) and the main difficulty for its use in the analysis of variable rules stems from the fact that the mathematics
of ANOVA have a basic requirement of equal cell counts. In terms
of a variable rule this corresponds to saying that the number of
observations per environment should be the same. Furthermore
there could not be any empty cells (T=0). This requirement cannot
be met in the analysis of linguistic data because it cannot be
predesigned and the occurrences of tokens in each environment
cannot be controlled.[4] The distribution tends to be very much
skewed in some cases and environments may occur where T=0, because they consist of linguistically impossible or improbable
configurations of features (Rousseau and Sankoff, 1978:60). Fortu-
nately,however, improvements in the technique of analysis of
variance now allow these restrictions to be relaxed under certain
conditions (Naro, 1981:70). The suitability of the additive model
for the analysis of variable rules was recently demonstrated by
Naro (1981) in a study of the subject-verb agreement variable
rule in Brazilian Portuguese. He analysed the data using two
methods based on the logistic and the additive models respectively, and arrived at parallel results. In both cases a good fit
between model and observations was found.

As already pointed out, the assumption underlying the additive model is that the effects of each factor present in an
environment accumulate additively. As the relative frequency of
rule application is expressed as a percentage, each variable
constraint is also associated with a quantity stated either as a
positive or negative percentage, that measures the effect of that
specific constraint. As Naro (1981:69) explains, 'the experimen-
tally determined percentage of rule application in any given
environment should tend,within the limits of statistical fluctuation, to be the sum of those percentages'. The overall frequency
of rule application, known as the grand mean, is added to the sum
in order to provide a non-arbitrary standard against which to
measure these effects. The model can be expressed by the equa-
tion:

$$f(t) = f(0) + f(1) + \ldots + f(n)$$

in which f(t) is the total frequency of the rule application in
the environment; f(0) is the grand mean, and f(1) ... f(n) are
the effects of n factors present in the context, stated as deviations from the grand mean.

In order to estimate the factorial deviations from the observed frequency distributions, by adjusting the raw deviation of
each for the effects of the other factors, a statistical technique known as multiple classification analysis (MCA) can be
used. The result of the MCA is called an adjusted deviation. (For
details, see Naro, 1981.)

The multiple classification analysis is used in conjunction
with the analysis of variance which provides a statistic known as
F-ratio for each group of factors as well as the level of statistical significance associated with the main effect of each group.
For this study the ANOVA subprogram (which includes the MCA) of
the SPSS package, version H, release 8.1, August 15, 1980, for
Burroughs large systems (Nie et al., 1975:410-22) was used. The
SPSS subprogram ANOVA can cope with unequal cell sizes as well as
with empty cells.

The primary interest for the analysis carried out in this book
was not the ANOVA output but the MCA table. When this is the case,
it is a recommended procedure to eliminate from the analysis two-
way and higher interactions among factors (Nie et al., 1975:416).
Then only the main effects of the factor groups appear in the
ANOVA summary table and all interaction effects are pooled into
the error sum of squares. On this issue it is also worth noting
with Naro (1981:71) that statistical significance of interaction
does not necessarily imply linguistic significance because when
we are dealing with large amounts of data, even minute interactions can be statistically significant.

The output of the MCA consists of (1) the grand mean of the
dependent variable, in this case the overall frequency of the
rule applications; (2) the number (N) of tokens for each factor
and (3) a table of factor means for each factor group expressed
as deviations from the grand mean, which reflect the magnitude
of the effect of each factor of a group. There are two types of
deviation values, namely, an unadjusted value and a value adjusted for the variation accounted for by all other factor

groups. The latter, referred to as adjusted deviation, allows for the assessment of the magnitude of factor effects for a given factor group that remains after variation due to other factor groups has been partialled out. The unadjusted values of factor effects are given together with a common correlation ratio - the eta value. Associated with the adjusted factor effect for each group is a partial correlation ratio, known as beta. The values of this partial beta vary from zero to one and indicate,when squared, the proportion of the total variation due to each group of factors with the influence of the other groups controlled. Finally, a statistic labelled multiple R is provided at the bottom of the table. It is a multiple correlation between the independent variable and all factor groups. It also varies from zero to one and indicates,when squared, the total proportion of variation explained by the additive effects of all the factors. For further details on the MCA output, see Nie et al. (1975:416-418).

A final word is in order here before we proceed to analyse the social constraints on the linguistic variables. As Labov and Sankoff (1980:xi) point out, the field of quantitative sociolinguistics has matured to the point that the advantages and disadvantages of the different methods of dealing with the data are well known and have received a great deal of discussion. Researchers are now 'free to concentrate upon the problem that they are confronting rather than on the suitability of the methods they are using'. The present study is not concerned with justifying the selected analytic method. The main purpose of the analysis is to assess the relative strength of the constraints. Furthermore, unlike other comparable studies that have dealt with data from Brazilian Portuguese, this study places a special emphasis upon the social constraints on the rules.

7.1.2 *Social constraints*

The social constraints included in the analysis of the linguistic variables in this book were sex, age, exposure to mass media and, in a few cases, occupational groups, also referred to as work category. These groups of sociodemographic factors will be briefly discussed below.

Almost every correlational sociolinguistic study carried out since the mid 1960s has investigated the covariance of linguistic norms with the parameter of sex. Their results have supported the widespread assumption that women are more status-conscious than men and therefore more likely to conform to prestige norms in both their actual speech and in their attitudes towards language. The phenomenon has been found in all social classes but is especially remarkable in lower middle-class and upper working-class, which are more beset by problems of linguistic insecurity. Trudgill (1972) suggests that such differences in the speech of men and women in complex urbanized societies could be associated with the two following socio-psychological factors. In the first place, the position of women in society is usually less secure than that of men and that might impose on the females a stronger necessity to adopt status signals, including prestige linguistic forms. In the second place nonstandard variables are probably used by males as symbols of masculinity and toughness. Men of whatever social class, at least in Trudgill's Norwich study, are likely to adhere to hidden values of this type (covert prestige) which favour the use of nonstandard forms.

In connection with the assumption above, it has been suggested that the sensitivity to prestige norms would put women in a position of initiating linguistic changes (Wolfram and Fasold, 1974: 94). Such a generalization would only necessarily hold, however, when the change is progressing in the direction of the prestige. In view of that, Milroy (1980:112) argues that sex seems to be a less important factor in determining leadership of a linguistic change than the social motivation of the change, which can be stronger in one subgroup than in another. This position is in accord with Labov's (1972a:303) statement that the correct generalization 'is not that women lead in linguistic change, but rather that the sexual differentiation of speech often plays a major role in the mechanism of linguistic evolution'.

Previous sociolinguistic studies carried out in Brazil do not point to sex differentiation as a decisive factor accounting for language variation. Most of them are based on data collected in the research project *Competências Básicas do Português* (Lemle and Naro, 1977) and, whenever the factor sex proved to be a relevant constraint, the results confirmed the tendency of women to favour

more standard forms. Guy (1981), for example, included sex as a
constraint in the analysis of four linguistic variables and found
that in the case of final s-deletion and noun phrase agreement,
women command a slightly greater stylistic range than men do. The
females in fact displayed a better control of style-shifting and
could avoid the nonstandard variants in formal styles more consistently than the men could. The sex effect in the analysis of
denasalization was more striking. Women were reported to use
proportionately 60 per cent more nasalized forms than men (Guy,
1981:234). As for the rule of subject-verb agreement, the sex effect was rather marginal but still women showed a slightly higher
tendency to use the plural marked forms. The probabilities of the
rule application for male and female speakers were .47 and .53,
respectively (Guy, 1981:269), and these results corroborate
Naro's results of sex effect on subject-verb agreement rule (Naro,
1981:85).

This evidence should be interpreted, however, in the light of
some information concerning the occupation of the informants of
the *Competências Básicas* project. Guy's analysis is based on data
gathered from nine women and eleven men with ages ranging from 15
to 54. Naro excluded from his analysis the data from one woman
and two men. In the whole sample, seven women have domestic jobs
and work as maids for middle-class families, one has never worked
and one is a custodian in a private Catholic school. The men, on
the other hand, hold a variety of jobs, such as helper in a
laundry, errand boy, soldier, janitor, gardener and doorman. This
information suggests that the female informants have regular contact with standard language speakers, whereas the male informants
do not. The social networks of those women are probably more
heterogeneous than the networks of the men and this fact must be
taken into account when the linguistic behaviour of the two
groups is considered. It is possible that the differences attributed to sex could be more properly explained in terms of the
characteristics of male and female social networks.

The situation of women in Brazlândia is of course very different. Most of them are housewives, some are locally employed and
very few have jobs outside the city. As discussed in chapter 6,
the female migrants are very much confined within the limits of

their homes and close neighbourhoods. Their social networks are usually restricted to kin and close neighbours. The only other possible recruitment framework for most women is the religious associations.

The male migrants, on the other hand, are likely to develop a network of friends outside their nuclear and extended families and will therefore be less dependent on kinship ties. They can more easily make new acquaintances such as working colleagues, playing and drinking mates, etc. with whom they meet in the streets and bars. The sociodemographic data reported in chapter 6 show, in some cases, striking differences between the behaviour and characteristics of men and women. Such differences have clear reflexes in linguistic behaviour, and in fact the analysis of the data in chapter 8 has shown that the process of dialect diffuse-ness is more advanced among the men than among the women.

Age is another variable that is usually contemplated in socio-linguistic studies. As regards the age factor, Wolfram and Fasold (1974:89) make a distinction between generation differ-ences and age-grading. Linguistic generation differences can be taken as evidence in apparent time of changes that are taking place in real time. A sound change in progress can be observed by comparing the differential behaviour of speakers in various age levels (Labov, 1972a:275). The age-grading, on the other hand, refers to appropriate behaviours for different stages in the life history of an individual. Teenagers,for instance, tend to be heavier users of nonstandard variables than their elders. But age-grading cannot be considered dissociated from a broader social matrix that includes the social values and conflicts characteristic of the specific speech community under study.

The results for generation differences in the studies based on the *Competências Básicas* data are somewhat confused and con-flicting. Votre's (1982) analysis of denasalization (see 3.2.1.2) has found a two-component diachronic drift that operates at dif-ferent rates in the two age groups. His conclusions support Naro's (1981:93) claim that, in the younger group, the loss of nasalization in regular verbs has two components, namely, the general trend that also affects nouns and a specific morphologi-cal shift in favour of singular suffixes. The results of the denasalization rule analysis, according to Naro's interpretation, corroborate the argument that the subject-verb agreement rule is undergoing a slow process of elimination from the grammar.

In his analysis of denasalization Guy (1981:233) divided the informants into three age groups, viz. teenagers (15-18), young adults (18-30) and older adults (30 +) but no systematic distribution in apparent time was traced. The same occurred with the rule of subject-verb agreement (1981:269), s-deletion (1981: 148) and noun-phrase agreement (1981:194). The author's general conclusion was that with respect to the age factor, the utter lack of any kind of systematicity is most apparent and 'this argues very strongly against any kind of change-in-progress' (1981:340). Further discussion on these two competing interpretations of the subject-verb agreement rule evolutionary course will be presented in chapter 8.

In the analysis carried out in this study two age groups have been considered, namely, adults and young people. The latter were defined as people aged from 15 to 25 years who have moved from the rural area as children.[5]

The data analysis has shown striking differences in the linguistic behaviour of the two age groups, but they cannot be interpreted as generation differences proper because the young people contrast with the adults in a number of ways. The younger group has a higher level of formal education, is more exposed to mass media, has more spatial mobility and shows a higher degree of political awareness. Every one of these variables is, we suspect, playing an important role in explaining linguistic variation when the two groups are compared.

The two other groups of social constraints included in this analysis were occupational groups and mass media exposure. The former was discussed in section 6.5. Mass media exposure has been an especially useful parameter in studies of modernization of peasant communities, but the importance of audio-visual media in language shift does not seem to have been very well established. Trudgill (1974:223) suggests that mass media are less influential than interpersonal contacts in language change. According to him, the media do play a part in the dissemination of new vocabulary and fashionable idioms but have no effect on phonological or grammatical change. The exposure to mass media in fact, he argues, only requires passive understanding on the part of the recipient who is not engaged in any active interaction with the innovator.

Douglas-Cowie (1978:38), in a study of bidialectalism in an Irish village, claims that better means of communication may have contributed to provide the villagers with a new sense of higher social values, showing them the disparity between their own linguistic behaviour and that of outsiders.

The main effect of mass media probably resides in influencing people's attitudes and establishing nation-wide referential networks rather than in altering linguistic habits as such. In any case, degree of media exposure proved to be a relevant constraint on the application of some linguistic rules, as will be shown in chapter 8.

7.2 *The network integration index*[6]

The analysis of sociometric data may be performed with the use of (1) charts or diagrams, such as sociograms and sociomatrices, or (2) by means of mathematical techniques, such as binary matrices, matrix multiplication, and graph theory (see 4.1.1). Each of these approaches, although not necessarily mutually exclusive, has its advantages and its limitations. It may be relatively easy, for example, to plot a sociogram or a sociomatrix of the communication patterns of a network of 40 or 50 persons, but be difficult to comprehend the data contained in it. Matrix multiplication and graph theory, on the other hand, as methods of data reduction, allow the formation of indices and of process variables, which in turn make possible, when dealing with relationship, a shift in the unit of analysis; from individuals to dyads, chains, cliques, and so on.[7]

A binary matrix is one with 0-1 entries, that is, a matrix with $a_{ij} = 1$ or 0 (the subscripts i and j represent the row and column, respectively, of the cell entry). The use of binary matrices opened up many analytical possibilities and stimulated the construction of various types of sociometric indices, centring on group or individual characteristics, such as group cohesiveness or choice status. One difficulty with these indices is that they only take into account direct connections between members of a network.

The matrix multiplication approach allows the identification of formally defined structures within a social network, but in addition it makes possible the analysis of both direct and indirect relations. The technique consists of raising the original binary matrix (0-1) to n-powers in order to determine n-chains among the network members, as well as the tendency towards subgroup formation.

If A is a square matrix, its powers can be formed:[8]

$$A^2 = AA, \quad A^3 = A^2A, \text{ etc., and } A^0 = 1$$

The entry of a square matrix, A^2, is:

$$A^2_{ij} = a_{i1} \, a_{1j} + a_{i2} \, a_{2j} + a_{in} \, a_{nj}$$

As an illustration, consider a simple hypothetical network of four persons (a, b, c, and d), whose relations are shown both in the sociogram and in the binary matrix, A, in figure 7.1. Assuming that the sociogram and its corresponding matrix, A, represent the communication patterns in the network, one can see clearly who relates to whom (in matrix A, by reading across the rows). By inspection one can, therefore, observe in matrix A, direct, one-step connections among the network members while the squared matrix, A^2, shows indirect, two-step connections among the network members. For example, in the squared matrix, A^2, one can see that cell ac has a value of 1 (in matrix A this cell has a value of 0). This means that a communicates with another person who communicates with c. In fact, the following relationships can be seen both in the sociogram and in matrix A: $a \rightarrow b \rightarrow c$. In cell ca of matrix A^2 one can also find a value of 1, indicating the relationship $c \rightarrow d \rightarrow a$.

Unlike matrix A, the squared matrix, A^2, has values other than zeros and ones. The values higher than 1 in matrix A^2 represent the number of two-chains by which two persons are connected.

Matrix A has zeros in its major diagonal (there were no self-communications). Matrix A^2, however, has 1's and 2's. These 1's and 2's represent the number of reciprocated interactions in the network. Cells <u>bb</u> and <u>dd</u> both have two mutual choices, while <u>aa</u> and <u>cc</u> have one each.

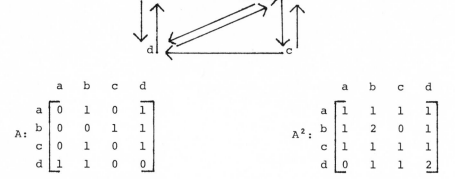

$$A: \quad \begin{array}{c} \\ a \\ b \\ c \\ d \end{array} \begin{array}{cccc} a & b & c & d \\ \left[\begin{array}{cccc} 0 & 1 & 0 & 1 \\ 0 & 0 & 1 & 1 \\ 0 & 1 & 0 & 1 \\ 1 & 1 & 0 & 0 \end{array}\right] \end{array} \qquad A^2: \quad \begin{array}{c} \\ a \\ b \\ c \\ d \end{array} \begin{array}{cccc} a & b & c & d \\ \left[\begin{array}{cccc} 1 & 1 & 1 & 1 \\ 1 & 2 & 0 & 1 \\ 1 & 1 & 1 & 1 \\ 0 & 1 & 1 & 2 \end{array}\right] \end{array}$$

Source: Guimarães (1970:40)

Figure 7.1 *Example of hypothetical network as represented by a sociogram, a binary matrix, A, and its corresponding squared matrix A^2*

Knowledge of the indirect connections within a network may also provide the criteria for classifying people according to their position along n-chains (i.e., one-step, two-steps, etc.), in regard to a given information input. The nth matrix can be partitioned into submatrices representing persons who exhibit similar (or different) characteristics along the n-chains dimension.

Despite its advantages over simply descriptive techniques, this procedure allows what has been called 'doubling back' or redundancy, that is, the same links may be counted more than once. To overcome such a problem, Guimarães (1970:61-3; 1972:64-9) devised alternative procedures, which use a distance matrix, DM, in connection with an adjacency matrix, A.

A distance matrix, DM, is constructed from an adjacency matrix, A, as follows; (1) enter 0's on the main diagonal of DM, so that $d_{ii}= 0$; (2) enter 1 in DM whenever $a_{ij}= 1$, so that $d_{ij}= 1$. For n-powers of A, enter $\underline{n}$ whenever $a_{ij}^{(n)}= 1$, and as long as there is no prior ij entry in DM, so that $d_{ij}= n$. In case any cells remain open on the DM after A^{n-1} power has been computed, the procedure is to enter 0's in all these.

Computer programs designed to perform the operations just

described have been available for some time. One version of such
programs is offered by Guimarães (1972) under the name 'network
routine'.

The main features of this program are:

1. Input: Sociometric data, or similar type of data that can be
reduced to a 0-1 matrix. The capacity of the present version is
400 subjects.

2. Output:

(1) A list of each nominator, i, and his respective nominee(s),j.

(2) A distance matrix, DM

(3) A reversed distance matrix, RDM. This is a square matrix
showing in its cells (ij) the entries of the distance matrix, in
inverted order. The cells which show the highest entries in DM
are assigned the lowest values in RDM; the cells with the second-
highest values in DM are assigned the second-lowest values in
RDM, and so forth. The reversed distance matrix, RDM, is constructed in order to obtain an accurate measure of the relative
integration index (defined below) of each individual in the network, as indicated by the averaged number of all their direct and
indirect links. The use of the distance matrix, DM, for the computation of this index would not correspond to each individual's
actual position in the network, since a given person may have
several relatively 'high' scores in his column cells (j) - say 5,
4, 6, etc. - but be in actuality relatively 'low' in integration
within the network structure, since the cell values correspond to
the number of steps through which a person is connected with the
others in the network. By the same token, persons with relatively
'low' values in their column cells (j) - say 1's and 2's - would
be 'low' in integration, when their scores are obtained from the
distance matrix, DM. In reality, however, the persons with 1's
and 2's in their column cells (j), in matrix DM, are relatively
'higher' in integration, as measured in terms of direct and two-
step contacts, than the persons with 5's and 6's, whose position
may be only peripheral in the network structure.

(4) The communication domain for each column j, and for each row
i. This is j's (or i's) number of direct and indirect links in
matrix DM.

(5) The sum of the length of all links in j's column and i's row.

(6) A <u>relative integration index</u> for each j's column (and for each i's row). This is the sum of the length of all links in j's column, or in i's row, in matrix RDM, divided by N-1 (the number of individuals in the matrix minus j, or i).

(7) A <u>network integration index</u>. This is the sum of j's or i's relative integration divided by N (the number of persons in the network).

(8) A list of <u>isolates</u> in the network, that is, persons who are not chosen or who do not choose any other person in the network.

Figure 7.2 illustrates the basic procedure for the computation of these indices.

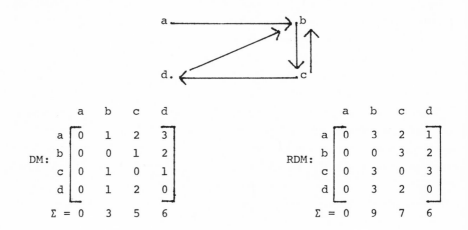

Subjects	Sum of column J	Communication domain J	Relative integration index, J	Network integration index
a_j	0	0	0/3=0.0	
b_j	9	3	9/3=3.0	
c_j	7	3	7/3=2.3	
d_j	6	3	6/3=2.0	7.3/4=1.825

Source: Guimarães (1972:68)

Figure 7.2 *Illustration of the basic procedures for the computation of indices by the network routine*

In addition to enabling the investigator to trace the patterns of relations in a network, from 1 to N-1 steps, the present

routine can be used as a technique of data reduction, thus allowing the formation of indices or process variables, which in
turn make possible a shift in the unit of analysis from the
individual to other units in the network or to the entire network.

The program described above, with some adaptation, was used to
compute the integration indices of the informants. As explained
in section 6.2, each of the 118 informants in the sample nominated three people with whom s/he talked most frequently, outside
of the home domain. These sociometric choices, reduced to a 118
by 118 matrix, were the input data for the program. It should be
noticed that, although the matrix includes the whole sample population, the indices obtained can be considered as representative
of the individuals' network integration only in the case of the
anchorage group members as the sample included all the people
nominated by them. People nominated by the first-order zone
group, unless they belonged to the anchorage group **or** to the
first-order zone group, were not included in the sample.

Another major adaptation in the program concerns the assessment of the integration index. The integration index of each
individual in the network corresponds to the averaged number of
the individual's direct and indirect links. The program can provide the direct links (one-step connections) and the indirect
links (from two-step connections up to (N-1)-step connections).
In the present study, however, only one-step and two-step links
were included in the computation of the network integration
index.

The integration indices of the 15 male informants of the
anchorage group range from zero to .21 (mean = .09).[9] The integration indices of the 17 female informants range from zero to
.10 (mean = .05).

The integration index is regarded here as an indicator of the
migrant's process of transition from an insulated network of
kins-folk and pre-migration acquaintances to a more heterogeneous
integrated network, and is treated as an independent variable in
the following hypothesis:

  The higher the migrant's integration index, the more advanced
  s/he is likely to be in the process of transition from an
  insulated into an integrated network, and consequently, the

more diffuse her/his rural dialect will tend to be.

The assumption here is that the increase in the number of the individual's social relations and the consequent increase in the complexity of his/her role relationship will foster the assimilation of more prestigious ways of speaking, which represents a movement away from the rural dialect.

The network routine was used in the past with relatively small groups in which an exhaustive sampling was feasible, i.e. every member of the group was included in the sample. An exhaustive sampling can be carried out when the units of study are pre-existing groups of any kind whose boundaries can be established. In such cases the reliability of the indices provided by the analysis technique is very high. In the present study it was impossible to establish the boundaries of any 'finite' group of speakers in the community in a non-arbitrary way for the simple reason that any natural urban community is not a rigidly self-contained group. An exhaustive sampling was therefore not feasible. For practical reasons the sample had to be limited to the anchorage group and their first-order zone relations, as explained above (see 6.2). A result of such limitation in the sampling procedure is that the indices become less immune from skewing.

We were aware of this potential problem but nonetheless we decided to use tentatively the integration index as a predictor of dialect diffuseness for two main reasons. Firstly, the relative integration index provides an assessment of the range[10] and, in an indirect way, of the heterogeneity of the migrants' network and that was deemed a crucial criterion to approach the rural-to-urban transition for the reasons discussed in chapter 5. If a person scores high on the relative integration index this is taken as an indication that his/her network has increased beyond the scope of the extended family and that the links are being recruited in more differentiated social contexts.

Secondly, we could only check the advantages and shortcomings of the integration index as a predictor of dialect diffuseness if we tested it. In fact, as will be shown in the next chapter, the integration index can be used as a predictor of dialect diffuseness, although some methodological improvements are recom-

mended in order to avoid the shortcomings that we were faced
with.

In any case, we decided to devise a supplementary network
index based on certain 'urbanized' characteristics of all the
direct and indirect relations of each migrant, which was labelled
the 'urbanization index'. The idea of combining a quantitative
measure of a person's network range, i.e. the number of people in
contact with ego (i.e. the person under study),with an analysis
in terms of the characteristics of the people to whom ego is
related was used by Wheeldon (1969). He says:'The range of a network is affected by two elements. These are, firstly, the absolute numbers of people with whom ego is observed to have a personal relationship, whatever its nature; and secondly, the numbers of people in his network who do not belong to broadly the
same socioeconomic group as himself' (Wheeldon, 1969:133).

The network urbanization index is described in the following
section.

7.3 *The urbanization index*

The urbanization index represents an 'urbanization' profile of
the members of each migrant's personal network. It is simply the
average of the migrant's network peers' scores on seven variables
that were considered diagnostic aspects of the degree of exposure
of the migrants to the urban culture. The migrant's personal network is defined as the set of people with whom s/he is related
through direct and indirect (two-step) links as provided by the
network routine program. The urbanization index can be expressed
by the formula below (i):

$$(i) \qquad \overline{X} = \frac{\sum\limits_{i=1}^{7} X_i}{7}$$

in which $\overline{X}_i$ is the mean of the scores of the members of the network on the ith variable, $\sum\limits_{i=1}^{7} \overline{X}_i$ is the sum of the seven means
($\overline{X}_1$ up to $\overline{X}_7$).

The variables selected as indicators of the rural-to-urban
transition were: schooling level, work category, spatial mobility, participation in urban events, media exposure, political

awareness and recruitment social framework. Except for the last, these variables have already been discussed in chapter 6. Recruitment social framework concerned the domain in which the link was actuated. 'Domains' were defined according to Southall (1973:74) as institutional spheres of action within a particular cultural system.[11] For the sake of the urbanization index, we made a basic distinction between a link recruited in the domain of kinship and pre-migration relations and a link recruited elsewhere.

The computation procedures were the following:
1. To list all the members of the personal network.
2. To assign each member a score (zero or one) on each variable as follows. In the case of the first six variables, if the person had a low score (corresponding to 0, 1 and 2 in the original scale in the questionnaire) s/he was assigned zero; if the person had a high score (corresponding to 3 and 4 in the original scale) s/he was assigned one. In the case of the recruitment social framework the score zero corresponded to a link that had been recruited in the domain of kinship and pre-migration relations; the score one corresponded to a link that had been recruited in another domain.
3. To compute the mean of the scores on each variable.
4. To compute the index according to the formula given in (i).

The urbanization index was treated as an independent variable in the following hypothesis:

The higher the migrant's urbanization index, the more advanced s/he is likely to be in the process of transition from an insulated into an integrated network, and consequently, the more diffuse his/her rural dialect will tend to be.

A basic assumption underlying this hypothesis is that speakers tend to adjust their linguistic behaviour in order to become more similar to those people with whom they interact. This assumption stems both from accommodation theory and from Le Page's theory of language variation and change as a function of group membership (see 4.3).

A high urbanization score indicates that the people with whom the migrant interacts are advanced in the process of rural-to-urban transition and are likely to show a high level of dialect diffuseness.

The urbanization indices for the 15 male informants of the anchorage group ranged from .33 to 4.5 (mean = 2.03) whereas for the 17 women the indices ranged from zero to 2.64 (mean = .84). As in the case of the integration indices, men scored significantly higher than women.

Notes

1   Quantitative methods are an essential requirement in a study of this type if we are to avoid purely impressionistic and subjective assessment of the phenomena in which we are interested. In essence, statistical techniques help us to demonstrate the degree to which relationships occur as a matter of chance or are predictable one from another. Here the crucial issue is the extent to which a relationship is significant, i.e. how far from mere chance its occurrence can be shown to be.
    In this study we have found levels of significance of .05 and below (i.e. chance can be held responsible for only 5 per cent, or less, of the occurrences of the measured phenomena) which are usually taken to be statistically reliable and significant. We also report levels of significance above .05 (i.e. chance plays a role beyond the 5 per cent threshold) which, though not technically significant, may be taken as indicators of trends rather than any strong causality (Dixon and Massey, 1957:89-99).

2   The methodology was put forward by Labov in 1969. It was mathematically revised and computationally refined by Cedergren and Sankoff (Cedergren and Sankoff, 1974; Labov, 1972b ch.3). Detailed discussion on the suitability of the paradigm as well as on the development of the computational methods is provided in the collection of papers edited by David Sankoff (1978) especially in chapters 2,4,5,6,7,8, and 18. On the same issue, see also Guy (1980) and Naro (1980, 1981).

3   It was our concern to code the data in such a way that they can also be fed into the VARBRUL 2 program.

4   A token is defined as the occurrence of any variant of the variable rule under study.

5   By the time of migration the ages of the young informants were as follows: 3 years old: 1 informant; 4 years old: 3 informants; 5 years old: 2 informants; 7 years old: 3 informants; 8 years old: 2 informants; 11 years old: 1 informant; 12 years old: 1 informant.

6   The description of the network analysis technique in this section is transcribed from Bortoni-Ricardo and Guimarães (1982: 17-22) and draws heavily on two pieces of work produced earlier by Guimarães (1970, 1972).

7   For detailed discussion of these analytical procedures see Guimarães (1970:30-49).

8   This means that the number which goes into the cell corresponding to row i and column j of the squared matrix, A^2, is obtained by multiplying each row i of the original matrix, A, by the corresponding cell in column j, and then adding up the product. The product will be different from zero only if a unit appears both in the i row and in the j column being

considered (Guimarães, 1970:39).

9 There are 16 male informants and 17 female informants in the anchorage group. In the reports of network indices, as well as in the analysis of individual linguistic scores, we will be referring to 15 male informants because there was one man who refused to nominate three interlocutors lest he might be unfair to his friends. We do not have, therefore, representative network indices for this informant. The data that he produced were included in the analysis of aggregated scores only.

10 The range of a network can be defined as the proportion of actual links among a specific set of persons with whom the person under study could possibly have contacts (Mitchell, 1969:19). In the present case, the integration index does not measure the size of a total personal network but indicates to what extent a person has contracted links in the new setting as compared to the other people in the group.

11 Southall (1973:74) proposes a taxonomy of five basic domains, namely, kinship or ethnic, economic or occupational, political, ritual or religious, and recreational. The concept of domain has been traditionally employed in sociolinguistics to refer to a cluster of social situations constrained by a common set of behavioural rules (e.g. the domain of home, work, religion etc.) which co-occur with major social institutions. See, on the issue, Fishman (1972:43); Bell (1976:102-5).

8.0 *Introduction*

This chapter contains the quantitative analysis of four linguistic variables that have been selected as potential indicators of the migrants' dialect diffuseness. In every case linguistic variation has been approached through two basic analytical procedures, which deal with aggregated scores and individual scores respectively. In the first case, the informants are divided into subgroups according to age, sex and other parameters and the mean linguistic scores of the subgroups are compared using the statistical techniques of analysis of variance and multiple classification analysis. In the second case, the individual linguistic scores were correlated with two network indices which were indicative of both the number and of some of the attributes of the people with whom each informant had personal relationships. Spearman rank-order correlation tests were used.

The purpose of both analytical procedures was to find out whether or not (and to what extent) each diagnostic variable is undergoing a process of change away from the highly focused rural dialect of the migrants. The results reported in the chapter show that the four variables behave differently in relation to such a process of dialect diffuseness.

The chapter is divided into three sections. Section 8.1 deals with the rule of vocalization of the alveopalatal lateral phoneme $|\lambda|$. The focus of section 8.2 is also a phonological rule, namely, the reduction of final rising diphthongs. Finally, section 8.3 is dedicated to the study of the subject-verb agreement rule with 3rd person and 1st person plural subjects.

8.1 *The vocalization of the alveopalatal lateral* $|\lambda|$

The vocalization of |λ| has become one of the most conspicuous
features of rural and rurban varieties in present-day Brazilian
Portuguese. It is a sharp feature in the dialect continuum and is
probably widespread in rural areas in every region of the country.
In some places a depalatalization rule (|λ| > |l|) co-occurs with
it (Elia, 1975:185-88) as in the examples below (i):

(i) |mu'λεr| : |mu'lεr| ∿ |muj'ʲε| mulher   (woman)

In the study of subjective reactions carried out by Head (1981)
in São Paulo, the feature was evaluated as the most stigmatized
(see 2.1).

Labov (1972a:180), in his discussion of the mechanism of linguistic change, calls these extremely stigmatized forms 'stereotypes'.[1] He observes that the stereotypes become the overt topic
of social comment and that they may eventually disappear. Vocalization of the alveopalatal lateral phoneme is a clear Caipira
stereotype in the mainstream culture in Brazil. In the rurban
speech communities it probably has the status of a 'stereotyped
marker' (see note 1), i.e. it is a variable which is diagnostic
of the speaker's rural background, is liable to stylistic variation, and, depending on how influential the mainstream culture
is in the community, is a topic of comment.

Standard language speakers only employ the rule either to
mimic the speech of rural dwellers or with a metaphorical purpose (to use the expression put forward by Blom and Gumperz,
1972; see 4.2.3). In the latter case, it conveys a flavour of infor-
mality that is suitable for the discussion of certain topics.
Such use is very common in TV sketches.

The phoneme |λ| occurs in inter-vocalic position only.[2] Its
origin can be traced back to the following Latin sequences of
phonemes:
(1) the cluster of the slit fricative |f| or a stop plus the
lateral |l|, e.g.

(ii)   speculum > speclum > espelho   (mirror) and,

(2) the sequence of the liquid |l| followed by |i|, e.g.

(iii)   palea > palia > palha   (straw).

Its vocalization has been a productive rule in Romance

languages. In French the vocalization of intervocalic |λ| fol-
lowing |i| probably started in the mid-seventeenth century and
two centuries later was a generalized feature of the language
(Amaral, 1920/1976; Teixeira, 1939; Melo, 1946/1971). It has also
occurred in some varieties of both European and American Spanish
and of Italian. In Galician, the merger of |λ| and |j| at the
expense of the former seems to be a feature in process of change
evidenced in apparent time. Vazquez Cuesta and Mendes da Luz
(1971:109) have observed that the vocalization rule is more productive among the younger generations. These authors attribute
the λ-vocalization in Galician to the Castilian influence,
and argue that the phenomenon is not encountered in any variety
of Continental Portuguese. Vasconcelos (1901/1970) points out,
however, that the vocalization rule is a widespread feature in
the Portuguese spoken in the Azores as well as in all Portuguese-
based creoles.

The origin of λ-vocalization in Caipira has been a controversial issue. Some authors relate it to the Romance drift whereas
others interpret it as an influence of either the language of the
aborigines or of the African slaves (Elia, 1975). The latter explanation seems more plausible considering that the vocalization
trend has never affected the standard varieties of European or
Brazilian Portuguese. This is indeed the interpretation of Mattoso Câmara (1975) thus stated:

> It is possible that the dialectal elimination of the inter-
> vocalic |λ| in Brazil, with the reduction to a consonantal
> |i| (*foia*, instead of folha, *oio*, instead of olho, etc.)
> can be explained by the Creole Portuguese of the black
> slaves or by the indigenous substrate, considering that
> there does not exist the opposition |l| - |r| in the
> indigenous languages and |λ|, like |l| may have been mis-
> interpreted. (Mattoso Câmara, 1975:57, footnote; translated
> from Portuguese)

Silva Neto (1950/1977:141) offers a similar assessment of the
phenomenon. He sees the vocalization of |λ| in Brazilian rural
varieties as a typical feature of Portuguese-based creoles.

The feature is fairly productive in the speech of the rural
migrants in Brazlândia and it was selected as an indicator of
dialect diffuseness because of its stereotypic character. It is
a source of much hypercorrection, as in the examples in (iv)

from the database (see also 3.2.3).

(iv) |maj'ʲɔr| : |ma'λɔr| maior (larger)
      |pi'ɔr| : |pi'λɔr| pior (worse)
      |'piʲa| : |'piλa| pia (kitchen sink)
      |'tejʲa| : |'teλa| teia (web)

An examination of the data as well as reflection on the phenomenon in other languages suggested the inclusion of a phonological constraint in the λ-vocalization analysis, namely, the
nature of the preceding vowel. A hypothesis that had to be tested
was whether the preceding high front vowel |i| would favour vo-
calization through a process of assimilation. The factor group
for this constraint included the following categories: (1) pre-
ceding |i| and (2) any other preceding vowel.

The analysis was based upon a total of 3,563 tokens and that
included all the occurrences of an assumed abstract intervocalic
|λ| whether or not realized as a lateral consonant. As explained
in section 3.1.2 the alveopalatal lateral |λ| can be also pro-
nounced as a |lj| sequence in any phonetic environment in
Brazilian Portuguese. As a result of this neutralization, words
in which the last unstressed syllable was either the sequence
|lja| or |lju|, (e.g. *família*, *mobília* and *óleo*) are eligible
environments for the application of the vocalization rule in Caipira and were therefore included in the data. Examples from this
set of words are given in (v).

(v) |fa'milja| ~ |fa'miλa| : |fa'miʲa| família (family)
     |mo'bilja| ~ |mo'biλa| : |mo'biʲa| mobília (furniture)
     |'ɔlju| ~ |'ɔλu| : |'ɔjʲu| óleo (oil)
     |ba'zilju| ~ |ba'ziλu| : |ba'ziʲu| Basílio (a man's
                                                       first name)

It should be noted, however, that words ending in the rising
diphthongs |ja| and |ju| can also undergo monophthongization
(see 8.2), as in the example below:

(vi) |ba'zilju| : |ba'ziʲu| ~ |ba'zilu|

This fact represented a problem for data codification and the
procedure adopted was as follows: (1) for the λ-vocalization
rule the monophthongized realizations of the |lja| and |lju|
sequences, e.g. |ba'zilu|, which represented a small amount of

the data, were excluded because in our interpretation if the monophthongization rule applies it blocks the application of the vocalization rule; (2) for the diphthong reduction analysis the vocalized realizations of |λ|, e.g. |fa'mi^{j}ja|, were not considered as an eligible environment. In sum, in the specific environment of word-final |lja| and |lju| the two low-level rules can apply but they are mutually exclusive. It was decided in this study to treat them separately as they seem to be conditioned by different sets of constraints. But the possibility of comparing the frequency of vocalization with the frequency of monophthongization in this specific set of words should not be discarded and can be the object of a feature study with a larger amount of data.

To summarize then, the environment where the vocalization rule never applied because it had previously undergone a process of diphthong reduction was excluded from the *corpus* at the outset and the following eligible environments for the rule application were considered:
(1) an abstract underlying intervocalic alveopalatal lateral |λ| that can be realized as an alveopalatal lateral, e.g. |mu'λɛr|, as an alveolar lateral, e.g. |mu'lɛr|, as a |lj| sequence, e.g. |mu'ljɛr|, or as a |j|, e.g. |muj'^{j}ɛ:|;
(2) the abstract underlying word-final sequences |lja| and |lju| in which the consonant can be realized as an alveopalatal lateral |λ| e.g. |fa'miλa|, as an alveolar lateral followed by a rising |j| diphthong, e.g. |fa'milja| or as a |j| followed by a vowel, e.g. |fa'mi^{j}a|.

As the analysis deals with dichotomous dependent variables a basic distinction was made between the realizations as a lateral phoneme and the realizations as a non-lateral phoneme. The frequency of the rule application was calculated according to the form:

lateral tokens / (lateral tokens + non-lateral tokens)

The data for the multivariate analysis of the aggregated scores for this variable, as well as for the other three linguistic variables to be discussed in the following sections, were produced by a sample of 46 informants divided into four groups, as indicated in table 8.1.

Table 8.1. *Distribution of informants according to sex and age*

	Male	Female
Adults	16	17
Youth	7	6

The overall frequency of the λ-vocalization rule application, i.e. the grand mean, was 1939/3563 = 54 per cent. The factor groups included in this analysis of variance were:

Sex: 1. Male
      2. Female

Age: 1. Youth
      2. Adults

Media Exposure: 1. Low
      2. High[3]

Work Category: 1. Low
      2. High[4]

Preceding Vowel: 1. V (any vowel except |i|)
      2. Y (|i|)

The ANOVA showed that the main effects of media exposure, age, preceding vowel, sex and work category factor groups were statistically significant at the .001 level. It is worth noticing again, however, that as we are dealing with very large amounts of data, the statistical significance of a group of factors does not necessarily imply that the contribution of this group of factors for the overall variation is indeed significant.

The results of the aggregated score analysis for the whole sample are presented in table 8.2. The first data column gives information on the raw frequencies; the second one presents the adjusted deviation for each factor together with the partial beta value of each group.

An important social constraint on the rule application is

Table 8.2. *Effect of all factor groups on the realization of |λ| as a lateral consonant (I)*

Factor group	Category	Frequency (%)	Adjusted deviation (%)	
Age:	1. Youth	491/600 = 81	+23	
	2. Adults	1448/2963 = 49	- 5	beta = .34
Media exposure:	1. Low	955/2164 = 44	- 8	
	2. High	984/1399 = 70	+12	beta = .32
Preceding vowel:	1. V	1498/2767 = 54	- 2	
	2. Y	441/796 = 55	+ 5	beta = .10
Work category:	1. Low	1421/2739 = 52	- 1	
	2. High	518/824 = 63	+ 5	beta = .09
Sex:	1. Male	1177/2148 = 55	- 2	
	2. Female	762/1415 = 54	+ 2	beta = .06
				(r = .54)

media exposure. The influence of the mass media on a variable that has become a stereotype in the mainstream culture can be easily understood. In fact the media are an extremely powerful vehicle of diffusion of the publicly accepted norms. Furthermore a high level of media exposure implies the ability to read fluently because access to newspapers, magazines and books had a very strong weight in the scale for the assessment of media exposure (see table 6.14.). And, of course, the contact with the written language can play an important role in changing speech habits, especially in the case of a phonological variation that has orthographic consequences. The correspondence between phonemes and graphemes in Portuguese is far from being isomorphic. In the case of the vowels, for example, the seven phonemes - which undergo much neutralization in unstressed syllables - are represented by five letters only and the diacritics that were employed to distinguish between grades 2 and 1 of medium vowels have been abolished in Brazil. The intervocalic consonant |λ|, however, is always represented by the digraph <u>lh</u> and the only possible orthographic problem stems from the neutralization with the sequence of letters -*lia* and -*lio*. The difference between

$|\lambda|$ and $|j|$ in the written language is therefore very conspicuous.

The influence of work category (beta = .09) and of sex (beta = .06) is not high and the effect of the preceding vowel is also small (beta = .10). It should be noted, however, that a preceding front high vowel slightly favours the realization of the target phoneme as a lateral consonant contrary to what would be antici- pated by the hypothesis of assimilation. It is very possible, however, that the difference attributed to the preceding vowel results from skewing by a particular set of lexical items, namely the verb *trabalhar* (to work) and cognate words, which were the most frequent items in the database and showed a large incidence of vocalization.[5] The most correct interpretation seems indeed to be that the vocalization rule is not constrained by any phonolog- ical environment. The rule seems to have completed its course of evolution and is now on its way to extinction. This argument is supported by the results of the age group of factors.

Age is the most important constraint on the application of the rule. The adults pronounce the phoneme as a lateral consonant 49 per cent of the time whereas the percentage for the youth group is 81. It seems evident that the rule of vocalization is undergoing a process of elimination from the repertoire of the migrants' children. This is indeed to be expected if one considers that (1) the feature is a rural stereotype and (2) the young people are more subject to urban influence than their elders.

The differences in the behaviour of the two age groups are even more striking if the individual scores of the young inform- ants are taken into consideration. In fact, the average for the group does not reflect very accurately the rule's position in the younger group's repertoire. We shall postpone discussion of the adults' individual scores until the results of the corre- lation tests are introduced. Table 8.3 gives the percentage of pronunciation of $|\lambda|$ as a lateral consonant for each young informant.[6]

Inspection of table 8.3. shows that for most of the girls the realization of $|\lambda|$ as a lateral consonant is practically a categorical rule. As for the boys, the first three cluster very closely, with their scores approaching the overall grand mean. The other four also cluster closely and in their repertoires the vocalization rule has almost completely disappeared.

Table 8.3. *Frequency of realization of $|\lambda|$ as a lateral consonant for the young informants*

	Male			Female	
Informant	*Age*	*%*	*Informant*	*Age*	*%*
AR	18	46	WI	15	86
AF	20	52	VM	16	96
GE	22	56	RI	24	100
SI	21	96	WA	15	100
AU	24	97	LI	18	100
JS	25	97	MO	15	100
JU	20	100			

What sort of factors could be at work to cause the deep differences between the two clusters of boys? Age is not, of course, a plausible candidate. Both AR and AF have dropped out of school. They belong to large extended families and do not seem to have contracted many links with non-relatives. They had already held urban unskilled jobs; at the time of the fieldwork they were unemployed but acted as casual labour working on a temporary basis on a neighbouring farm.

GE is the older brother of JU. The two boys are orphans and live together but there is a striking difference in their behaviour, linguistically and otherwise. JU is a very hard-working student and has plans to go to university. He is a member of a *Vicentino* Conference and his friends are school mates or colleagues from the Conference. There were several recorded group sessions in which the two brothers participated and in all of them JU always maintained a somewhat solemn countenance and a careful speech style.

GE is the opposite of his brother. He had meningitis when he was a boy and did not attend school regularly. By the time of the fieldwork he was going to night school. He has held many different types of unskilled jobs. His speech is marked by a high frequency of nonstandard variables and an irreverent lexicon typical of a 'tough guy'. He is very much oriented towards *machismo* values, an illustration of which is one of his favourite statements that 'the honour of a betrayed husband can only be washed with blood'. GE does not belong to any religious associations and his closest friend is a neighbour.

The high frequency of λ-vocalization in the repertoire of AR, AF and GE can probably be explained in the light of their social network characteristics. As has been suggested in the previous chapters the friendship recruitment framework for the young people is basically the school and the religious and sports associations. In the case of the three informants, they have not been able to contract stable links in such domains. AR and AF are still enmeshed in a network of kin and fellow-migrants. GE does not have a large network of relatives and unlike his brother he is not integrated in any institutional recruitment framework. As a consequence of that he lives very much on his own. Compared to the other boys of the sample, he can be considered an isolate.

In order to check whether the data from the youth group could have skewed the overall result, a second run was made with the data yielded by the adults only. Table 8.4. reports the results. The grand mean was: 1452/2963 = 49 per cent.

Table 8.4.   *Effect of all factor groups on the realization of*
|λ| as a lateral consonant (II)(Adult informants)

Factor group	Category	Frequency (%)	Adjusted deviation (%)	
Media exposure:	1. *Low*	853/1986 = 43	− 6	
	2. *High*	599/977 = 61	+11	*beta = .28*
Preceding vowel:	1. *V*	1063/2226 = 48	− 2	
	2. *Y*	389/737 = 53	+ 5	*beta = .11*
Work category:	1. *Low*	1034/2244 = 46	− 1	
	2. *High*	418/719 = 58	+ 5	*beta = .09*
Sex:	1. *Male*	846/1707 = 49	− 1	
	2. *Female*	606/1256 = 48	+ 1	*beta = .03*
				(r = .33)

The results do not differ much from those of table 8.2. It should be noted furthermore that this analysis of aggregated scores is not capable of accounting for the large range of intra-

group variation that obtains in the case of the λ-vocalization
variable. It should therefore be supplemented with an analytic
procedure in which the informants are treated individually. What
follows is an analysis based on individual scores.

Table 8.5. *Rank order of male informants by frequency of*
|λ| pronunciation as a lateral consonant

Informant	Age	Frequency (%)
JO	38(37)	2/32 = 6
FS	51(41)	3/48 = 6
JD	50(35)	12/148 = 8
JM	43(42)	6/63 = 9
JP	59(44)	20/202 = 9
AR	47(23)	13/37 = 35
AG	65(30)	17/39 = 43
NS	43(26)	91/171 = 53
RC	51(37)	149/253 = 59
FM	54(30)	86/133 = 65
BS	42(29)	94/130 = 72
AV	46(34)	120/164 = 73
PD	32(28)	77/89 = 86
LU	42(29)	57/61 = 93
FD	34(28)	23/24 = 96

Table 8.5. reports the frequency of the rule application in
both phonological environments for fifteen male informants.
Information on the women's scores will be provided later. In the
age column, the first number refers to the present age and the
number in parentheses to the informant's age at the time of migration.

An informal inspection of the data in table 8.5. allows the
identification of three different groups of informants. At the
most nonstandard end of the spectrum we find five informants,
viz. JO, FS, JD, JM and JP clustering closely. At the opposite
end PD, LU and FD also cluster closely, the incidence of λ-vocalization in their speech being very low. As for the other
seven informants, viz. AR, AG, NS, RC, FM, BS, and AV, the rule
application ranges from 35 per cent to 73 per cent.

The most intriguing fact seems to be the results for the
standard end cluster as the three informants are not long-term
established migrants. PD and FD are brothers and they are the
youngest adult male informants. They belong to a large extended

family and both work in Brasília. PD is one member of the Caipira
duo and as such has the opportunity of travelling around to participate in amateur singer shows. He hopes to become a professional singer. The high incidence of the standard variant of the
λ-rule in the two brothers' speech could be in part explained by
their age and by the fact that they are permanently exposed to
cross-cultural interaction in their work setting. It should be
noted that JO, the informant with the lowest score, is also their
brother but, unlike PD and FD, he has moved recently from the
rural area.

LU is clearly an isolate in the community although he participated for a while in the dance group. He has had to retire
from work prematurely (he is in his early forties). On both
phonological variables studied he scored high and yet he lived
in the rural area up to the age of 29 and had little formal
education. Very much more has to be discovered about his life
story if we seek to provide an adequate explanation of his atypical linguistic behaviour.

What about the nonstandard end cluster? JO and JM have recently arrived from the country and can be considered as paradigmatic
migrants embedded in the isolated type of network. FS's network
is also of the isolated type. He works on his own small farm and
travels to Brazlândia occasionally to visit his family. JD and JP
are long-term established migrants. JD is well adjusted to the
city life but he scored low on the network integration index as
he is very much family oriented and does not participate in any
voluntary religious or non-religious associations. JP is the
leader of the folk dance club and, as might be expected, he scored
high on the network integration index but it should be noted that
his preferred friends are his fellow-migrants and kin. Unlike the
majority of the informants, he does not show any preference for
the urban life and in fact would like to go back to his place of
origin. His motivation for carrying out the dance group activities stems from his high esteem for the rural way of life.

The informants that cluster at the middle of the spectrum are
all long-term established migrants. Four of them, viz. NS, FM, BS
and AV are *Vicentino* Conference leaders with high integration
and urbanization network scores.

The brief analysis above is mainly based on ethnographic data. A more accurate assessment of the relationship between intra-group variation and the characteristics of the informants' social networks was provided, however, by a series of rank-order correlation tests. The SPSS subprogram NONPAR CORR that computes the Spearman rank-order correlation coefficient was used (Nie et al. 1975:276-92). This correlation coefficient indicates the degree to which variation in the frequency of the linguistic rule is related to variation in the network integration and urbanization scores, respectively. The results of the correlation tests include the variable pair; r_s: the correlation coefficient (Spearman's rho); N: the number of cases used to calculate the correlation and sig.: the significance level of the correlation coefficient.

The first tests that were run correlated the two scores of each one of the 15 male informants for the λ-variable (the frequency of the rule in environment (V) and in environment (Y)) with the integration index and with the urbanization index, respectively. The results are reported below in (1) and (2).

(1)	Variable pair	r_s	N	sig.
	λ-rule scores with integration indices	0.1664	30	.190 (not significant)

(2)	Variable pair	r_s	N	sig.
	λ-rule scores with urbanization indices	0.3304	30	.037

The correlation of the λ-rule scores with the integration indices was not statistically significant, but the correlation with the urbanization indices was significant at a .03 level.

We decided then to exclude from the analysis the data of the two youngest informants, PD and FD, as well as of LU whose behaviour was considered atypical; two more tests were carried out and the results are the following:

(3)	Variable pair	r_s	N	sig.
	λ-rule scores with integration indices	0.6080	24	.001

(4) <u>Variable pair</u> r_s N   sig.

	r_s	N	sig.
λ-rule scores with urbanization indices	0.5120	24	.005

As the correlation proved to be highly significant, we decided to test the individual scores in each phonological environment separately for the twelve informants. It should be noted that as the N decreases the test becomes more stringent but in spite of that, very high correlation coefficients were obtained:

(5) <u>Variable pair</u>

	r_s	N	sig.
λ-rule scores (environment V) with integration indices	0.6830	12	.007

(6) <u>Variable pair</u>

	r_s	N	sig.
λ-rule scores (environment V) with urbanization indices	0.6902	12	.006

(7) <u>Variable pair</u>

	r_s	N	sig.
λ-rule scores (environment Y) with integration indices	0.5429	12	.034

(8) <u>Variable pair</u>

	r_s	N	sig.
λ-rule scores (environment Y) with urbanization indices	0.4507	12	.071

Correlation tests between the integration and the urbanization indices of the male informants were carried out and whether we included 15 or 12 informants, a positive correlation coefficient was found, as shown in (9) below.

(9) <u>Variable pair</u>

	r_s	N	sig.
Integration indices with urbanization indices	0.4991	12	.04

The results of the correlation tests clearly show that in the case of the male adult migrants the large range of intra-group variation in the application of the λ-rule can be accounted for

by network scores. These results, in fact, argue in favour of a
strong relationship between the process of the migrants' dialect
diffuseness and both the quantitative and qualitative characteristics of their networks.

So far the discussion has been restricted to men's scores and
a natural question at this point would be whether or not good
correlations between the λ-rule scores and network indices obtain
in the case of the whole adult sample, and in the case of the
women. In order to answer the first part of the question the following tests were carried out.

(10) Variable pair r_s N   sig.

λ-rule scores
(environment V)
with integra-
tion indices   0.2054   32   .130
                              (15 men and   (not significant)
                              17 women)

(11) Variable pair r_s N   sig.

λ-rule scores
(environment V)
with urbaniza-
tion indices   0.2508   32   .083

(12) Variable pair r_s N   sig.

λ-rule scores
(environment Y)
with integra-
tion indices   0.0490   32   .395
                                                  (not significant)

(13) Variable pair r_s N   sig.

λ-rule scores
(environment Y)
with urbaniza-
tion indices   0.2884   32   .055

No significant correlation was found in the case of the integration indices. As for the urbanization indices, the coefficient
in (11) indicates a trend towards a positive correlation, and in
(13) a significant correlation. No significant correlation was
encountered,however,between the integration and the urbanization
scores. The next step was to examine the women's scores. Table
8.6. presents the rank order of female informants by frequency of
application of the rule in both environments.

Here again a simple inspection allows for the identification

Table 8.6.   *Rank order of female informants by frequency*
of |λ| pronunciation as a lateral consonant

Informant	Age	Frequency (%)
BP	40(20)	8/70 = 11
MO	38(37)	11/75 = 15
MD	71(68)	13/87 = 15
MT	44(40)	14/45 = 31
TE	46(31)	37/108 = 34
GR	28(22)	5/18 = 36
MP	24(19)	51/139 = 37
TS	40(16)	38/92 = 41
GP	47(38)	34/81 = 42
JJ	56(38)	61/106 = 57
JL	40(28)	22/38 = 58
MR	59(37)	77/133 = 58
LA	27(26)	9/15 = 60
CV	45(33)	62/75 = 83
MC	47(32)	69/76 = 90
LS	47(34)	31/33 = 94
CL	42(16)	61/64 = 95

of three clusters of informants. At the most nonstandard end we
find three women, viz. BP, MO and MD. The latter two are newly-
arrived migrants. It should be noted,however,that LA, MD's
daughter-in-law, has a score of 60 per cent and she is also a
new-comer to the urban environment. The four women at the standard end of the spectrum are long-term established migrants but
several of the women whose scores cluster at the middle of the
spectrum are also long-term established migrants. In fact, a
perusal of the rank order does not show clear patterns of relation between the women's network characteristics and their adherence to the standard variants of the λ-rule.

A series of eight correlation tests - equivalent to the ones
carried out for the male scores - were performed, but no significant correlation indices were found. As for the urbanization indices, a significant correlation was encountered when the scores in
environment V were considered separately. The results are reported in (14).

(14) | Variable pair | r_s | N | sig. |
|---|---|---|---|
| λ- rule scores (environment V) with urbaniza- tion indices | 0.4520 | 17 | .034 |

The most interesting information that emerged from the series of tests with the female scores was a consistent negative correlation between the integration and the urbanization indices as reported below:

(15) | Variable pair | r_s | N | sig. |
|---|---|---|---|
| Integration indices with urbanization indices | -0.4083 | 17 | .05 |

We have seen that for the men the two network measurements correlated positively and both were good predictors of dialect diffuseness as regards the λ-vocalization rule. But, surprisingly, for the women the urbanization index was a fair indicator of dialect diffuseness, while the integration index was not.

Why did the integration and urbanization indices correlate positively for the men, but negatively for the women? In order to answer this question some of the assumptions underlying the network scores must be recalled. For devising the integration index it has been assumed that the higher the migrant's communication domain, defined as the number of persons with whom s/he is directly or indirectly connected through interpersonal channels, the more advanced s/he is likely to be in the process of transition from an insulated into an integrated network, and consequently, the more diffuse her/his rural dialect will tend to be. The increase in the number of the individual's social relations will imply an increase in the complexity of her/his rule relationships and a higher degree of flexibility in the verbal repertoire regarding the control of standard variants.

The urbanization index, on the other hand, is meant to provide an urbanization profile of all the relations in each migrant's network. It is the average of his peers' scores on several variables deemed to be good indicators of the rural-urban transition process.

In the case of male migrants, the integration index seems to be an accurate means for measuring the dynamics of the insulated-integrated transition. The more adjusted a male migrant is in his new social environment, the larger his communication domain tends to be.

As discussed in chapter 6, most of the adult female informants

remain embedded in insulated networks of kin and pre-migration
ties and their new acquaintances tend to be restricted to their
close neighbours. As a result of that, a relatively high integration index is not indicative of expansion and heterogeneity in
the woman's network but is merely a consequence of the high level
of symmetry and transitivity that obtains in close-knit networks.
In other words, the high levels of density and multiplexity (see
4.1.2) of their insulated networks skew their integration index.
Consequently the women who belong to large extended families,
within which they are very much confined, scored high on integration but low on urbanization, as their network peers are likely
to be women with low scores on the urbanization variables.[7]

At this point the following question may occur to the reader:
if the network integration index is not a good indicator of the
women's dialect diffuseness what kind of socializing parameters
can be used to account for the large range of variation displayed
in table 8.6.? Or putting it in another way, what are the characteristics of those women who have relatively high urbanization
indices and also show a higher degree of dialect diffuseness as
far as the λ-variable is concerned?

A high level of the standard variant for the females seems to
be related to the condition of the woman having a large family of
grown-up children who attend school regularly and display a typical urban linguistic behaviour. Most women with relatively high
urbanization scores are married to men who scored high on both
the integration and urbanization indices. It seems plausible to
suggest therefore that the socializing process of the migrant
women is very much dependent on their relationship with their
husbands and children. The women seem to be mostly exposed to the
mainstream culture in an indirect way, through their family members. One could argue that they do not 'go' into the city, but
the city 'enters' into their homes. This state of affairs should
indeed be taken into consideration in the selection of criteria
to be used in constructing network scales in future studies.

To summarize then, both the integration and urbanization indices are useful in the assessment of dialect diffuseness in the
case of the men. In the case of the women, only the latter can be
of some utility. A positive correlation was found between the

λ-vocalization scores and urbanization indices, but this was not
a consistent pattern with the other linguistic variables, as will
be shown in the following sections. We have to recognize, therefore, that in order to make an accurate assessment of dialect
diffuseness in the speech of the female migrants we would need
supplementary indicators based on criteria which have not been
formally adopted in this study. In view of that, we shall not concern ourselves with examining in detail the female individual
scores. The main focus of the following analyses will be the phenomenon of dialect diffuseness in the speech of the male informants.

8.2 *Diphthong reduction*

A feature of rural and rurban varieties that seems to define a
sharp stratification in the dialect continuum is the reduction of
|j| rising diphthongs in word-end unstressed syllables. The phe-
nomenon has been also registered in European dialects (see 3.2.2.
1). The |w| rising diphthongs in this environment are less fre-
quent and in rural and rurban varieties can undergo a process of
metathesis, as in (i):

(i)	|'agwa|	:	|'awga|	água	(water)
	|is'tatwa|	:	|is'tawta|	estátua	(statue)
	|'tabwa|	:	|'tawba|	tábua	(board)

Both reduction processes operating with the |j| and the |w|
rising diphthongs are related to the language tendency of
avoiding proparoxytone words. On this issue Vasconcelos (1901/
1970:101) makes the following remark concerning Southern dialects
in Portugal: 'Accent a une grande influence sur la destinée des
voyelles ... Dans le langage du Sud, l'action de l'accent se fait
sentir d'une manière remarquable dans les proparoxytons, que se
éduisent à des paroxytons: *paciença* = *paciência*; *coida* = *códia* =
codea; *tauba* = *tábua*.'

The monophthongization of the final |j| rising diphthongs is
very productive in the repertoire of the adult sample population
and was selected as another indicator of dialect diffuseness.
Despite being a feature that seems to show a sharp stratifica-
tion, the final |j| rising diphthong reduction rule (henceforth

diphthong rule), unlike the λ-vocalization, does not appear to be a stereotype, since it is not an overt topic of social comment. It is instructive to observe that the feature was not even included in Head's (1981) attitudinal study (see 2.1). In fact, many standard language speakers are unaware of its existence. Nonetheless the rule can give rise to hypercorrection as the examples in (ii) show:

(ii) |'frãnsa| : |'frãsja| França   (France)
      |na'sẽsa| : |na'sẽsja| nascença   (birth)
      |o'fẽsa| : |o'fẽsja| ofensa   (offence)
      |i'mẽsa| : |i'mẽsja| imensa   (immense)

For the multivariate analysis of the diphthong rule in the speech of the Brazlândia migrants one phonological constraint, namely, the nature of the preceding consonant, was considered in addition to the sociodemographic groups of factors. Lemle (1978: 67-8) has observed that the preceding consonants |s| and |r| favour reduction, whereas the labial stops, fricatives and the nasals inhibit it. An examination of the dataset has shown, however, that the slit fricative |v| and the nasal |m| also seemed to be favourable environments for the rule application and that there were a few consonants that never occurred preceding a |j| rising diphthong. It was decided then that the preceding consonant constraint group should include three categories as follows: (1) the following fricative and sonorant consonants: |r|, |s|, |z|, |š|, |ž|, |m|, and |v| as in examples (iii). This category was labelled (J).

(iii) |ar'marju| : |ar'maru| armário   (cupboard)
      |ne'gɔsju| : |ne'gɔsu| negócio   (commerce)
      |'duzja| : |'duza| dúzia   (dozen)
      |'žemju| : |'žemu| gêmeo   (twin)
      |a'livju| : |a'livu| alívio   (relief)
      |'sɛržju| : |'sɛržu| Sérgio   (a man's first name)

(2) the following stops: |p|, |b|, |k|, and |g| and the clusters |tr| and |dr| as in examples (iv). The category was labelled (K).

(iv) |prĩ'sipju| : |prĩ'sipu| princípio (beginning)
      |'labju| : |'labu| lábio   (lip)

|ĩ'dustrja| : |ĩ'dustra| indústria (industry)
|ews'takju| : |os'taku| Eustáquio (a man's first name)

(3) the third category, labelled (L), comprised a special class
of consonants that are assimilated in palatalization to the fol-
lowing |j| as shown below:

$$|n| \rightarrow |ñ| \quad / - |j|$$
$$|l| \rightarrow |\lambda| \quad / - |j|$$
$$|t| \rightarrow |tš| \quad / - |j|$$
$$|d| \rightarrow |dž| \quad / - |j|$$

Examples of this category are given in (v):

(v) |ã'tõnju| : |ã'tõñu| Antônio   (a man's first
     |bra'zilja| : |bra'ziλa| Brasília   name)
     |braz'lãdja| : |braz'lãdžja| Brazlândia

In the case of category (L) the application of the reduction rule
blocks the application of the palatalization rule, as in examples
(vi):

(vi) |bra'zilja| : |bra'zila| Brasília
      |ã'tõnju| : |ã'tõnu| Antônio
      |kõte'xãnju| : |kõte'xãnu| conterrâneo (fellow-
                                                 townsman)

In the examples of the three categories above, the reduction
pattern implied deletion of the non-syllabic |j|. Another reduc-
tion possibility, however, is deletion of the syllabic vowel, as
in the example list (vii). These cases were computed, but as they
were marginal in quantity, were excluded from the final analysis.

(vii) |ĩ'dustrja| : |ĩ'dustri| indústria (industry)
       |'žemju| : |'žemi| gêmeo   (twin)
       |ne'gɔsju| : |ne'gɔsi| negócio   (commerce)
       |a'livju| : |a'livi| alívio   (relief)
       |xe'mɛdžju| : |xe'mɛdži| remédio   (remedy)

The working hypothesis concerning the postulation of the three
categories was that category (J) was the most favourable environment for reduction. Both categories (K) and (L) were considered
to inhibit the rule application.

The data for the analysis of variance included 2,843 tokens

and the frequency of rule application was computed according to
the following form:

diphthongized tokens / (diphthongized tokens + reduced tokens)

and the grand mean was: 1791/2843 = 63 per cent.

The analysis of variance has shown that the main effect of all
factor groups   was statistically significant at the .001 level.
Table 8.7. shows the effects of all factor groups on diphthong
retention.

Table 8.7.   *Effect of all factor groups on retention
of the diphthong (I)*

Factor group	Category	Frequency (%)	Adjusted deviation (%)	
Age:	1. *Youth*	707/802 = 88	+28	
	2. *Adults*	1084/2041 = 53	−11	beta = .58
Preceding consonant:	1. *J*	780/1557 = 50	−15	
	2. *K*	60/112 = 54	− 1	
	3. *L*	951/1174 = 81	+20	beta = .57
Sex:	1. *Male*	1111/1826 = 61	− 3	
	2. *Female*	680/1017 = 67	+ 6	beta = .15
Work category:	1. *Low*	1361/2199 = 62	− 1	
	2. *High*	430/644 = 67	+ 4	beta = .07
Media exposure:	1. *Low*	848/1459 = 58	− 2	
	2. *High*	943/1384 = 68	+ 2	beta = .05
				(r = .78)

A powerful constraint on the rule is the nature of the preceding consonant. A preceding fricative and sonorant is the most
favourable environment for reduction (adj.dev.= − 15%), but a
preceding stop (adj.dev.= − 1%) does not in fact block the reduction rule as seems to happen in the nonstandard variety of Rio de
Janeiro (Lemle, 1978). As was expected the consonants that are
assimilated to the following |j| favour the maintenance of the
diphthong (adj.dev.= 20%).

Age is the most important constraint on the rule. The raw

frequency of diphthong retention for the youth group is 88 per
cent (adj.dev. = + 28%), whereas for the adults it is 53 per cent
(adj.dev. = - 11%).

The women's scores are, surprisingly, slightly higher than
men's. So, at least in regard to the diphthong rule, the women
are closer to the standard than men. The effects of work category
and media exposure are negligible. It is interesting to observe
that media exposure has no influence on the diphthong rule whereas in the case of the λ-vocalization rule it proved to be an
important constraint.

Since the inhibiting effect of the (L) environment was so
strong, we decided to carry out another test, this time excluding
the data of category L from the *corpus*. Table 8.8. reports the
results.

Table 8.8. *Effect of all factor groups on retention
            of the diphthong (II)*

Factor group	Category	Frequency (%)	Adjusted deviation (%)	
Age:	1. Youth	451/537 = 84	+34	
	2. Adults	384/1132 = 34	-16	beta = .79
Preceding consonant:	1. J	776/1557 = 50	- 1	
	2. K	59/112 = 53	+16	beta = .14
Sex:	1. Male	525/1081 = 49	- 3	
	2. Female	310/588 = 53	+ 6	beta = .14
Media exposure:	1. Low	321/783 = 41	- 3	
	2. High	514/886 = 58	+ 3	beta = .10
Work category	1. Low	635/1288 = 49	- 1	
	2. High	200/381 = 52	+ 2	beta = .04
				(r = .81)

The grand mean was 835/1669 = 50%, and the effect of age was
even more striking (beta = .79) than in the first test (beta =
.57), but the effect of sex was slightly weakened (beta = .14).
As age is clearly an important factor in the application of the rule,
the examination of the young people individual scores can be

very instructive. Table 8.9. reports the frequencies of rule
application in environment (J) for each young informant.

Table 8.9. *Frequency of retention of the diphthong
for the young informants*

Male			Female		
Informant	*Age*	*%*	*Informant*	*Age*	*%*
AR	18	60	MO	15	70
GE	22	66	WA	15	83
AF	20	86	WI	15	88
SI	21	93	RI	24	96
AU	24	96	VM	16	98
JS	25	96	LI	18	100
JU	20	100			

The rule is categorical for two young people only but for the
majority of them the incidence of diphthong reduction is very
low. The results follow the same pattern of the λ-vocalization
rule shown in table 8.3.

For the male and female adult informants, however, the rank
order of the diphthong rule scores did not correlate with the
rank order of the λ-vocalization scores.

Furthermore a long series of correlation tests between diphthong rule scores and network integration and urbanization indices was carried out but no significant coefficient was encountered.
Unlike the λ-vocalization rule, no systematic relationship seems
to exist between variation of the diphthong rule in the adult
migrants' repertoire and the characteristics of their social networks. In view of the results obtained for the previous rule,
this evidence may seem rather surprising.

It has been suggested that the diphthong rule is a sharp feature in the dialect continuum, and the results for the two age
groups argue in favour of this assertion: the retention of the
diphthongs is an almost categorical rule in the speech of those young
people who have been extensively exposed to the urban standard.
In spite of that, the rule does not seem to have reached the
stage of a marker among the adult migrants, i.e. the feature is
below the level of social awareness and shows no systematic
pattern of stylistic variation (Labov, 1972a: 178). In other

words, the adult migrants do not seem to be aware of the stigmatized character of the monophthongized variant. The rule in their
repertoire is strongly conditioned by a phonological constraint
and does not appear to be undergoing a process of diffuseness
similar to what is occurring with the λ-vocalization rule. It
seems reasonable to suggest that the diphthong rule is more resistant to the standardizing influence because in the migrants'
speech community it does not have a clear social significance. We
have to conclude therefore that at the present stage the diphthong reduction rule is almost completely absent from the speech
of the youths who attend school regularly but in the case of the
illiterate or semi-literate adults with a rural background there
are no signs that the rule is following a trend towards elimination from their grammar.

On this issue it is instructive to observe the distribution of
the scores of both the λ-vocalization rule and the diphthong rule
(environment J) along a spectrum ranging from 0 to 100 (Figure 8.
1 below).

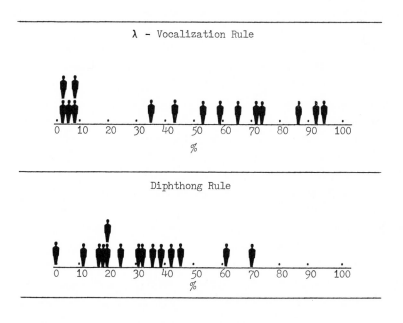

Figure 8.1 *Male scores for the phonological rules*

The inspection of figure 8.1 shows that, in the case of the λ-vocalization rule, the scores are distributed along the whole spectrum, ranging from 6 to 96. The mean is 47.53 and the standard deviation is 1,102. The standard deviation is a measure of dispersion which shows how the observations are spread out from the average. In the case of the diphthong rule the range of variability goes from 0 to 70. The mean is 31.6 and the standard deviation is 342.25.

The two different patterns of distribution are rather revealing of the course of evolution of the two rules in the repertoire of the male migrants. In the case of the λ-vocalization rule, the linguistic behaviour of the fifteen informants is much more heterogeneous and this heterogeneity can be explained in terms of their socialization patterns, i.e. in terms of their social network characteristics. The rule seems to be susceptible to change in the repertoire of the adult male speakers as they move from an insulated into an integrated type of network.

The diphthong rule, on the other hand, seems to be less susceptible to change in the repertoire of the adult male migrants. Here their behaviour is less heterogeneous and there is no evidence that an adult speaker will consistently decrease the number of monophthongized final rising diphthongs as he becomes more enmeshed in a larger and more heterogeneous network.

8.3 *The subject-verb agreement rule*

In Standard Portuguese, subject-verb agreement is a categorical rule. The only case where the rule is optional is with the inflected infinitives. All other verbs are marked to agree with the number of the subject, regardless of the fact that the subject may be present or deleted and, whenever the former case obtains, may conform with the canonical order (subject-verb-object) or not, i.e. occur after the verb.

One of the most conspicuous features of Brazilian Portuguese *vis à vis* the European varieties is the simplification of the inflectional system of the verbs. European Portuguese has maintained the Latin system of six distinct person-number categories, i.e. first, second and third persons and two numbers: singular and plural. In most varieties of Brazilian Portuguese, however, the

second person forms are not used any more and third person verbs
are employed for both second and third person subjects. As Guy
(1981:234) observes, the system is reduced in those varieties to
four distinctive categories, namely, first singular, first plural, nonfirst singular and nonfirst plural, in which the first is
the marked person and the plural is the marked number. The completely unmarked case is then the nonfirst singular. All first
person plural verbs end in *-mos* |-mus| and all nonfirst person
plural verbs end in a nasalized vowel or diphthong.

In addition to the reduction in person-number categories which
is now a generalized feature of standard and nonstandard Brazilian Portuguese (the second person forms having survived in some
regional varieties only), there has been in the nonstandard
varieties a levelling of verb suffixes at the expense of the
marked plural forms. Subject-verb agreement has therefore become
a variable rule and very often first and nonfirst plural subjects
co-occur with the unmarked verb form, as in examples below:

Standard	Nonstandard	
Nós queríamos ir.	Nós queria ir	(We wanted to go)
Eles queriam ir	Eles queria ir.	(They wanted to go)

The variable rule of third person plural agreement will be discussed in the next section while the variable rule of first person plural subjects will be dealt with in section 8.3.2.

8.3.1 Subject-verb agreement with third person plural
There are a number of recent studies that deal with the subject-
verb variable rule agreement with third person plural subjects
(henceforth SVA-3 rule) in Brazilian Portuguese. These studies
are based upon the hypothesis put forward by Naro and Lemle
(1976) that the lack of agreement is more likely to occur with
those verb forms in which it matters least, in the sense that
the levelling of the suffixes is hardly noticeable or salient to
the native speakers. The authors argue that the lack of agreement is more salient when the phonetic segments that realize the
singular/plural opposition are more different. Taking into
account the phonetic distinction between the marked plural form

and unmarked form a multilevel scale of phonetic salience of the singular/plural opposition was set up. Furthermore it was observed that lack of agreement was more salient when the subject preceded the verb than when it occurred after the verb or was separated from the verb by intervening elements (Naro, 1981:67-8). On the basis of these observations another scale of salience was set up and both the phonetic and positional scales of salience were treated as constraint groups in the multivariate analysis of the variable rule.

In the case of the phonetic salience hierarchy some alternative arrays of morphological classes containing slightly different classification criteria have been tested through successive recodifications and reanalyses (Naro and Lemle, 1976; Lemle and Naro, 1977; Naro 1981; Guy, 1981).[8] In the most recent of these studies two main component features of salience (i.e. two main forces that operate simultaneously to produce salience) have been treated as two separate factor groups, namely, a stress feature group and a 'material differentiation' factor group (Naro, 1981: 78). For the former the classification criterion was whether or not the inflectional suffix was stressed; 'material differentiation', considered as a secondary constraint, concerned the degree of phonetic distinction between the singular and the plural forms. The stress factor group proved to be the most important determinant of agreement. The effects of these two factor groups, reported in Naro (1981:85),were as follows. For the stress factor group there was a sharp polarization between unstressed endings (probability = .24; adjusted deviation = - 20.5%) and stressed endings (probability = .77; adjusted deviation = + 26.7%). The beta value of the group was .69. The 'material differentiation' group had a beta value of .20 and the probability and the adjusted deviation values of the 'minor', 'greater' and 'complete' differentiation categories were, respectively, .34 (- 11%); .54 (+ 2.3%); .61 (+ 6.9%).

Guy (1981:268) argues, however, that stress, considered as a major dimension for oppositional salience, should not be seen as an independent constraint on the agreement rule but rather as a reflection of the denasalization rule (see 3.2.1.2). The sharp polarization that obtains in the analysis reflects, he argues, a distinction between those verbs whose plurals can be changed into superficial singular through the phonological rule of denasalization and those in which denasalization alone cannot make the singular and plural forms homophonous.

As was mentioned above, SVA-3 in Brazilian Portuguese has been extensively studied. Why then, the reader may wonder, was this variable rule analysis included in this study? There were two reasons for selecting SVA-3 as one of the features of the migrants' dialect that should receive a quantitative treatment. Firstly, the very concept of salience, which is of fundamental importance in the assessment of this morphosyntactic rule, seems to be rooted in the function of the standard language as a frame of reference, i.e. the speakers' awareness of the 'correct usage' as Garvin (1959) called it. The lack of agreement is more or less 'salient' to a native speaker depending on how much the nonstandard form is deviant from the expected standard form.

In a study that we carried out in 1977, briefly discussed in section 2.1 (Bortoni-Ricardo, 1981), it was found that whereas university students in Brasília exhibited a full awareness of the correct usage of the agreement rule, lower-class night school adult students did not appear to perceive consistently the social significance of the variants of the rule. It seemed reasonable therefore to wonder whether the salience scales would be an operational constraint on the speech of rural migrants who have never been fully exposed to the standard language. It should be noted that the *Competências Básicas* informants were illiterate but had spent their whole life in a metropolitan area in contact with the mainstream culture, whereas the Brazlândia adult migrants were born and bred in the countryside. Moreover, if our hypothesis of the salience principle being rooted in the frame-of-reference function of the standard language were correct, then the control of the standard variant of the agreement rule ought to be a good indicator of the migrants' dialect diffuseness. In other words, there should be a positive correlation between the ability of the migrants to use the standard variant of the rule and their process of transition from an insulated into an integrated network. The results of the analysis in fact confirmed this expectation.

A second reason for including SVA-3 analysis in the present study stemmed from the controversies regarding the course of the rule's evolution in Brazilian Portuguese. Taking into account the fact that older informants showed a higher rate of agreement than younger informants (probabilities of .58 and .42 respectively), Naro (1981:85-8) argued that the age-grading in apparent time was a synchronic reflex of a slow process of elimination of the rule from the grammar. However, the results of another social factor group, namely, the cultural orientation of the informant, assessed through their habits of television viewing, provided conflicting evidence. The results of the orientation variable (which had a much greater effect than the age variable) showed that the speakers who participated vicariously in an upper-class socio-cultural context exhibited a higher rate of agreement than those who did not. The probabilities of rule application for the two groups were .69 and .31, respectively. In view of this, Naro concluded that the relative strength of the age and the orientation constraints reflected a conflict between opposing evolutionary trends. The age variable indicated a continuation of a slow process of rule death; the orientation variable, on the other hand, reflected a resurgence in the use of the rule that depended upon the speaker's cultural orientation. The long-term linguistic outcome of these opposing forces can only be speculated on for the moment.

Working with the same data, Guy (1981:340) found no evidence of systematic age-grading in SVA-3 and strongly argued against Naro's hypothesis that change is presently diffusing through the language along a dimension of salience. Guy suggested instead that variation related to the different salience categories could be explained as the result of an earlier period of decreolization in which the most salient features of the standard were borrowed earliest.

In view of these competing assessments of the phenomenon, we carried out an SVA-3 analysis of the Brazlândia dataset with the expectation that it might be able to provide evidence of an ongoing change process of recovery of verbal endings that could be occurring as the migrants come under the influence of the standard language. The basic issues that had to be investigated concerned both the differences in the behaviour of the two age groups, and the possible correlation between the rule application and the characteristics of the informants' social networks.

	Code	Examples	Description
Unstressed endings	N	come - comem |'kɔmi|-|kɔmĩ|	*The singular-plural opposition is* |iɲĩ| *or* |iɲẽj̃|. *Present of the 2nd and 3rd conjugations.*
	M	fala - falam |'fala|-|'falũ|	*The singular-plural opposition is* |aɲũ|, |aɲu| *or* |aɲãw̃|. *Present of the 1st conjugation.*
	F	faz - fazem |'fas|-|'fazẽj̃| quer - querem |'kɛr|-|'kɛrẽj̃|	*The singular-plural opposition is* ɸɲ|ẽj̃|, ɸɲ|ĩ| *or* ɸɲ|i|. *Present of the 2nd and 3rd conjugation irregular verbs ending in -r or -z.*
Stressed endings	G	dá - dão |'da|-|'dãw̃| está - estão |is'ta|-|is'tãw̃|	*The singular-plural opposition is* |aɲãw̃| *in the stressed syllable.*
	R	comeu - comeram |ko'meu|-|ko'meru| sumiu - sumiram |su'miw|-|su'miru| foi - foram |'foj|-|'forũ|	*The singular-plural opposition is* |ewɲ'eru| *or* |ewɲ'erãw̃| *for the preterites of the 2nd conjugation and* |iwɲ'iru| *or* |iwɲ'irãw̃| *for the preterites of the 3rd conjugation. No change of the stressed theme vowel. This class also includes the pair* **foi-foram** *which is the preterite of both* **ser** *(to be) and* **ir** *(to go).*
	I	falou - falaram |fa'lou|-|fa'laru| fez - fizeram |'fes|-|fi'zɛrãw̃| é - são |'ɛ|-|'sãw̃|	*This class embodies the preterites of 1st conjugation in which the stressed theme vowel changes, the preterites of irregular verbs and the pair* **é-são**, *which is the present of* **ser** *(to be).*

Figure 8.2 *The six-category salience hierarchy of morphological classes*

The SVA-3 multivariate analysis used two linguistic factor groups, namely, morphological class and position of subject, in addition to the sociodemographic factor groups. The morphological class group included six categories postulated by Naro (1981). At the outset of his study Naro had set up an array of eight morphological classes, but as some of them (which were found to be similar in behaviour) were amalgamated, the group was reduced to six categories, as described in figure 8.2. The position of subject factor group included four categories, as described in figure 8.3.

	Code	Examples	Description
Within a single surface sentence	A	*Preposed subject* *Eles vivem* *(they live)*	*The subject immediately precedes the determined verb or is separated from it by short words (up to 5 syllables).*
	D	*Distant preposed subject* *Eles ... vivem*	*The preceding subject is separated from the determined verb by relative clauses, adverbial phrases, etc.*
	P	*Postposed subject* *Vivem eles*	*The subject follows the verb.*
Cross-sentential	O	*Deleted subject* *... vivem*	*The subject is deleted from the sentence, occurring earlier in the discourse.*

Figure 8.3 *The four-category salience hierarchy of position of subject*

The data for the analysis of variance included 2,295 tokens.

The grand mean of application of the agreement rule was 806/2,295 = 35 per cent. The ANOVA showed that the main effect of every factor group was significant at a .001 level. The effect of all factor group on SVA-3 for the whole sample population (adults and youth) is shown in table 8.10.

Table 8.10. *Effect of all factor groups on SVA-3*

Factor group	Category	Frequency (%)	Adjusted deviation (%)	
Morphological class:	1. *N*	*28/177 = 16*	-20	
	2. *M*	*105/657 = 16*	-18	
	3. *F*	*18/122 = 15*	-20	
	4. *G*	*150/341 = 44*	+10	
	5. *R*	*70/226 = 31*	- 4	
	6. *I*	*435/772 = 56*	+20	*beta = .51*
Age:	1. *Youth*	*319/496 = 64*	+27	
	2. *Adults*	*487/1799 = 27*	- 7	*beta = .41*
Position of subject:	1. *A*	*431/1347 = 32*	0	
	2. *D*	*49/175 = 28*	- 8	
	3. *P*	*49/198 = 25*	-18	
	4. *0*	*277/575 = 48*	+ 9	*beta = .22*
Media exposure:	1. *Low*	*296/1113 = 26*	- 5	
	2. *High*	*510/1182 = 43*	+ 5	*beta = .13*
Sex:	1. *Male*	*508/1302 = 39*	+ 2	
	2. *Female*	*298/993 = 30*	- 2	*beta = .05*
				(r = .72)

The morphological class constraint group is the most impor-tant determinant of agreement (beta = .51). The results show a clear polarization between the verbs with unstressed singular-plural opposition (categories N,M and F) and the verbs with stressed singular-plural opposition (categories G,R and I). In the former group, lack of agreement can be accounted for by a low-level phonological rule of denasalization which applies to final unstressed nasal vowels (Guy, 1981:260-2). Except for category R (the preterites of regular verbs) the ordering of constraints is similar to the results reported by Naro (1981:77)

in the study carried out in Rio de Janeiro. In table 8.11. the
results of the two studies for the morphological class constraint
are compared. The grand mean in the Rio de Janeiro study was
47.6 per cent.

Table 8.11. *Comparison of the Rio de Janeiro and the
Brazlândia results for the morphological
class constraint*

Classes	Rio de Janeiro		Brazlândia	
	Frequency(%)	Adj.dev.(%)	Frequency(%)	Adj.dev.(%)
N come/comem	110/755=14.6	-33.7	28/177=16	-22
M fala/falam	763/2540=30.0	-18.2	105/657=16	-18
F faz/fazem	99/273=36.3	-11.3	18/122=15	-22
G dá/dão	604/927=65.2	+17.9	150/341=44	+10
R comeu/comeram	266/365=72.9	+25.5	70/226=31	- 4
I falou/falaram	1160/1450=80.0	+33.6	435/772=56	+21

In contrast to the Rio de Janeiro results, the Brazlândia
results do not show any significant ordering within the unstressed group of verbs (categories N,M and F). On the basis of
this evidence it seems reasonable to conclude that the three
level salience hierarchy within the group of verbs with unstressed singular-plural opposition is not operational in the
rural migrants' speech community. The salience hierarchy seems
to be well defined in their repertoire,though,in the case of the
verbs with stressed singular-plural opposition. The constraint
ordering in this group of verbs does not differ much from the
Rio de Janeiro results. The main difference lies in the fact
that for the rural migrants category G is a more favourable
environment for agreement than category R. For the moment we do
not see any plausible explanation for such an incongruence. Yet
it is possible that an analysis with a larger amount of data

will shed light on this issue.

As **regards** the positional salience hierarchy, the ordering of **constraints is** the same in both studies. Postposed subjects are the least favourable environment for agreement. Non-agreement with postposed subjects is in fact rather frequent in the reper- toire of Brazilian standard speakers and it seems to occur also in European Portuguese. The second least favourable environment is the distant preposed subject. With immediately preposed sub- ject the agreement rule is more likely to apply. Finally, the most favourable situation for the rule application is that of the deleted subject. But this is in fact a special case because if the subject is not present in the sentence, the verbal suffix is the only mark of number and the structural link between the **extra-sentential** subject and the verb can only be accomplished through the agency of agreement (see on the issue Naro (1981:80) and Guy (1981:240-9)).

The results for the social factor groups in table 8.10. are also interesting. Generation differences play an important role in the application of the agreement rule: the youth show a much higher rate of agreement than the adults. These results argue in favour of the hypothesis that young speakers of dialect Portu- guese are likely to recover the inflectional suffixes as they come under the influence of the standard language mainly through formal education. The media exposure and the sex parameters have relatively minor effect but it should be noted that women are further from the standard than men.

We have seen so far that both the phonetic and the positional salience scales are important constraints on SVA-3 in the speech of the rural migrants, even though the phonetic scale is appar- ently less complex than it seems to be in the speech of urban dwellers. It has also been demonstrated that the migrants' children, who are more exposed to the standard language than their elders, show a higher rate of agreement. Still a main issue remains unanswered, viz: is there any evidence that adult speakers, born and bred in the countryside,will be engaged in a process of acquisition of the verbal endings as their degree of exposure to the mainstream language in the urban setting increases? In order to answer this question we sought for a

consistent relationship between the migrants' scores for SVA-3
and their degree of exposure to the mainstream culture assessed
by means of their social network indices.

Out of the 24 different linguistic environments in which the
rule application was analysed (i.e. 6 morphological classes x 4
subject positions) we picked up the one with the largest amount
of data, namely, the preterites of irregular verbs (class I)
occurring with preposed subjects (class A), in order to examine
the intra-group range of variation.

There were data in this environment for 12 male adults, whose
scores for agreement ranged from zero to 92 per cent.[9] The range
of SVA-3 variation in this specific environment is shown in
figure 8.4.

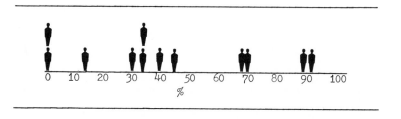

Figure 8.4 *Male scores for SVA-3*

Figure 8.4 shows that the scores are distributed along the
whole spectrum. The arithmetic mean of the scores is 42.7 per
cent and the standard deviation is 970.8. The three informants
that cluster closely at the nonstandard end of the spectrum are
migrants whose social networks are of the insulated type. The
two informants located at the standard end are FM and BS, the
two *Vicentino* leaders whose discourse was analysed in section
5.2 (excerpts number (6), (7) and (8)).

The next step was to carry out correlation tests between the
SVA-3 scores and the network indices for the male and female
adult informants. Rank-order correlation tests were run for the
SVA-3 scores in each one of the 24 environments separately, and
in the case of morphological class I (preterites of irregular
verbs) significant coefficients were found. The results for the
whole sample (men and women) are reported in (1) and (2). (All

the results that show a significant correlation or indicate a trend towards correlation are reported.)

(1) Variable pair $\qquad$ r_s $\qquad$ N $\qquad$ sig.

SVA-3 scores (morphological class:I) (subject position:A) with urbanization indices   0.2546   30   .08
          (14 men)
          (16 women)

(2) Variable pair $\qquad$ r_s $\qquad$ N $\qquad$ sig.

SVA-3 scores (morphological class:I) (subject position:A) with integration indices   0.2436   30   .09
          (14 men)
          (16 women)

The results for the male group are reported in (3), (4) and (5) below.[10]

(3) Variable pair $\qquad$ r_s $\qquad$ N $\qquad$ sig.

SVA-3 scores (morphological class:I) (subject position:A) with urbanization indices   0.6108   14   .01
          (men)

(4) Variable pair $\qquad$ r_s $\qquad$ N $\qquad$ sig.

SVA-3 scores (morphological class:I) (subject position;A) with integration indices   0.4273   14   .06
          (men)

A positive correlation between the urbanization and the integration indices of these 14 informants was found at a .01 significance level.

(5) Variable pair $\qquad$ r_s $\qquad$ N $\qquad$ sig.

SVA-3 scores (morphological class:I) (subject position:O) with urbanization indices   0.4613   12   .06
          (men)

The results for the female group are reported in (6) below.

(6) <u>Variable pair</u> r_s N   sig.
   SVA-3 scores
   (morphological
   class:I) (subject
   position:A) with ur-
   banization indices   0.3593   16   .08
                                              (women)

A negative correlation between the urbanization and the integration indices of these 16 informants was found at a .06 significance level.

The results for the two groups follow approximately the same
pattern found in the case of the λ-vocalization rule, i.e. there
is a good positive correlation between the linguistic and the
network scores for the men but not for the women. For the latter,
however, the urbanization indices show a trend towards a relationship with the linguistic scores.

At this point it is worth pointing out that a significant correlation between agreement rates and network scores obtained only
with verbs of class I. This morphological class of verbs showed
in fact the highest rate of agreement (table 8.10.). It was
furthermore the most salient class in the phonetic salience
scale. Pulling the individual lines of the argument together, we
can conclude with confidence that as the rural migrants become
more enmeshed in the mainstream culture they are likely to display a better control of the standard agreement rule. Such a
gradual process of recovery of verbal suffixes is constrained by
a scale of salience, i.e. verbal forms which show the most conspicuous singular-plural oppositions are the earliest to acquire
the inflections. At the present stage of the rural-to-urban
transition in the community, only in the case of the most salient
verbal class is the SVA-3 rule consistently associated with
social significance, and functions as a good indicator of dialect
diffuseness. With the less salient classes the process of suffix
recovery is less advanced and the social function of agreement
as an urbanization marker has not been consistently established
yet.

8.3.2 Subject-verb agreement with first person plural

Subject-verb agreement with first person plural (henceforth

SVA-1) is also a variable rule in nonstandard Brazilian Portuguese. The first person plural suffix *-mos* - |mus| in the standard language - can be realized as |mu| or be simply deleted. In the latter case the unmarked nonfirst singular is substituted. In Caipira the variant |mu| usually co-occurs with a change of the root vowel (|a| > |e|) in the preterites of the first conjugation, as in (i) below.

(i) Standard   Nonstandard

     nós falamos   nós falemu   (we talked)
     nós andamos   nós andemu   (we walked)
     nós paramos   nós paremu   (we stopped)

In present-day Brazilian Portuguese there is a general trend towards using the expression *a gente* (which corresponds to the French impersonal *on*) instead of the first person plural pronoun *nós*. According to the standard agreement rule the subject *nós* determines the use of the verbal suffix *-mos*, but the subject *a gente* co-occurs with the unmarked nonfirst singular form. In the nonstandard varieties, however, the two rules are likely to merge and the following agreement patterns obtain:

(ii) Standard   Nonstandard

     nós falamos   nós fala
     a gente fala   a gente falamos

A study of SVA-1 according to the variable rule paradigm is being carried out in Rio de Janeiro as part of the project *Censo da variação lingüística no Estado do Rio de Janeiro* (Naro, 1982). The hypothesis that variation could be constrained by the degree of salience of the singular-plural opposition was tested but the available results have shown that the main constraint is not simply the salience but the relation that the salience scale holds with verbal tenses. Naro observes that children below the age of 10 years show an overwhelming tendency to use the suffix *-mos* with both the subject *nós* and *a gente* in the past tense, and to delete the suffix with both subject forms in the present tense, as in (iii) below.

(iii) Nós (or) a gente fala   (we talk)
      Nós (or) a gente falamos   (we talked)

In the present study we decided not to consider the occur-

rences of the subject *a gente* as eligible environments for the
rule application because the frequency of inflected verbal forms
with this subject is relatively low in the dataset. As we had to
work with a dichotomous   dependent variable we postulated a
basic distinction between maintenance and deletion of the suffix
-mos. The former group included the realizations |mus| and |mu|
whether the theme vowel was changed or not.

Table 8.12. *Effect of all factor groups on SVA-1*

Factor group	Category	Frequency (%)	Adjusted deviation (%)	
Stress:	1. *T*	670/1077 = 62	+ 6	
	2. *X*	15/147 = 10	-41	
				beta = .41
Position of subject:	1. *A*	417/888 = 47	- 9	
	2. *D*	4/12 = 34	-22	
	3. *P*	4/14 = 29	-31	
	4. *O*	260/310 = 84	+19	
				beta = .32
Age:	1. *Youth*	244/298 = 82	+18	
	2. *Adults*	441/926 = 48	- 6	
				beta = .28
Sex:	1. *Male*	473/719 = 66	+ 6	
	2. *Female*	212/505 = 42	- 9	
				beta = .20
Media exposure:	1. *Low*	304/594 = 51	- 0	
	2. *High*	381/630 = 60	+ 0	
				beta = .01
				(r = .71)

Two linguistic factor groups were included in the multivariate
analysis: position of subject and stress placement in the verbal
form. The position of subject group was set up in the same way as
in the SVA-3 analysis. As regards stress placement, the verbal
forms were divided into two categories: firstly, paroxytone words
(T), in which the suffix *-mos* follows the stressed syllable, e.g.
falamos, andamos, and secondly, proparoxytone words (X), in which
there is a syllable between the stressed syllable and the suffix,
e.g. *falávamos, andávamos.* Deletion of the suffix was expected to
occur at higher rates in class X considering that there is in the
dialect a productive phonological rule of final unstressed

syllable deletion which affects the proparoxytone words (see
3.2.2.2). Table 8.12. reports the results of the multivariate
analysis. The main effect of every factor group was significant
at a .001 level, except for mass media exposure, the main effect
of which was not statistically significant. The grand mean of
rule application was 685/1224 = 56 per cent.

Both linguistic factor groups are important constraints on the
application of the rule. The results for stress placement confirm
what was anticipated by the proparoxytone reduction hypothesis.
The results of the position of subject group follow the same
pattern found for the SVA-3 rule. The rate of agreement in those
cases in which the verb agrees with an extra-sentential subject
(class 0 of deleted subjects) is, however, much higher than in
the equivalent cases in SVA-3.

The most striking information given in table 8.12. is related
to the parameters of sex and age (beta values of .20 and .28
respectively). The explanation for the wide gap between men's
and women's control of the SVA-1 rule seems indeed to stem from
the differences in the situation of the two groups in relation to
the rural-to-urban transition. We have been arguing throughout
this study (mainly in sections 6.4 and 7.1.2) that the male migrants are in the lead in the process of adjustment to the new
urban environment, as well as being more exposed to the mainstream culture than the female migrants. The SVA-1 rule can be
considered as the best linguistic diagnostic variable of this
state of affairs of all the four variables that were included in
the present study.

The range of intra-group variation was assessed in the environment of paroxytone verb forms occurring with preposed subject,
as this was the environment with the largest amount of available
data. The male informants' scores in this environment ranged from
zero to 74 per cent as shown in figure 8.5.

The mean of the scores was 45.2 and the standard deviation
was 672.7.

Rank-order correlation tests between SVA-1 scores in each
environment and network index were carried out. The results of
those tests in which a significant correlation was found are
reported below.

(1) <u>Variable pair</u> r_s N   sig.

SVA-1 scores
(stress class:T)
(position of
subject:A) with
integration indices   0.3037   31   .04
                                     (15 men)
                                     (16 women)

(2) <u>Variable pair</u> r_s N   sig.

SVA-1 scores
(stress class:T)
(position of
subject:A) with ur-
banization indices   0.3743   31   .01
                                     (15 men)
                                     (16 women)

(3) <u>Variable pair</u> r_s N   sig.

SVA-1 scores
(stress class:T)
(position of
subject:A) with ur-
banization indices   0.6031   15   .009
                                     (men)

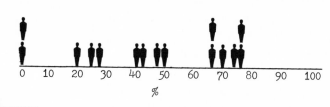

Figure 8.5 *Male scores for SVA-1*

For the fifteen male informants a highly significant correlation (sig. = .009) was also found between the urbanization and
the integration indices. For the 16 female informants a negative
correlation between the urbanization and the integration indices
was found at a .06 level of significance. As no significant
correlation coefficient was found between the linguistic scores
and integration indices either for the men or for the women,
the correlation reported in (1) for all informants is attributa-

ble to the larger N.

In sum, there is a reliable relationship between men's network urbanization indices and their control of the SVA-1 rule. The feature seems in fact to be a good indicator of dialect diffuseness for the men. As for the women, the process of acquisition of first person plural inflection is less advanced and the feature does not appear to have acquired a consistent significance as a marker of urbanization. The female individual scores are fairly low, but four women scored high on this variable (scores of 73%, 75%, 83% and 100%). Every one of them belongs to a large nuclear family and is very much exposed to interactions with young people (her own children and their friends) in her home. Although in this study we have not formally treated such inter-generation degree of contact as a condition that might foster dialect diffuseness we can firmly suggest that the assessment of linguistic changes in the women's repertoire must take into consideration their indirect exposure to the mainstream culture through their husbands and, to a larger extent, their children.

Notes

1 Labov (1972a:178-80) proposes a typology of linguistic variables taking into account the social import associated with them, that can be thus summarized: an 'indicator' is a variable that correlates with sociodemographic parameters but is not subject to stylistic variation in the speech community. When the members of the speech community consistently use the variable to mark differences in speech style, the variable is considered to have reached the stage of a 'marker'. Finally, a 'stereotype' is a variable which is subject to extreme stigmatization. A useful revision of this classification is provided by Bell in the third printing of his Sociolinguistics (1976/1983). According to Bell, stereotypes are variables which are commented upon by the speech community whether or not they are immune from the influence of style-shifting. An advantage of the revised typology is that a stereotype is viewed as a category which is not mutually exclusive with the other two variable types, viz. indicators and markers. This allows for the assessment of a given variable as a marker and a stereotype or as an indicator and a stereotype, something which is not possible with Labov's categories, which are deemed to be isomorphic with successive stages in the evolutionary course of the variable.
An assumption in the reviewed scheme is that a stereotype does not necessarily have to be associated with a negative evaluation in the speech community. It seems to us, however, that the situation of a variable immune from the influence of style shifting (an indicator) becoming a stereotype is

more likely to obtain with regional dialect features than with
social dialect features. The latter situation seems unrealistic considering that a socially-diagnostic variable that is
the object of metalinguistic comments is likely to be salient,
i.e. to be recognized as a sign of significant social differences, and consequently to be liable to the influence of
style shifting. A regional feature, on the other hand, can be
the object of metalinguistic comment, and still not be associated with any negative evaluation in the specific speech
community (although it may be stigmatized at a nation-wide
level). In such a case it would not function as a stylistic
marker in the specific community.

2   The occurrence of $|\lambda|$ in **word-initial** position is restricted
to a few loan words and to the clitics *lhe* and *lhes*, the third
person indirect object pronouns.

3   As in tables 6.12. and 6.13.

4   The low category corresponds to categories A and B in table
6.4. and the high category corresponds to categories C,D and
E in the same table (see 6.4).

5   In a one-hour interview with JP, for example, the different
forms of the verb *trabalhar* and cognate nouns occurred 32
times and the vocalization rule applied in every case. The
total number of tokens in that interview was 85.

6   The frequencies reported in table 8.3. include tokens in an
environment of preceding vowel (V), i.e. any preceding vowel
except $|i|$. The tokens in environment (Y) were not computed
because there were no data in this specific environment for
three informants.

7   It should be noted also that the range of variation of network
integration scores for women (.0 to .10; mean = .055) is much
smaller than that of men (.0 to .21; mean = .089) (see 7.2).

8   Except for the first study (Naro and Lemle, 1976) the others
were based on data of the project *Competências básicas do
Português*.

9   It   should not be inferred from this information that there
are speakers for whom lack of agreement is a categorical rule.
The overall frequency of rule application for the two informants with zero scores in the environment of class I verbs with
preposed subjects was 15% and 14% respectively. In fact for
every informant in the sample SVA-3 is a variable rule.

10 The range of variation in figure 8.4 was calculated for 12
informants and not for 14 informants as indicated in the
correlation results (3) because the scores of two informants,
with negligible values (1/1 = 100; 0/1 = 0), were excluded.

9.0   *Introduction*

The reduction of the linguistic dissimilarities between the
researcher's Standard Portuguese and the informants' dialect was
a major strategy during the fieldwork. Such an effort towards
linguistic convergence was crucial in order to avoid communication mismatches as well as to maintain a good rapport between the
two parties. In spite of this there were many occurrences of
communication problems which are typical of cross-cultural interaction events. In the present chapter some instances of such
misunderstandings are reported and briefly commented upon. The
purpose is mainly to demonstrate that in a situation of monolingualism fluent intelligibility between speakers of different
social dialects should not be taken for granted. Lack of recognition of communication problems can only contribute to increasing
the disadvantage of the speakers of nonstandard varieties.

The chapter is divided into two sections. In the first the
interviewer-informant interaction is discussed in the light of
information drawn from the fields of pragmatics and discourse
analysis. Our intention in this section is merely to show a
potentially fruitful area for future investigation in Brazilian
sociolinguistics.

The second section deals with the difficult cases of miscommunication, and aims at exposing shortcomings in the fieldwork
and discussing the strategies that were used to overcome them.

9.1   *The interviewer-informant interaction*

As was pointed out in chapter 2, perfect intelligibility
between speakers of different varieties of Portuguese in Brazil
is taken for granted. Quite often in informal, or even formal,

218 *The urbanization of rural dialect speakers*

discussions of this issue people argue that the term dialect is
not applicable to the varieties of the language because it implies to varying degrees barriers of communication which, they
claim, do not exist in the Brazilian situation. The purpose of
this chapter is to make a plea for a revision of such attitudes.

A number of instances of miscommunication which occurred
during the fieldwork, mostly in the structured interviews, have
been selected and will be analysed throughout the chapter with
emphasis upon the identification of the probable sources of the
communication breakdown and the strategies employed by the
speakers for both requesting and providing clarification. The
speech situation of middle-class, college graduate fieldworkers
interviewing lower-class migrants of rural background is considered to be a good example of cross-cultural interaction, despite
the fact that Portuguese is the mother tongue of all the participants. We feel, with Thomas (1983), that the category of cross-
cultural communication should include any communication between
two people who, in any particular domain, do not share a common
linguistic or cultural background.

That the interview is a speech event with very singular characteristics is a well-known and often discussed fact in sociolinguistics. Some authors even discard it as a useful method of
linguistic data collecting on the grounds of its artificiality
(Wolfson, 1976). Other researchers recognize its usefulness but
are concerned with strategies that can be used in order to make
the informant's speech approach, as much as possible, a colloquial style (Wolfram and Fasold, 1974; Labov, 1981). These two
positions share a common assumption: that the situation of an
interview is rather artificial and uncommon in people's daily
life. If this were the case, then it could be argued that the
instances of misunderstanding recorded during the interviews are
not representative of the speakers' ability to handle routine
linguistic situations, and therefore should not be considered as
a serious handicap.

We would like to make a claim,however,that interview-like
events can occur rather frequently in the life of these informants. They are likely to be questioned in a very similar way
during a doctor-patient interaction, a visit of a social worker,

an appointment with their children's teacher or the school
principal, an incident with the police, a job interview, a trial
and so on. One piece of evidence of the informants' familiarity
with interviews is that at the beginning the fieldworker was
often taken for a social worker. There had been a large survey in
the community conducted by the Social Service Secretary personnel
the year before with the purpose of identifying the families who
did not own the houses where they lived. In fact, visits of this
type are regularly carried out in the area. Life in the city
indeed provides many opportunities for cross-cultural interaction
and the migrants' failure to maintain a fluent communication
during the research fieldwork should not be seen therefore as an
isolated phenomenon but rather as the manifestation of a routine
problem.

Before we proceed to examine the *corpus* it is worthwhile
discussing briefly the characteristics of an interview as a
speech event. Taking advantage of Goffman's (1976) analysis of
conversational organization, we may distinguish between the
system constraints and the ritual constraints on the interview.
The former represent the requirements on the dialogic format,
while the latter refer to the management of conversational inter-
play in any particular social situation.

An interview differs from trivial conversation because it
adheres more tightly to patterned sequencing rules. There is a
preallocated system of turn-taking (Sacks *et al.*, 1974) and the
elicitation-reply format is rarely broken, resulting in a regular
sequence of adjacency pairs (Coulthard, 1977). The most interesting features,however,are related to the ritual constraints.
As Goffman (1976:269) points out, such constraints mark the
physical and social accessibility of two individuals to each
other and carry implications concerning the character of the
speaker and his evaluation of the recipients, as well as the
relationship between them. Pêcheux (1978) suggests that a
speaker develops an imaginary formation, i.e. a mental image of
his own and of his interlocutor's social role. Underlying this
imaginary formation are the answers to some questions that are
implicit in the discourse process: 'Who am I to talk to him like
this?', 'Who is he so that I talk to him like this?'

Three characteristics of the structured interviews which are related to the social relationships of the interlocutors to each other as well as to their recognition of the rules governing the event   seem to be crucial in determining the ritual constraints on the interview, namely, the asymmetrical position of the participants, the predisposition of both parties to converge their speech and the linguistic insecurity of many informants. The second and the third characteristics, of course, derive from the first.

The situation is structurally asymmetrical from a social point of view, with the informant occupying a one-down position. One member of the dyad is either a middle-class university teacher or a university student, and the other is a working-class illiterate or semi-literate person with a rural background. The serious efforts and concern of the fieldworkers to establish a good rapport with the informants can minimize the asymmetry but do not override it.

Furthermore, according to the rules of the event, the interviewer is the dominant participant who has most of the control over the discourse. The roles are defined *a priori* and normally there is a unilateral right to ask questions and to introduce topics. Unlike other types of dialogues, the informant usually has a very restricted latitude concerning the questions he can turn down, as they are not posed to him as requests that can be declined once he has agreed to be interviewed.

Such a state of affairs may lead to an invasion of the informants' territoriality if the researcher does not behave tactfully. Baugh (1979:21) observes that it is imperative that the fieldworker develop a 'heightened ethnographic awareness', which he calls 'ethnosensitivity'. This will enable him to deal with the situation of dominance, referred to above, without any patronizing attitude, compensating for the unavoidable intrusion into the informant's privacy so that the latter will not consider himself exploited.

Wolfson (1976) claims that it is difficult to switch from a structured to a spontaneous interview because whereas the informants have clear expectations regarding the former, the latter will seem to them a truly unnatural speech situation

insofar as people are just not used to holding a natural conversation with strangers. In fact this may be true in the first or
second contact between researcher and informant, but after long-
term participant observation in a community, the fieldworker can
easily perform the transition from a structured interview to a
spontaneous conversation. This was used in Brazlândia as a
strategy to allow a change-over of positions regarding the right
of asking questions and constraining topic selection. Whenever
the fieldworkers succeeded in establishing an atmosphere of
mutual confidence and relaxation the informants would frequently
ask them questions on general topics or on private matters. These
occasional intrusions into the interviewers' privacy helped to
compensate for their constant position of dominance (see 6.3).

The interview event was frequently marked by the willingness
of both participants to converge their speech. As discussed in
section 4.3, speech convergence is part of the accommodation
process whereby the speakers shift their speech style to become
more similar to that of their interlocutors (Giles, 1980). While
the interviewer would make an effort of downward convergence, the
informants would be engaged in an effort of upward convergence.
Evidence of the latter can be seen in the occurrence of hypercorrections in their speech and their willingness to recall information and episodes which they imagined could be relevant for the
research.

The fieldworkers, on the other hand, employed a number of convergence strategies, manifest in different dimensions. The most
obvious was a quite natural style-shifting, which followed consistent but rather spontaneous rules. Most of the fieldworkers
did not use any of the sharp features characteristic of Caipira,
which do not belong to their repertoires, but the occurrence of
gradient features, which in their speech function as markers of
colloquial style, increased meaningfully during the interactions.
In the case of a fieldworker who was born and raised in the
region where the anchorage group informants come from, a few
sharp features, such as the vocalization of $|\lambda|$, sometimes
emerged in his speech. In some interviews there was no conspicuous difference between his and the informant's dialects. Another
one unconsciously recovered the retroflex $|\dot{r}|$ of her childhood

222 The urbanization of rural dialect speakers

in Minas Gerais, which had now almost disappeared from her repertoire.

Two episodes during an interview with the same informant illustrate the convergence strategies. In the first one, the fieldworker (FW) uses the acronyms 'INPS' and 'FUNRURAL' which are two different institutions of social security, but she anticipates the possibility of a misunderstanding and provides further information. The informant still does not understand and requests clarification. The fieldworker then substitutes the word *Instituto*, which is more usual among that population, for the acronym. The last two moves help clarify the question a little further. (The first number in parentheses following the informant's initials refers to the age at the time of the fieldwork, the second to the age at which she moved from the rural area to the city.)

(1)FW:And from the INPS, or the FUNRURAL, have you received any benefit? For example, if you were sick, received assistance, anything like that?

MO:(38)(37) What do you mean?

FW:From the Institute. Over there on the farm, you didn't have the Institute, right?

MO:Over there, you mean, receiving (money)?

FW:Or having free medical care.

(1)FW:E do INPS, ou do FUNRURAL, você já recebeu algum benefício? Assim que você estivesse doente, tivesse assistência alguma coisa assim?

MO:(38)(37) Como que a senhora fala?

FW:Do Instituto. Lá na roça vocês não tinham Instituto, não é?

MO:Lá? Assim de ganhá?

FW:Assim de tê médico de graça...

In example (2) the fieldworker switches from a more unusual verb *participar* (to participate, to belong to) to the verb *freqüentar* (to frequent, to go to constantly, to attend) and then to the verb *ir* (to go).

(2)FW:Do you belong to any association here in Brazlândia, the *Vicentinos*, prayer group, mothers' club, dance group, residents' association? Do you

(2)FW:Você participa de alguma associação aqui em Brazlândia, os Vicentinos, clube de mães, grupo de dança, associação de moradores? Você participa de alguma

take part in any of these?	delas?
MO:(38)(37) If is...	MO:Se tã...
FW:Do you attend those meetings? Do you attend, are you going to those meetings?	FW:Você está freqüentando essas reuniões? Você está freqüentando, você está indo nessas reuniões?
MO:I always go there to the Saint Vincent.	MO:Eu sempre vou lá no São Vicente.

Another strategy of convergence was the use of what Duncan (1974:166) has called 'back channels', employed by the auditor to provide the speaker with useful information as the turn progresses. They may have the form of head nods or approval noises ('mm - hmm', *ẽ*), of sentence completions, when the recipient provides the end of an utterance that the speaker has begun, of brief requests for clarification or for restatements of a preceding thought expressed by the speaker. During the interview they were used to convey agreement and functioned as a positive reinforcement for the flow of conversation. They were in fact very useful to encourage the informant, to show sympathy and develop a good rapport.

The fieldworkers' efforts at accommodation, however, could not prevent occurrences of miscommunication. The comprehension failures derive in part from the linguistic insecurity of the informant and, in a vicious circle, may contribute to increase it. Goffman (1976:296) observes that failing to hear need expose the recipient to nothing more deprecatory than the imputation of lack of attention. The recognition of a misunderstanding, however, can be the source of much embarrassment to the recipient. These circumstances require from the fieldworker an ability to handle the situation satisfactorily.

Not all the informants would manifest overtly a feeling of embarrassment or insecurity regarding mismatches in the communication. Women, especially the older ones, were more likely to verbalize such feelings. Interestingly, though, they did not refer directly or indirectly to dialect differences. They attributed their failure to understand to problems of memory or to deficiencies of their 'heads'. The following excerpts illustrate the point.

(3)FW:Did the doctor say what
it was?

LS:(47)(34) He didn't...
yes he did, but I don't
understand very well, I
forget, it's a funny
little name, I don't
know what it is.

(4)FW:But, is there a special
programme (on the radio)
that you like?

MT:(44)(40) Yes, there is,
but I don't understand
those things, I see them
talk, I forget, my 'head'
is too bad.

(5)FW:And so, the religious
groups, dance groups,
do you take part in any
of those?

MD:(71)(68) I do.

FW:Which one?

MD:Oh, I'm silly. I don't
know which one, how
I should answer you.

(3)FW:O médico já disse o que
é?

LS:(47)(34) Num disse...
disse sim, mais eu num
compreendo muito bem, eu
me esqueço, é um nome-
zinho esquisito, num sei
bem o que é não.

(4)FW:Mas tem um programa especial que a senhora
gosta (no rádio)?

MT:(44)(40) Tem, maisi, eu
num entendo daquilo, eu
vejo eles falá, eu
esqueço, tô c'a cabeça
ruim.

(5)FW:E assim, de grupos de
igreja, de dança, a
senhora participa de
alguma coisa?

MD:(71)(68) Participo.

FW:De quê?

MD:Ah... eu sô boba, eu
num sei de que que é,
cumé que é que responde
a senhora.

Actually the informant provided the first answer without
understanding the question. When the fieldworker asked for
details, she admitted the failure, justifying it with a severe
self depreciation.

The questions about mass media exposure elicited some
evidence of the informants' difficulty in comprehending
broadcast Portuguese. The following are examples:

(6)FW:Didn't you hear the news
on the telly about the
minister who was ousted,
they pushed him out from
...

MD:(71)(68) No, I didn't.
Ah love, I tell you I'm
deaf; things happen here,
they talk about it there,
I seem to hear everything,
but I don't understand, I
don't understand what it
is about.

(7)MR:(59)(37) Recently, what I

(6)FW:A senhora num ouviu falá
na televisão da notícia
do ministro que caiu,
tiraru ele du...

MD:(71)(68) Não senhora.
Ah, mia fia, eu num tô
dizenu pa senhora, eu
sô surda, aqui passa as
coisa, tá falanu lá
eu tô escutanu, mais
num tô entendenu como é
que é.

(7)MR:(59)(37) O qu'eu tô

seem to understand is this business of news. I follow the news programmes, radio news. telly news. You see, I'm learning now, I had never used a TV before. We used to live in the country, and even here, only a short time ago could my children afford to buy a radio.	comprendenu de poco tempo pra cã é negoçu di reporti. Qu'eu cumpanho nutiça, reporti no rãdio e televisão, que agora qu'eu to aprendenu, nunca tinha usado nem televisão, que a gente morava na roça, e mesmo aqui né, mesmo aqui, é de pocos tempo pra cã que us menino deu conta de comprã um rãdio.

We may state in conclusion that the informant is clearly at a disadvantage both from the social and from the dialogic organization points of view. Yet the clear disposition of the interviewers towards a linguistic accommodation as well as their ethnosensitivity make the situation more comfortable for the informants than it might be in other types of cross-cultural interaction. Their disadvantaged position may well be more crucial if the interlocutor is neither sympathetic nor conscious of potential dialect mismatches.

9.2 *Analysis of the sources of miscommunications*

In order to communicate meaningfully two people must share interpretative rules which are part of their communicative competence (Hymes, 1972). Some of these rules are stored in their linguistic competence, e.g. their shared knowledge of segmental and suprasegmental phonology, of grammar and semantics. Another set of these rules refers to their shared knowledge of the world, which is crucial for an effective use of language in context. This second group is being considered as a broad category including extra-textual or pragmatic principles that assign illocutionary force to the utterance and allow for pragmatic inferencing.

Most of the miscommunication occurrences during the interviews seem to derive from dialect differences at the phonological, grammatical and semantic levels. In other words, the hearer fails to understand the sense/reference of the speaker's utterance in the specific context because he is not familiar with (1) a certain phonological rule which alters a given word, (2) a certain grammatical variant, (3) the sense of a given word which differs from the sense the word has in his own dialect, or (4) the object

or the state of affairs that is identified by means of the word.
Pragmatic failures, in the sense used by Thomas (1983) i.e. mis-
interpretation of the intended pragmatic force of an utterance,
can also occur, but are most often related to a syntactic or
lexical mismatch between the two varieties. The following example
from Magalhães (in progress) illustrates the point. It is part of
a dialogue between the fieldworker and a practitioner (*benzedeira*). The topic is the contributions of the patients to the *benzedeira*'s domestic income. The researcher wants to check the use of
the term *agrado* - a gift that is offered to the *benzedeira* in
payment for her curing services.

(8)1. B (benzedeira):Others bring a little *agrado*, a soap... right?	(8)1. B (benzedeira):Outros traz um agradinho, um sabão assim... não é?
2.FW:Do they bring what?	2.FW:Traz o quê?
3. B:They bring a little *agra-do* of - food, right?	3. B:Traz um agradinho de alimento nê?
4.FW:How do you call (it)?	4.FW:Como é que a senhora chama?
5. B:Conceição Moreira!	5. B:Conceição Moreira!
6.FW:No.	6.FW:Não.
7. B:Ah!	7. B:Ah!

The *benzedeira*'s third move (nº 5) is apparently a violation
of the Gricean Cooperation Principle, more specifically of the
maxim 'Be relevant' (Grice, 1975). Her contribution is absolutely
not pertinent and breaks the rules of a coherent discourse. Yet
the *benzedeira* had no intention of being uncooperative. Quite the
contrary, the informants in these situations, both in Magalhães'
and in Brazlândia fieldwork, were usually eager to collaborate.
The problem lies, in fact, in the ambiguity of the fieldworker's
question: *'Como é que a senhora chama?'* (nº 4). The utterance has
two possible meanings:

(i)   What's your name?

(ii) How do you call it?

The fieldworker of course had the second meaning in mind but the
informant understood the first one. Considering that the two participants already knew each other well enough, for that was not
the first visit to the informant's house, it may seem amazing

that the *benzedeira* would pick out the least likely sense of the utterance in that context. Yet her response can be easily understood from a dialect mismatch point of view.

In the fieldworker's standard dialect, in order to convey the first sense the verb *chamar* (to name, to call, to be named, to be called) is usually accompanied by a verbal clitic:

(iii)   'Como a senhora se chama?'

In the informant's dialect, on the other hand, the verb *chamar* is used without the clitic and conveys the first sense. In the second sense the verb *falar* (to say, to speak) is usually substituted.

The fieldworker might have avoided the ambiguity if she had added a verb complement:

(iv)   How do you call it?   (iv)   Como a senhora chama isso?

which is, in the informant's dialect, equivalent to:

(v)   How do you say it?   (v)   Como a senhora fala isso?

The cases of misunderstanding during the interviews fall into five groups. In the first, the origin of the problem lies in the application of phonological rules, some of which are not productive in the researcher's dialect. In the second group the difficulty is related to morpho-syntactic rules. The three last embody different types of communication mismatches at the lexical level and imply semantic-pragmatic rules. The following two examples belong to the first group.

(9)1.FW:What does our success depend on? For us to achieve something, what does it depend on? Who does it depend on?

2.MP:(47)(32) Well, it depends on... on our 'sistence and good will, right? If you don't give up, and always...

3.FW:But what type of assistance would that be? Assistance, let's say, from someone?

4.MP:No, assistance, let's say, when we say: I'm

(9)1.FW:Depende de que o sucesso da gente? Pra gente conseguir alguma coisa, depende de quê, de quem?

2.MP:(47)(32) Uai, depende da... da sistença da gente e da boa vontade, né? Num disisti daquilo, i sempri...

3.FW:Mas que tipo de assistência seria essa? Assistência assim de alguém?

4MP:Não, assistença assim da gente mesmo falá:

going to do that, that that I want to do, right? to work to... to get that... and we work and get that, or we do what we want to do, right?	i'eu vô fazê aquilo, aquilo qui i'eu tenho vontade, né, de traba- lhã pra... pra se con- sigui aquilo, a gente trabalha e consegue, o faiz aquilo que a gen- te tem vontade de fazê, né?

In the informant's first move (nº 2) the word *insistência*
(insistence) suffered aphaeresis of the initial syllable and
reduction of the rising diphthong in the last unstressed syllable
Both rules are very productive in the dialect (see 3.3.5 and 8.2).
The fieldworker interpreted *sistença* as a variant of *assistência*
(assistance) and asked for clarification (nº 3). In nº 4, the
informant recovered the initial syllable of the word, as pronounced by the fieldworker - behaviour that may have been motivated by her insecurity - but when she rephrases her answer, she
leaves it clear that the word in question was *insistência* and not
assistência.

(10)1.FW:In your opinion, is it easier to bring up male or female children?	(10)1.FW:Na sua opinião, o que é mais fácil criar: os filhos homens ou as filhas mulheres?
2.JJ:(56)(38) Oh, dear! Now that's... they're all the same. Daughters are easier to bring up, I think.	2.JJ:(56)(38) Ah, meu Deus! Agora é que tá... São tudo igual As filha mulhé é mais faci. Eu acho.
3.FW:Why?	3.FW:Por quê?
4.JJ:Because daughters spend more time at home. Daughters are more 'acurteous' with their mothers at home.	4.JJ:Porque as filha mulhé fica mais em casa. As filha mulhé é mais acurteis com as mãe em casa.
5.FW:What did you say about daughters?	5.FW:Que que tem as filha mulher?
6.JJ:Daughters are more courteous at home.	6.JJ:As filha mulhé é mais curteis em casa.

In the move nº 4 the word *cortês* |kor'tes| (courteous) was
pronounced with the prothesis of an initial |a|, narrowing of the
back vowel and diphthongization of the final vowel followed by
the sibilant consonant: |akur'tejs|. The first rule is very pro-
ductive in Caipira (see 3.3.5). The narrowing of pretonic vowels

is a productive rule in Brazilian Portuguese but it is more
likely to apply to common and frequent words (see 3.2.1). In *cor-
tês* the mid vowel is maintained in the standard variety. The
diphthongization of stressed vowels followed by a sibilant is a
gradient feature in the language, which occurs also in the standard variety. The fieldworker did not recognize the word and asked
for clarification in nº 5. It is interesting to observe that in
nº 6 the informant repeats the word without the prothetic |a| in
an effort at accommodation.

Another source of miscommunication in the interviews is found
in the use by the fieldworker of syntactic variants which, apparently, do not belong to the informant's repertoire. In the following excerpt of a sociolinguistic interview, the informant, an
81-year-old cattleman, did not understand the irregular form of
the past participle of the verb *ganhar* (to receive).[1]

(11) FW: Had or hadn't you ever won a prize before?

    C: (Cattleman) What?

    FW: Is this the first prize you've got or had you already got one before?

    C: No, this was the first one.

(11) FW: O senhor já tinha ganho um prêmio antes, ou não?

    C: (Cattleman) Cuma?

    FW: É o primeiro prêmio que o senhor ganha ou já ganhou outro antes?

    C: Não o primeiro foi esse.

Most of the communication breakdowns during the fieldwork in
Brazlândia are associated with the comprehension of lexical
items. In some cases the interviewer used a bookish lexicon
characteristic of formal styles, but even current words, frequently used in the colloquial styles of Standard language
speakers, were sometimes misunderstood. In these circumstances,
the strategy employed was to shift the style, substituting a more
common synonym for the crucial word or rephrasing the utterance.
The following dialogues (12 to 19) illustrate the situation.

(12) FD: (31)(4) (pointing to her cheek) This here, see, I can't even stand the effort of speaking, it is hard. This here was so swollen that... not even water... Now

(12) FD: (31)(4) (apontando a bochecha) Isso aqui, ó, eu num tô aguentanu fa-lá direito, tá duro. Isso aqui inchô tanto que nem... nem água. Agora já tô conseguino

I can eat again, like this, food.	cumê, assim, comida.
FW:The antibiotic is having the intended effect, isn't it?	FW:O antibiótico já tá fazendo efeito, né?
FD:Uhm?	FD:Uhm?
FW:The medicine you're taking...	FW:O remédio que você tá tomando...
FD:Yes, it is. It's coming back to normal.	FD:Tá, tá desinchanu.
(13)1.FW:D. Maria, in the next ten years, what do you intend to do?	(13)1.FW:D. Maria, nos próximos dez anos, o que a senhora pretende fazê?
2.MT:(44)(40) Ten years now or...	2.MT:(44)(40) Dez anu agora ou...
3.FW:Yes, in the next ten years.	3.FW:É, nos próximos dez anos.
4.MT:Up to now?	4.MT:Pra trais?
5.FW:No, from now on.	5.FW:Não, daqui pra frente.

The move nº 2 is in fact a request for clarification. Very often the speaker uses the disjunctive operator *ou* (or) to ask a question, offering the first alternative and finishing the utterance with a non-terminal pitch. The expectation is that the auditor will provide the conclusion.The fieldworker, however, failed to perceive that *próximo* (next) was a crucial item and repeated the question (nº 3). The informant then changed the strategy and risked an interpretation (nº 4). In nº 5 the fieldworker finally provided the information.

In the following example (14), the negotiation between the interlocutors was expedited because the informant selected directly the strategy of risking an interpretation.[2]

(14)1.FW:But in the next five or ten years, what would you really like to do in your life in the next years?	(14)1.FW:Mas nos próximos cinco ou dez anos, o que a senhora tem mais vontade de fazê ainda na vida da senhora nos próximos anu?
2.GP:(47)(38) From now on, right?	2.GP:(47)(38) Pa frente, é?
3.FW:Yes.	3.FW:É.

4.GP:Oh dear!

5.FW:Something you find most
important, something
you always thought
about doing.

6.GP:Well, in this next...
within this period of
time I'd like to
build my house, right?

4.GP:Ichi!

5.FW:Uma coisa que a se-
nhora acha mais im-
portante, sempre
pensou em fazê.

6.GP:Ah, é... nesses pró-
ximu... nesse prazo
aí eu tinha vontade
de construí minha
casa, né?

The informant in nº 6 tries to use the word *próximos* but
hesitates and chooses a more familiar word.

A request for clarification can be manifested in many different ways. It is sometimes an explicit question, as in (15) and
(16); it can consist of the repetition of the unknown word (17);
or be presented as a combination of the two former devices (18
and 19), or else be a meaningful silence (20).

(15)FW:The nursery is closed,
but only temporarily,
isn't it?

RC:(51)(37) What?

FW:It'll start again
soon, won't it?

RC:Yes, it is closed for
repairs.

(15)FW:A creche está parada,
mas é temporário,
né?

RC:(51)(37) Comu?

FW:Volta logo, né?

RC:É, tá parada pra reparo.

(16)FW:Do you frequently go
to Taguating?

CF:(72)(42) Uhm?

FW:Do you always go to
Taguatinga?

CF:Yes, you see, I was
there the day before
yesterday.

(16)FW:O senhor vai freqüen-
temente à Taguatinga?

CF:(72)(42) Uhm?

FW:O senhor vai muito à
Taguatinga?

CF:Vô, ainda antonte mes-
mo eu vim de lá.

(17)FW:How about piped water,
haven't you got it?

MO:(38)(37) Piped?

FW:Water in the sink...

MO:Only in the sink out-
side the house.

(17)FW:E água encanada, vocês
não têm?

MO:(38)(37) Encanada?

FW:Água na pia...

MO:Somente na pia lá fora.

(18)FW:Who's your favourite
singer?

JJ:(56)(38) Favouri...
the one I like the most?

(18)FW:Qual o seu cantor pre-
dileto?

JJ:(56)(38) Predilei...
que eu gosto mais?

FW:The one you like the most

FW:Que gosta mais.

(19)FW:Do you take part in any association here in Brazlândia?

FS:(71)(63) Asso... What?

FW:Do you take part in any *Vicentino* conference, prayer group, or something like that?

FS:No, no.

(19)FW:A senhora participa de alguma associação aqui em Brazlândia?

FS:(71)(63) Assa... o quê?

FW:A senhora participa de alguma associação de Vicentinos, de oração, alguma coisa?

FS:Não, não.

(20)FW:In your opinion, if someone is born poor, can he improve his economic condition?

MC:(42)(40) ???

FW:Do you think this person can manage to improve his economic condition ?Can he become rich, can he at least lead a good and carefree life?

MC:There are some who improve their situation, right? The person may be poor, but in the end things come to him, right?

(20)FW:Na sua opinião, uma pessoa que nasce pobre, pode melhorar sua condição econômica?

MC:(42)(40) ???

FW:O senhor acha que ela pode melhorar sua condição econômica? Pode vir a ser rica, pode pelo menos ter vida boa, folgada?

MC:Tem e'as que miora a situação, né, a pessoa é pobre, mas no fim ganha as coisa, né?

Interestingly,though, the informants very seldom ask for clarification with an explicit metalinguistic question of the type: 'What does X mean?' But the strategy is frequently used by the fieldworkers, as in example (21).

(21)JP:(59)(44) I'm a *confrade*.

FW:Are you a *Vicentino*?

JP:I'm a *confrade* of the youth conference.

FW:I see. What does *confrade* mean?

JP:*Confrade* is a person who belongs to a conference. That means I'm a *confrade*.

(21)JP:(59)(44) Sô confrade.

FW:O senhor é Vicentino?

JP:Eu sô confrade do grupo jovi.

FW:Sei. O que quer dizer confrade?

JP:Confrade é aquele que faz parte daquele grupo. Quê dizê que eu sô confrade.

An alternative way out of the communication problem was used by the informants when they did not acknowledge their failure to understand the question and provided an affirmative answer randomly. When this happens the difficulty may be misassessed or even be unnoticed, unless some kind of further information is required, as in example (5) above. Another possibility is for the informant to give a random answer, and a few seconds afterwards, to realize the sense of the question and to correct the answer. The following dialogue (22) is an example of such cases.

(22)1.FW:Is Brasilândia part
       of João Pinheiro?

   2.RC:(51)(37) It is part
       of João Pinheiro.

   3.FW:Is it a city?

   4.RC:It is.

   5.FW:Is it now autonomous?

   6.RC:Yes it is... no it
       isn't emancipated yet.

   7.FW:It isn't emancipated
       yet, is it?

   8.RC:No, it is part of
       João Pinheiro.

(22)1.FW:Brasilândia é municí-
       pio de João Pinheiro?

   2.RC:(51)(37) É municipu
       di João Pinheiro.

   3.FW:Ou já é cidade?

   4.RC:É uma cidade.

   5.FW:Agora já é autônoma?

   6.RC:É já tá... Não, não é
       mancipada ainda não.

   7.FW:Não é emancipada ain-
       da não, né?

   8.RC:Não, pertence João
       Pinheiro.

The question in nº 3 is ambiguous. What the fieldworker wanted to know was whether the town had already become the seat of a county. The move nº 5 was added in order to clarify the ambiguity. But the informant does not realize immediately the meaning of the word *autônoma* (autonomous) and gives an affirmative answer, which he soon corrects, introducing the word *emancipada* (emancipated) which is indeed more adequate in that context.

A little different from the cases discussed above are those in which the difficulty lies in the polysemy of some lexemes, i.e. a **lexeme with** different related senses. The most usual sense of the lexeme in the variety spoken by the informant may be different from that prevailing in the fieldworker's repertoire. Some words like *desejo* (desire, wish) and *sucesso* (success) were the source of this polysemy problem as is illustrated in examples (23) to (26).

(23)FW:And to succeed in life,
      what do you think one
      needs?

   BS:(42)(29) I think you

(23)FW:E pra ter sucesso na
      vida, o que o senhor
      acha que a pessoa
      precisa?

   BS:(42)(29) Eu acho que

have to be lucky as well,
right, because artists
are already born with
that gift. The person
who was not born to sing,
he tries to sing and
never succeeds, right?
It's like that in other
arts as well.

Tem que tê sorte tam-
bém, né, porque artista
já nasce com aquele
dom. A pessoa que não
nasceu pra cantá, ele
tenta cantá e não con-
segue nunca, né? E
assim é otas arte tam-
bém.

In the informant's repertoire the sense of the word *sucesso* seems to be restricted to the success of singers and actors.

(24)1.FW:What is your biggest
wish in life?

2.AP:(18)(12) This 'wish'
you used is...

3.FW:Biggest wish like,
what you would
like to be, what
you always dream
of.

4.AP:My biggest wish in
life is to be rich.

(24)1.FW:Qual o maior desejo
da sua vida?

2.AP:(18)(12) Desejo que
você fala é...

3.FW:Maior desejo assim, o
que você gostaria de
ser, o que você sem-
pre sonhou fazer,
alguma coisa.

4.AP:O maió desejo da mi-
nha vida é sê rico.

The informant had to ask clarification in n° 2 because the widespread sense of *desejo* (desire) in his dialect is the extravagant appetite that pregnant women frequently have for unusual foods.

(25)1.FW:What is your biggest
wish in life?

2.MO:(38)(37) 'Wish' that
I...

3.FW:What do you want to
get done, the biggest
'influence' you have,
what do you especial-
ly want to get done?

4.MO:Ah...

5.FW:If you could choose
one thing today, what
would you choose?

6.MO:Are you talking about,
for example, a tool?

7.FW:Anything.

8.MO:Anything...

9.FW:If we, if you think

(25)1.FW:Qual é o maior desejo
da sua vida?

2.MO:(38)(37) Desejo qu'eu
...

3.FW:Que vontade, a maior
influência que você
tem, qual é a maior
vontade de alguma
coisa que você quer
fazer?

4:MO:Ah...

5.FW:Se você pudesse esco-
lher uma coisa hoje,
o que você escolhia?

6.MO:A senhora fala assim
de ferramenta?

7.FW:De qualquer coisa.

8.MO:Qualqué coisa...

9.FW:Se a gente, se você

about something you really want, what is it that you really want?	pudesse pensar numa coisa que você quer muito, o que que é uma coisa que você deseja muito?
10.MO:I, it's about that tool, I want a machine.	10.MO:Eu, sobre o negoci de ferramenta, eu quero uma máquina.
11.FW:A machine!?	11.FW:Uma máquina!
12.MO:It's a wish I have in my life, besides a, uhm, how do you say, besides my husband's and children's love.	12.MO:É uma vontade na mi- nha vida, a num sê a, u..., cuma diz, o amor do marido e dos fiu.

This episode represents a moment of great difficulty of communication notwithstanding the accommodation efforts of both parties. In nº 2, the informant requests clarification, clearly identifying the crucial lexical item. In the next move, the fieldworker rephrases the question and risks the use of the word *influência* (influence) which in the informant's dialect is synonymous with 'willingness', 'inclination', 'disposition'. In nº 6, the informant contributes an interpretation, but she introduces the word *ferramenta* (tool) which in her repertoire is also used to refer to household appliances. The fieldworker however is not familiar with this sense and does not realize it until the informant refers to a (sewing) machine (nº 10).

In the following dialogue (26) the source of difficulty was the word *constipação* (constipation). For the fieldworker, this word means bowel constipation, but in the informant's dialect, it can be used to refer to a large range of pathological conditions. A long negotiation was necessary in order to clarify the issue.

(26)AV:(46)(34) ... then my father got constipated and, it was during that condition that he took all the medicines pre- scribed by every single healer in the neighbour- hood, you know... when the doctor examined him, he said that if the con- dition had lasted three days more, the swelling would have reached the heart, then he would die,	(26)AV:(46)(34) ... aí meu pai sofreu uma constipação, que, justamente aquela qu'ele tomô us remédio cum tudo quanto é cura- dô, sabe... o médico inxaminô, falô, ó, se demora mais treis dia a inchação já tava ataca- no o coração, aí ele iã pifá, ia morrê, né, aí feiz operação, feiz ... tirô podriguera que não foi mole.

then he was operated on,
he was... they rid him of
a lot of waste.

FW:But was it the bowels?
What was it?

AV:No, it was a real con-
stipation, you know.

FW:???

AV:No, constipation. I
think it was in the
leg, you know... it was
in the leg, he couldn't
move his arm, either,
you know.

FW:Then he was operated on?

AV:He was operated on, he
was massaged, you know
until...

FW:And he got rid of...?

AV:Yes, he did. And, I
shouldn't even talk
about that, but he got
rid of five litres of
pus in a single day.

FW:He actually had an
inflammation!

AV:Yes, an infection. Then
what hapened was the
following. He left the
hospital after about
forty days he was there.
But he was still
crippled.

FW:Mas era intestino? Era
o quê?

AV:Não, constipação mesmo,
sabe?

FW:???

AV:Não constipação me pa-
rece que foi na perna,
sabe... foi na perna,
que ele entrevô a per-
na e entrevô us braço,
sabe?

FW:Ai feiz operação?

AV:Feiz operação, feiz
massagi, nê, atê que
...

FW:Ele tirô?

AV:Tirô. E nem ê bom nem
falá, mais tirô cinco
litro de pus num dia.

FW:Ele estava era com in-
flamação mesmo!

AV:É, infecção. Então é o
seguinte, ele vei du
hospital cum uns qua-
renta dia que ele tava
internado. Mas inda
voltô alejado.

In the dialogue (27) the miscomprehension is not associated
with polysemy but rather with the homonymy of the adjective *presente* (present) and the noun *presente* (present, gift).

(27)FW:Were you present at
the last two
novenas?

FS:(71)(63) If I...

FW:Yes.

FS:No.

FW:Didn't you go?

(The informant's
daughter interferes):
You did go to that last

(27)FW:A senhora esteve presente nas duas últimas
reuniões da novena?

FS:(71)(63) Se eu tive?

FW:É.

FS:Não.

FW:A senhora não foi?

(Interferência da fi-
lha da informante): E
a senhora não foi na-

novena, did you not?	quela última novena, não?
FS:I was at the novena, but I didn't get any present.	FS:Tive na novena, mas não tive presente!

The informant probably is not familiar with the expression *estar presente* (to be present) and interpreted it as *ganhar presente* (to receive a present).

In a last group of instances of miscommunication one finds cases in which the informant is unfamiliar not only with a certain word but also with the object, class of objects or state of affairs to which the word refers. The word referent or *significatum* (Lyons, 1977:96-7) does not belong to the life experience of the speaker. Examples (28) and (29) illustrate the point.

(28)FW:Do you take part in any residents' association?	(28)FW:A senhora participa de alguma associação de moradores?
BP:(40)(20) Residents?	BP:(40)(20) Moradô?
FW:Perhaps there isn't one here, a residents' association, is there?	BP:Capaiz que aqui não devi tê não, associação de moradores, tem?
BP:Yes there is.	BP:Tem.
FW:Do you take part in it?	FW:A senhora participa?
BP:I do. What is this, this residents' association?	BP:Participo sim. O que é isso associação de moradores?
(29)FW:Do you take part in any trade union activity?	(29)FW:A senhora participa de algum sindicato?
BP:Trade union?	BP:Sindicato?
FW:Yes.	FW:É.
BP:What is this like?	BP:Como é esse negócio?

The purpose of this chapter was twofold: firstly to expose shortcomings in the fieldwork and discuss the strategies employed to overcome them; secondly, to present evidence of the situation of disadvantage of the nonstandard dialect speakers *vis-à-vis* the dominant code and culture. Brazilian society has not yet paid much attention to the language heterogeneity. Much emphasis is placed on the country's monolingualism at the expense of a clear consciousness of the language differences and their social import. In particular overestimation of the language uniformity has thrown into a limbo of irrelevant and non-pertinent issues the discussion of cross-cultural communication problems. This brief analysis of communication breakdowns should be viewed, therefore, as a small contribution towards the revision of these attitudes.

Notes

1   The verb *ganhar* (to receive, to earn, to gain) has a regular past participle: *ganhado,* and an irregular one: *ganho*. The interview was carried out by Eneida Oliveira in Pernambuco, a northeastern state in Brazil.
2   Jefferson (1972) suggests that the negotiation required whenever a misapprehension obtains embodies a three-part structure (which she calls a side-sequence) inserted in a larger sequence in the following way:

```
                      - statement
                    ┌ - misapprehension
side-sequence ┤ - clarification
                    └ - termination
                      - continuation
```

In the example discussed in this section, the minimal clarification side-sequence is made up of two parts, as follows:

1. (Elicitation):What is the biggest desire in your life?
               (Qual o maior desejo de sua vida?)

2. (Misapprehension):Like what?
               (Assim como?)

3. (Clarification):Something that you want most in life.
               (O que você mais quer na vida.)

4. (Answer):I really don't know.
               (Eu num sei mesmo.)

10.0 *Introduction*

Writing a final chapter is usually a difficult task with multiple purposes. The present chapter is divided into four sections according to the main goals that we intend to achieve. In the first section, a synthesis of the important issues that have been touched upon is provided and the findings are discussed. In the second section we are concerned with the question of the methods employed and we make a few suggestions that may represent method-ological improvements in future similar studies. The third section reports briefly what we consider to be the main contributions of this study to the area of speech community studies, and in particular, to the development of linguistic indices to other social processes. The last section advances suggestions for future related research.

10.1 *The language-network relationship*

This study was concerned with the process of dialect diffuseness in the repertoire of speakers of Brazilian Portuguese who have moved from the rural hinterland into the city. Dialect diffuse-ness is viewed, according to Le Page (1980), as a result of geo-graphical and eventually social mobility. In the community studied migrants with varying degrees of exposure to the standard language are brought into contact with each other, and their highly focused rural dialects tend to become more diffuse, i.e. the occurrence of typical Caipira lexical items decreases and some of the nonstandard rules of their repertoire which were almost categorical tend to become variable. Diffuseness should not be viewed as an assimilation of the standard urban language but rather as a movement away from the stigmatized Caipira dialect.

Systematic description of variation in a situation of diffuseness is considerably more difficult than in a situation in which a norm has emerged as the result of dialect focusing and variability follows systematic patterns. One might argue that in the former case heterogeneity is less orderly than in the latter. Moreover, the analysis of aggregated scores, which is frequently carried out in sociolinguistic studies of language variation and change, is more likely to be effective when the former situation obtains. Whenever there is a large range of intra-group variation, the phenomenon should be approached through analytical procedures that can account for individual differences.

The theoretical framework and the methodology employed in this study rely basically on the assumption that an individual's behaviour, linguistically and otherwise, can be accounted for by the characteristics of his/her social network. Following a tradition of social anthropology, we believe that there are regularly patterned relations, amenable to statistical assessment, between network characteristics and individual linguistic behaviour. Network characteristics, such as the number and the character of people with whom an individual has personal relationships of different kinds, and the institutional framework where the links are activated, can constrain the individual's choice of the reference group that will be taken as model for his/her linguistic behaviour.

In the case of the rural migrants whose speech was the object of study here, we have assumed that dialect diffuseness is likely to be fostered when the migrant becomes more subject to the influence of a prestigious exterior reference group. In a first stage of the rural-to-urban physical and psychological transition process the migrants are usually enmeshed in insulated networks in which kinship and pre-migration relations constitute their reference group. In a later stage of the process they are likely to switch from the insulated networks into larger and more heterogeneous integrated networks in which they will be more exposed to the mainstream urban culture and language and more susceptible to the influence of an exterior reference group.

Our basic goal was to find systematic patterns of variation

in a situation of dialect diffuseness and we believed that a migrant's network characteristics, assessed by means of two indices which were indicative of both the number and of some of the attributes of the people with whom s/he had personal relationships, could be used as predictors of the degree of dialect diffuseness. These indices were labelled 'integration index' and 'urbanization index' respectively and will be briefly discussed in the next section. The question that must concern us here is whether or not (and to what extent) network indices are useful predictors of dialect diffuseness.

A major finding of this study is that in a rurban community of migrants such as Brazlândia the process of dialect diffuseness can follow rather different tracks for men and for women. In the case of male migrants it can be accounted for by the number and characteristics of their interpersonal relations in a public sphere, i.e. outside of their home domain. As both the integration and the urbanization indices dealt with personal relations which were contracted in the public and not in the private social sphere, they were good predictors of dialect diffuseness for the men, although their capacity as predictors varied according to the linguistic nonstandard rules that were studied.

The arena where women's dialect diffuseness must be investigated is, in contrast, not in the public but in the private sphere of social relations. The female migrants remain still very much confined within their kinship and neighbour network and as a consequence of that are not directly exposed to the mainstream culture via interpersonal links with strangers. In spite of that, their dialects undergo a process of diffuseness which in the case of some variables follows the same rate observed for men. This is the case of the λ-vocalization rule. In relation to the diphthong reduction rule, the women are, surprisingly, a little ahead of the men in the acquisition of the standard variant. As for the morphosyntactic rules that were studied, viz. subject-verb agreement with third and with first person plural, the men are clearly in the lead in the acquisition of the standard forms. In sum, the women are not directly exposed to the standardizing influence but nonetheless their speech does not remain immune to change. The rate of change in their repertoire is, however, slower than in the repertoire of men, at least in the case of some linguistic rules. The main factor that seems to foster the women's dialect diffuseness is the inter-generation contact which takes place within the home domain, through their relationship with their grown-up children.

We have been arguing that network characteristics can be good predictors of linguistic behaviour because they exert an influence on the speakers' choice of the social groups with whom they want to be identified. At this point it may be interesting to examine the results of the quantitative analysis of the linguistic rules in the light of Le Page's (1975/1980) theory of language change as a function of group membership. According to this linguist, the speakers create their rules so as to resemble as closely as possible the members of the groups with which they wish to identify themselves from time to time. The process is constrained however by the following prerequisites:

1. the extent to which they can identify the model groups;
2. the extent to which they have access to such groups;
3. the weight of various (possibly conflicting) motivations towards one or another model group, and
4. the ability to modify their linguistic behaviour.

We shall comment on each of the above conditions in regard to our findings.

As concerns the first item, we can assert that the ability to identify the model group varies according to the salience of the rule. A rule is considered to be salient when it is recognized by the community as a sign of significant social differences. The results of the correlation tests demonstrated that the λ-vocalization rule is salient but the diphthong rule is not. Salient variables (like the λ-vocalization rule, the SVA-3 rule with some morphological classes and the SVA-1 rule) are more susceptible to change in the repertoire of adult speakers. They are subject to what Labov (1972a:179) called sporadic and irregular correction of the changed forms towards the prestige model. This informal correction stems from the value system prevailing in the speech community. The variables that are not salient, such as the diphthong rule, are less susceptible to change in the adults' speech. They are not subject to informal correction but only to formal correction provided by school and by exposure to the written language. Consequently, illiterate and semi-literate adult migrants are likely to maintain the feature regardless of their degree of integration in the urban *modus vivendi*, whereas the youth, who are systematically exposed to formal correction, drop it.

Le Page's second rider refers to the speakers' access to the model group. Such access in the case of the rural migrants varies according to the parameters of sex, of age, of media exposure and, in the case of the men, according to their network characteristics as insulated or integrated. A comparison of the scores of two male informants for the four variables shows the influence of network characteristics on access to the model groups (table 10.1.).

Table 10.1. *Comparison of two informants' scores for the four variables (I)*

Inform-ant	Age	Urbani-zation index	Integra-tion index	λ-voc. %	Diph-thong %	SVA-3 %	SVA-1 %
PD	32(28)	1.89	.09	86	61	30	70
JO	38(37)	.33	.00	6	25	0	20

The two informants are brothers and have the same occupation. PD has been living in the city for four years and has succeeded in **making** a transition from an insulated to an integrated net-work, whereas JO is still enmeshed in an insulated network.

The third condition postulated by Le Page concerns possibly conflicting motivations towards one or another model group. The rural-to-urban transition is, in fact, a complex process during which the migrant will be permanently faced with ambivalence between an out-group identification, motivated by pragmatic reasons, and the need for the in-group psychological and social support. The emphasis of this study was mainly on the trend towards out-group identification, but the opposite phenomenon cannot be overlooked. The influence of in-group or solidarity

orientation in dialect maintenance can be illustrated by the
behaviour of JP. Table 10.2. compares his scores with the scores
of his close friend AV. Both men have contracted many links in
the urban setting, as indicated by their integration indices,
but they have very different urbanization scores.

Table 10.2. *Comparison of two informants' scores for the
four variables (II)*

Inform-ant	Age	Urbani-zation index	Integra-tion index	λ-voc. %	Diph-thong %	SVA-3 %	SVA-1 %
JP	59(44)	1.80	.19	9	12	44	42
AV	46(34)	2.65	.21	73	18	70	73

The two informants have been living in the city for approximately the same length of time, but whereas AV is a *Vicentino*
leader clearly oriented towards urban values, JP, the dance
group leader, is rural oriented. He maintains a Caipira identity, which he actualizes mainly through the folk dance activities
and linguistic behaviour, probably because it allows him to
exert a strong leadership power within the limited sphere of the
newly-arrived migrants who participate in the group.

The last rider to Le Page's hypothesis refers to the ability
to modify linguistic behaviour. The most striking evidence for
this stems from the results for the two age groups. Although
the differences here can also be accounted for by level of
schooling there is no doubt that age is playing an important
role in the acquisition of the standard forms. Children and
adolescents can more easily learn a second language or dialect
than adults. Another fact that argues in favour of this condition is the high rate of the standard variant of the λ-vocalization rule in the speech of the two youngest adult male informants.

10.2 *Suggestions for methodological improvements*
Milroy (1980:141) comments on the requirements that must be met
by a reliable network index. Devising network measures to be

used in quantitative studies may in fact be difficult. In this study two network indices were devised in order to be used as potential predictors of dialect diffuseness. Such indices are intended to reflect two conditions that were considered crucial for the assessment of the rural-to-urban transition, namely, the number of links contracted by the migrant in the urban environment (integration index) and the degree to which the people with whom the migrant is directly or indirectly related are exposed to the urban influence (urbanization index). As discussed in chapter 7, the impossibility of using an exhaustive sampling can give rise to skewing in the integration index. We want to discuss in this section some methodological improvements that may help minimize the effect of skewing as well as improve the goodness of fit in the correlation tests.

The skewing of the integration index occurred with the female scores. It can be argued in the first place that the measure is not really suited to the situation of women's interpersonal relations, which tend to be restricted to the domain of home. However, it does not seem appropriate to use different network measures for men and women in the same community, since this would deprive us of any grounds for comparison. A better alternative seems to be the use of supplementary network measures that take into consideration the following conditions: firstly, the distinction between interpersonal contacts in the public and in the private spheres of social relations, and secondly, the degree of inter-generation contact in the different domains.

Even so, we will probably be able to improve the goodness of fit in the correlation tests in future studies if we include an analysis of distribution of network indices across age subgroups. In the case of the λ-vocalization rule, it seems clear that age is a variable that should have been controlled. We did not divide the adult group into subsets according to age, however, because we were dealing with a very small sample.

Two other minor improvements that can be easily adopted are: firstly, to correlate the network indices with the overall frequency of rule application for each informant, i.e. the application of the rule in all environments in addition to correlating them with the frequencies in each environment separately;

secondly, to correlate the linguistic variables one with another.

10.3   *Major contributions of the study*

It was pointed out in the introduction that the sociolinguistic situation in Brazil is rather peculiar and extremely complex. Although it cannot be treated as a post-creole continuum we are attracted to the idea of displaying the varieties on a hypothetical spectrum ranging from the isolated rural vernacular at one extreme to the urban standard of the upper classes at the other. A crucial distinction that must be made then is between the features that show a gradient stratification along the continuum and those that indicate a sharp stratification between rural and urban speech. In this work we have provided a tentative classification of sharp and gradient nonstandard features.

When Brazilian Portuguese is compared with European Portuguese a striking difference is the tendency in the former towards simplification of the inflectional system in the number agreement rule within the noun phrase and in subject-verb agreement. In both cases redundant plural markers are simply deleted. Two recent studies of these grammatical rules, carried out by Naro (1981) and Guy (1981), have provided different assessments of their evolutionary trend. Naro's basic argument is that there is a slow drift in the language towards elimination of redundant number agreement from the grammar. Guy argues against this hypothesis and suggests that variation related to different salience categories results from an earlier period of decreolization in which the most salient features of the standard language were acquired earliest. In this study we have provided evidence of an ongoing change involving the process of verbal ending recovery when we compare the rate of SVA-3 rule in the speech of migrants who are at different stages of the rural-to-urban transition. The results of the correlation tests for both the SVA-3 and SVA-1 rules provide evidence in favour of the hypothesis that adult speakers tend to acquire the verbal endings as they come under the influence of standardizing pressures. Such a gradual process of recovery of verbal suffixes is constrained by a scale of salience, i.e. verbal forms which deviate the most from the standard form are the earliest to be recovered.

As regards the methods used in this study, an important contribution to the study of speech communities is the development of network indices designed to deal with dialect diffuseness rather than with dialect focusing. In the latter case two reliable indicators are the levels of density and multiplexity in the network, but for dealing with dialect diffuseness there were no well established measurement techniques.

It should be pointed out finally that this study has succeeded in showing a consistent relationship between network structure and linguistic behaviour in a very fluid situation of dialect contact undergoing rapid change.

10.4 *Suggestions for future investigation*

We have pointed out in the introduction to this book that an important sociolinguistic issue to be investigated in Brazil is the conflict between two opposing trends, namely, standardization pressures (which are part of the homogenization phenomenon of modern societies) and the maintenance of nonstandard forms as signs of group identity. The analysis of the motivations underlying the migrants' dialect diffuseness hinges on this issue, but much more inquiry is required in this area. In partioular, the maintenance of what we have labelled rurban varieties or their evolution towards the urban standard need to be studied, with emphasis upon the processes of dialect focusing in long-term established communities.

The study of dialect focusing in different speech communities should necessarily include an assessment of the extent to which the population is aware of linguistic differences. As we see the phenomenon in Brazil currently, linguistic differences related to geographic region can be more easily assessed than those related to social groups.

The investigation of language focusing or diffuseness suggested above entails the study of the evolutionary trend of many nonstandard features of Brazilian Portuguese. The available studies have focused on a small set of them and in some cases the results are partial and inconclusive.

The influence of literacy on language change and, conversely, information on patterns of language variation as an aid in establishing a democratic educational policy in the country represent crucial areas requiring much sociolinguistic research. A related area concerns misunderstanding and stigmatization in cross-cultural communication. Investigating the dynamics of unequal encounters is indeed another fruitful area for study in Brazilian society.

The field of Brazilian sociolinguistics offers, in fact, a huge number of possibilities for investigation, which are relevant not only for scientific and academic reasons, but also (and maybe most importantly) because sociolinguistic research can certainly perform 'therapeutic' functions, which may contribute to a major goal to be pursued: the advancement of a more egalitarian society in the country. We regard the present work as a small contribution to the carrying out of this task.

Network indices and linguistic variable scores

Male Informant	Age[1]	Urbanization Index	Integration Index	λ -vocalization %	Diphthong Rules[2] %	SVA-3[3] %	SVA-1[4] %
FM	54(30)	4.15	.08	86/133=65	36/78=46	8/9=89	10/21=48
NS	43(26)	3.40	.17	91/171=53	13/41=32	6/18=33	37/50=74
BS	42(29)	3.20	.17	94/130=72	12/63=19	11/12=92	5/10=50
AV	46(34)	2.65	.21	120/164=73	12/67=18	7/10=70	27/37=73
AG	65(30)	2.50	.02	17/39=43	3/7=43	1/3=33	3/11=27
JD	50(35)	2.11	.08	12/148=8	19/48=39	4/10=40	9/21=43
PD	32(28)	1.89	.09	77/89=86	19/31=61	3/10=30	21/30=70
JP	59(44)	1.80	.19	20/202=9	13/111=12	11/25=44	20/47=42
RC	51(37)	1.65	.18	149/253=59	22/112=20	35/53=67	17/23=74
FS	51(41)	1.65	.00	3/48=6	0/9=0	*1/1=100	0/6=0
AR	47(23)	1.50	.02	13/37=35	1/5=20	*0/1=0	2/3=66
FD	34(28)	1.47	.04	23/24=96	3/9=33	*0/0=0	2/3=66
JM	43(42)	1.20	.03	6/63=9	4/11=36	1/15=14	2/8=25
LU	42(29)	1.00	.03	57/61=93	9/13=70	0/5=0	*0/1=0
JO	38(37)	0.33	.00	2/32=6	2/8=25	0/3=0	1/5=20
Female Informant							
JL	40(28)	2.64	.02	22/38=58	2/4=50	4/5=80	*1/1=100
MR	59(37)	2.50	.00	77/133=58	33/106=31	11/37=30	3/47=6
LA	27(26)	1.00	.02	9/15=60	*0/0=0	*1/1=100	*0/1=0
TE	46(31)	1.00	.02	37/108=34	4/20=20	4/9=44	5/8=62
TS	40(16)	0.99	.02	38/92=41	6/18=33	7/18=39	15/78=19
LS	47(34)	0.99	.10	31/33=94	3/7=43	*1/2=50	6/8=75
BP	40(20)	0.99	.02	8/70=11	14/15=93	*1/1=100	*1/1=100
CV	45(33)	0.77	.10	62/75=83	4/12=33	6/9=66	12/12=100
CL	42(16)	0.66	.02	61/64=95	13/25=52	3/8=37	5/6=83
JJ	56(38)	0.66	.02	61/106=57	5/29=17	2/14=14	3/12=25
MC	47(32)	0.49	.07	69/76=90	12/14=86	2/3=66	1/5=20
GP	47(38)	0.49	.09	34/81=42	13/26=50	7/14=50	8/11=73
MD	71(68)	0.33	.09	13/87=15	7/14=50	*0/0=0	3/20=15
MP	24(19)	0.33	.00	51/139=37	17/57=30	4/11=33	4/22=18
GR	28(22)	0.28	.06	5/18=36	6/7=86	*1/1=100	*0/0=0
MO	38(37)	0.14	.09	11/75=15	7/27=26	1/7=14	2/18=11
MT	44(40)	0.00	.06	14/45=31	*0/1=0	*0/1=0	0/4=0

(1) Present age and age by the time of migration.

(2) In environment (J)

(3) In environment (IA).

(4) In environment (TA).

(*) The percentage is not representative.

BIBLIOGRAPHY

Abaurre-Gnerre, M.B. 1981. Processos fonológicos segmentais como índices de padrões prosódicos diversos nos estilos formal e casual do Português do Brasil. *Cadernos de Estudos Lingüísticos* (Unicamp) 2:23-43.

Afendras, E.A. 1974. Network concepts in the sociology of language. Paper presented at the *IXth International Congress of Anthropological and Ethnological Sciences*. CIRB.

Ali, M.I.S. 1964. *Gramática Secundária e Gramática Histórica da Língua Portuguesa*. Brasília: Editora Universidade de Brasília (first published in 1931).

Almeida, A. 1976. The Portuguese nasal vowels: Phonetics and phonemics. In J. Schmidt-Radefeldt (ed.), *Readings in Portuguese Linguistics*, Amsterdam: North Holland.

Amaral, A. 1976. *O Dialeto Caipira*. São Paulo: Hucitec (first published in 1920).

Aronson, D.R. (ed.) 1970. *The Canadian Review of Sociology and Anthropology* 7(4).

Banton, M. 1973. Urbanization and role analysis. In Southall (ed.).

Barnes, J.A. 1954. Class and committees in a Norwegian Island Parish. *Human Relations* 7(1):39-58.

    1969. Network and political process. In Mitchell (ed.).

Baugh, J.G., Jr. 1979. *Linguistic style-shifting in Black English*. Ph.D. Thesis, University of Pennsylvania.

Bavelas, A. 1948. A mathematical model for group structures. *Applied Anthropology* 7:16-30.

Bell, R.T. 1976. *Sociolinguistics*. London: B.T. Batsford.

Berlinck, M.T. 1977. *Marginalidade Social e Relações de Classe em São Paulo*. Petrópolis: Vozes.

Berreman, G.D. 1964. Aleut reference group alienation, mobility and acculturation. *American Anthropologist* 66(2):231-250.

Bickerton, D. 1977. Pidginization and creolization: language acquisition and language universals. In A. Valdman (ed.), *Pidgin and Creole Linguistics*, Bloomington: Indiana University Press.

Bisol, L. 1981. *Harmonia vocálica: uma regra variável*. Doctoral Thesis, Universidade Federal do Rio de Janeiro.

Blom, J.-P. & Gumperz, J.J. 1972. Social meaning in linguistic structures: code switching in Norway. In Gumperz & Hymes (eds.).

Boissevain, J. & Mitchell, J.C.(eds.) 1973. *Network Analysis: Studies in Human Interaction*. The Hague: Mouton.

Bortoni-Ricardo, S. 1981. On nonstandard subject-verb agreement in Portuguese. In W. Gutwinski & G. Jolly (eds.), *The Eighth LACUS Forum 1981*. Columbia: Hornbeam.

Bortoni-Ricardo, S. & Guimarães, L.L. 1982. Language change and social networks: an exploration study of rural migrants in Brasília. Paper presented at the *X World Congress of Sociology*, Mexico City, 16-21 August 1982.

Bott, E. 1957. *Family and Social Network*. London: Tavistock.

Braga, M.L. 1977. *A concordância de número no sintagma nominal no Triângulo Mineiro*. MA Dissertation, Pontifícia Universidade Católica do Rio de Janeiro.

Cagliari, L.C. 1980. Investigando o ritmo da fala. *Anais do V Encontro Nacional de Lingüística*, vol. II:290-304. (Rio de Janeiro: PUC)

Camacho, R.H. 1978. A variação lingüística. *Variação Lingüística e Ensino da Língua Materna*. São Paulo: Secretaria de Educação, Coordenadoria de Estudos e Normas Pedagógicas.

Cândido, A. 1964. *Os Parceiros do Rio Bonito*. Rio de Janeiro: José Olympio.

Cardoso de Oliveira, R. 1968. *Urbanização e Tribalismo*. Rio de Janeiro: Zahar.

    1981. Movimentos indigenas e indigenismo em Brasil. *America Indigena* 41(3):399-405.

    1983. *Enigmas e Soluções*. Rio de Janeiro: Tempo Brasileiro/ Universidade Federal do Ceará.

Carvalho, J.G.H. de 1969. Nota sobre o vocalismo antigo
   português : valor dos grafemas E e O em sílaba átona. In his
   Estudos Lingüísticos, vol. 2. Coimbra-Atlântida.
Cedergren, H.J. & Sankoff, D. 1974. Variable rules: performance
   as a statistical reflection of competence. *Language* 50:333-55.
Chediak, A.J. 1958. Aspectos da linguagem do Espraiado. *Anais
   do Primeiro Congresso Brasileiro de Língua Falada no Teatro*.
   Rio de Janeiro:Ministério da Educação e Cultura.
Costa, M.A. (ed.) 1975. *Estudos de Demografia Urbana*. Rio de
   Janeiro: IPEA/INPES.
Coulthard, M. 1978. *An Introduction to Discourse Analysis*.
   London: Longman.
Couto, H. do 1974. O falar capelinhense. Mimeo
Cunha, C. 1977. *Língua Portuguesa e Realidade Brasileira*. Rio de
   Janeiro: Tempo Brasileiro.
   1985. *A Questão da Norma Culta Brasileira*. Rio de Janeiro:
   Tempo Brasileiro.
Dixon, W.J. & Massey, F.J., Jr. 1957. *Introduction to
   Statistical Analysis*. New York: McGraw-Hill.
Douglas-Cowie, E. 1978. Linguistic code-switching in a Northern
   Irish village: Social interaction and social ambition. In P.
   Trudgill (ed.), *Sociolinguistic Patterns in British English*.
   London: Arnold.
Dourado, A. 1981. Língua, linguagem e poder. *Jornal do Brasil*,
   7 June 1981, Especial, p. 2.
Duncan Jr., S. 1974. On the structure of speaker-auditor
   interaction during speaking turns. *Language in Society* 3(2):
   161-180.
Elia, S. 1975. *Ensaios de Filologia e Lingüística*. Rio de
   Janeiro: Grifo.
Ferguson, C. & de Bose, C. 1977. Simplified registers, broken
   language and pidginization. In A. Valdman (ed.), *Pidgin and
   Creole Linguistics*. Bloomington: Indiana University Press.
Fishman, J.A. 1972. *The Sociology of Language*. Rowley: Newbury
   House.
   1980. Bilingualism and biculturism as individual and as
   societal phenomena. *Journal of Multilingual and Multicultural
   Development* 1(1):3-15.

Franco de Sá, F. 1915. *A Língua Portuguesa (Dificuldades e Dúvidas)*. Maranhão: Imprensa Oficial.

Freire, G. 1968. *Sobrados e Mucambos*. Rio de Janeiro: José Olympio. (First published in 1936.)

Gal, S. 1978. Variation and change in patterns of speaking: language shift in Austria. In Sankoff (ed.).

        1979. *Language Shift: Social Determinants of Linguistic Change in Bilingual Austria*. New York: Academic Press.

Garvin, P.L. 1959. The standard language problem - concepts and methods. *Anthropological Linguistics* 1(2): 28-31.

Giles, H. 1980. Accommodation theory: some new directions. *York Papers in Linguistics* 9:105-136.

Giles, H. & Powesland, P.F. 1975. Speech style and perceived status: some conceptual distinctions. In H. Giles & P.F. Powesland (eds.), *Speech Style and Social Evaluation*. London: Academic Press.

Giles, H. & Smith, P.M. 1979. Accommodation theory: optimal levels of convergence. In H. Giles & R. St Clair (eds.), *Language and Social Psychology*. Oxford: Basil Blackwell.

Goffman, E. 1976. Replies and responses. *Language in Society* 5: 257-313.

Gonçalves Viana, A.R. 1973. Essai de phonétique et de phonologie de la langue portugaise d'après le dialecte actuel de Lisbonne. In his *Estudos de Fonética Portuguesa*. Lisboa: Imprensa Nacional. (First published in 1883.)

Gonzales, E. & Bastos, M.I. 1975. Migração para Brasília: uma análise dos migrantes de baixa renda. *Série Sociologia* 7. Departamento de Ciências Sociais, Universidade de Brasília.

Goulart, M. 1975. *A Escravidão Africana no Brasil*. São Paulo: Alfa Ômega.

Grice, H.P. 1975. Logic and conversation. In P. Cole & J.L. Morgan (eds.), *Syntax and Semantics*, vol. 3. New York: Academic Press.

Guimarães, L.L. 1970. Network analysis: an approach to the study of communication systems. *Technical Report* 12. Department of Communication, Michigan State University.

        1972. *Communication integration in modern and traditional social systems: a comparative analysis across twenty*

communities of Minas Gerais, Brazil. Ph.D. Thesis, Michigan
State University.

Gumperz, J.J. 1968. The speech community. In J.B. Pride & S.
Holmes (eds.), *Sociolinguistics*. Harmondsworth: Penguin.
1972. Introduction to Gumperz and Hymes (eds.).
1976a. Social network and language shift. *Working Paper* 46.
Language Behavior Laboratory, Berkeley.
1976b. The sociolinguistic significance of conversational
code-switching. *Working Paper* 46. Language Behavior Research
Laboratory, Berkeley.
1980. Language, social knowledge and interpersonal relations.
York Papers in Linguistics 9:137-150.

Gumperz, J.J. & Hymes, D. (eds.) 1972. *Directions in Sociolinguistics*. New York: Holt, Rinehart & Winston.

Guy, G.R. 1980. Variation in the group and the individual: the
case of final stop deletion. In Labov (ed.).
1981. *Linguistic variation in Brazilian Portuguese: aspects of
the phonology, syntax, and language history*. Ph.D. Thesis,
University of Pennsylvania.

Halliday, M.A.K. 1978. *Language as Social Semiotic*. Baltimore:
University of Park Press.

Halpern, J.M. 1967. *The Changing Village Community*. Englewood
Cliffs: Prentice Hall.

Hart, T.R., Jr. 1955. Notes on sixteenth century Portuguese
pronunciation. *Word* 2:404-15.

Haugen, E. 1956. *Bilingualism in the Americas*. University of
Alabama.

Head, B. 1981. Social factors in the perception of phonetic
differences. *Cadernos de Estudos Lingüísticos* (Unicamp) 2:
158-166.

Hockett, C.F. 1958. *A Course in Modern Linguistics*. New York:
Macmillan.

Hogan, D. & Berlinck, M.T. 1976. Conditions of migration, access
to information and first jobs: a study of migrant adaptation
in São Paulo, Brazil. In A. Richmond & D. Kubat (eds.),
Internal Migration - The New World and the Third World.
London: Sage.

Houaiss, A. 1958. Tentativa de descrição do sistema vocálico do

português culto na área dita carioca. *Anais do Primeiro
Congresso Brasileiro de Língua Falada no Teatro*. Rio de
Janeiro: Ministério da Educação e Cultura.

Hymes, D. 1972. On communicative competence. In J.B. Pride &
J. Holmes (eds.), *Sociolinguistics*. Harmondsworth: Penguin.

1974. *Foundations of sociolinguistics: an ethnographic
approach*. Philadelphia: University of Pennsylvania Press.

Jefferson,G. 1972. Side sequences. In D.N. Sudnow (ed.), *Studies
in social interaction*. New York: Free Press.

Kemper, R.V. 1975. Social factors in migration: the case of
Tzintzuntzeños in Mexico City. In B. Du Toit & H. Safa (eds.),
Migration and urbanization: models and adaptive strategies.
The Hague: Mouton.

Labov, W. 1966. The effect of social mobility on linguistic
behavior. *Sociological Inquiry* 36:186-203.

1972a. *Sociolinguistic patterns*. Philadelphia: Pennsylvania
University Press.

1972b. *Language in the inner city*. Philadelphia: Pennsylvania
University Press.

1980. (ed.). *Locating language in time and space*. New York:
Academic Press.

1980. Is there a Creole speech community? In A. Valdman &
H. Highfield (eds.), *Theoretical orientation in Creole
studies*. New York: Academic Press.

1981. Field methods of the project on linguistic change and
variation. *Working Paper in Sociolinguistics*. Austin, Texas:
Southwest Educational Development Laboratory.

Labov, W. & Sankoff, D. 1980. Preface in Labov (ed.).

Lemle, M. 1978. Heterogeneidade dialetal: um apelo à pesquisa.
L. Lobato (ed.), *Lingüística e ensino do vernáculo*. Rio de
Janeiro: Tempo Brasileiro.

Lemle, M. & Naro A:J. 1977. *Competências básicas do Português*.
Rio de Janeiro: Fundação Movimento Brasileiro de
Alfabetização.

Le Page, R.B. 1980. Projection, focussing and diffusion. *York
Papers in Linguistics* 9:9-31 (first published in 1975).

Lessa, L.C. 1976. *O modernismo brasileiro e a língua portuguesa*.
2nd ed. Rio de Janeiro: Grifo.

Lewis, O. 1973. Some perspectives on urbanization with special reference to Mexico City. In Southall (ed.).

Lomnitz,L. A. 1977. *Network and marginality*. New York: Academic Press.

Lyons, J. 1977. *Semantics.* 2v. Cambridge: Cambridge University Press.

Magalhães, M.I. The 'reza': a curing speech event. In progress.

Matta Machado, M.T. 1981. *Étude articulatoire et acoustique des voyelles nasales du portugais de Rio de Janeiro*. Doctoral Thesis, Université des Sciences Humaines de Strasbourg.

Mattoso Câmara, J., Jr. 1970. *Estrutura da Língua Portuguesa*. Petrópolis: Vozes.

1972. Ele como acusativo no Português no Brasil. In his *Dispersos*. Rio de Janeiro: Fundação Getúlio Vargas.

1975. *História e estrutura da língua portuguesa*. Rio de Janeiro: Padrão.

1977. *Para o estudo da fonêmica portuguesa*. Rio de Janeiro: Organização Simões (first published in 1953).

1978. *Dicionário de lingüística*. Petrópolis: Vozes (first published in 1956).

Melo, G.C. de 1971. *A língua do Brasil*. Rio de Janeiro: Fundação Getúlio Vargas (first published in 1946).

Milroy, L. 1980. *Language and social networks*. Oxford: Basil Blackwell.

1982. Social networks and linguistic focusing. In S. Romaine (ed.), *Sociolinguistic variation in speech communities*. London: Arnold.

Milroy, L. & Margrain, S. 1980. Vernacular language loyalty and social network. *Language in Society*. 9:43-70.

Mitchell, J.C. (ed.) 1969. *Social networks in urban situations*. Manchester: Manchester University Press.

1969. The concept and use of social networks. In Mitchell (ed.).

1973. Networks, norms and institutions. In Boissevain and Mitchell (eds.).

Moreno, J. 1953. *Who shall survive? Foundations of Sociometry, Group Psychotherapy and Sociodrama*. New. York: Beacon House.

Nagel, E. 1961. *The Structure of Science - Problems in the Logic of Scientific Explanation*. New York: Harcourt, Brace and World Ltd.

Naro, A.J. 1971. The history of e and o in Portuguese: a study in linguistic drift. *Language* 47(3):615-45.

⎯⎯⎯ 1980. Review article on linguistic variation: models and methods, ed. by David Sankoff. *Language* 56:158-170.

⎯⎯⎯ 1981. The social and structural dimensions of a syntactic change. *Language* 57(1):63-98.

⎯⎯⎯ 1982. Projeto censo da variação lingüística no Estado do Rio de Janeiro. Paper presented at the *Seminário Aprendizagem da Língua Materna*. Brasília: MEC/INEP, 3-5 November 1982.

Naro, A.J. & Lemle, M. 1976. Syntactic diffusion. *Ciência e Cultura* 29:259-68.

Nie,N. H., et al. 1975. SPSS: *Statistical Package for the Social Sciences*. 2nd ed. New York: McGraw-Hill.

Oliveira, F. de 1975. *A Gramática da Linguagem Portuguesa*. (Introdução, leitura atualizada e notas por Maria Leonor Carvalho Buescu.) Lisboa: Imprensa Nacional, Casa da Moeda (first published in 1536).

Oliven, R.G. 1982. *Urbanização e Mudança no Brasil*. Petrópolis: Vozes.

Pêcheux. M. 1978. *Hacia el Analisis Automatico del Discurso*. Madrid: Gredos.

Penha, J.A. 1974. Aspectos da linguagem de São Domingos: tentativa de descrição da linguagem rural brasileira. *Alfa* 20/21:81-115.

Pereira de Queiroz, M.I. 1978. *Cultura, Sociedade Rural, Sociedade Urbana no Brasil*. Rio de Janeiro: Livros Técnicos e Científicos; São Paulo: EDUSP.

Pike, K. 1945. *The Intonation of American English*. Ann Arbor: University of Michigan Press.

Révah, I.S. 1958. L'Evolution de la prononciation au Portugal et au Brésil du XVIe siècle à nos jours. *Anais do Primeiro Congresso Brasileiro de Língua Falada no Teatro*. Rio de Janeiro: Ministério da Educação e Cultura.

Ridley, D.C. 1979. *Uma mão lavando a outra e as duas banhando o rosto*. M.A. dissertation: Universidade de Brasília.

Riley, M.W. 1963. *Sociological Research*. New York: Harcourt.

Rodrigues, A.D. 1967. Problemas relativos à descrição do português contemporâneo como língua padrão no Brasil. Paper presented to the *I Simpósio Luso-Brasileiro sobre a Língua Portuguesa Contemporânea*. Coimbra, 1967.

Rodrigues, A.N. 1974. *O dialeto Caipira na Região de Piracicaba*. São Paulo: Ática.

Romaine, S. 1981. The status of variable rules in sociolinguistic theory. *Journal of Linguistics* 17:93-119.

Rousseau, P. & Sankoff, D. 1978. Advances in variable rule methodology. In Sankoff (ed.).

Ryan, E.B. 1979. Why do low-prestige language varieties persist? In H. Giles & R. St Clair (eds.), *Language and social Psychology*. Oxford: Basil Blackwell.

Sacks H., Schegloff, E.A. & Jefferson, G. 1974. A simplest systematics for the organization of turn-taking conversation. *Language* 50(4):696-753.

Sankoff, D. (ed.) 1978. *Linguistic Variation Models and Methods*. New York: Academic Press.

Sankoff, D. & Labov, W. 1979. On the use of variable rules. *Language in Society* 8(2):189-223.

Santos, A. P.A. 1982. *A redução do ditongo decrescente na linguagem de migrantes de origem rural*. M.A. Dissertation: Universidade de Brasília.

Scherre, M.M.P. 1978. *A regra de concordância nominal de número no sintagma nominal em Português*. M.A. Dissertation: Pontifícia Universidade Católica do Rio de Janeiro.

Schühly, G.F. 1981. *Marginalidade*. Rio de Janeiro: PUC & Agir.

Silva Neto, S. da.1977. *Introdução ao estudo da língua portuguesa no Brasil*. Rio de Janeiro: Presença (first published in 1950).

Sousa da Silveira. 1964. *Lições de Português*. Rio de Janeiro: Livros de Portugal (first published in 1923).

Southall, A. (ed.) 1973. *Urban Anthropology*. London: Oxford University Press.

1973. The density of role relationship as a universal index of urbanization. In Southall (ed.).

Teixeira, J.A. 1938. *O Falar Mineiro*. Separata da Revista do

Arquivo Municipal de São Paulo, n.45.

1944. *Estudos de Dialetologia Portuguesa: Linguagem de Goiás*. São Paulo: Anchieta.

Thomas, J. 1983. Cross-cultural pragmatic failure. *Applied Linguistics* 4(2):92-110.

Trudgill, P. 1972. Sex, covert prestige and linguistic change in the urban British English of Norwich. *Language in Society* 1:179-95.

1974. Linguistic change and diffusion: description and explanation in sociolinguistic dialect geography. *Language in Society* 2:215-46.

Vasconcelos, J.L. de 1970. *Esquisse d'une dialectologie Portugaise*. 2nd ed. Lisboa: Centro de Estudos Filológicos (first published in 1901).

Vasquez Cuesta, P. & Luz, A.M. 1971. *Gramática Portuguesa*. vol. 1. Madrid: Gredos.

Votre, S.J. 1978. *Variação fonológica na fala dos mobralenses da área do Rio de Janeiro*. Doctoral Thesis, Pontifícia Universidade Católica do Rio de Janeiro.

1982. Phonological and syntactic aspects of denasalization in spoken Brazilian Portuguese. In D. Sankoff & H.J. Cedergren (eds.), *Variation Omnibus*. Montreal.

Wagley, C. 1971. *An Introduction to Brazil*. New York: Columbia University Press.

Weinreich, U. 1953. *Languages in Contact*. The Hague: Mouton.

Wheeldon, P.D. 1969. The operation of voluntary associations and personal networks in the political processes of an inter-ethnic community. In Mitchell (ed.).

Wolfram, W. & Fasold, R.W. 1974. *The study of social dialects in American English*. Englewood Cliffs: Prentice-Hall.

Wolfson, N. 1976. Speech events and natural speech: some implications for sociolinguistic methodology. *Language in Society* 5:189-209.